On the Road with
DAVID
THOMPSON

JOYCE AND
PETER MCCART

FIFTH
HOUSE
PUBLISHERS

Front cover photograph © and design by John Luckhurst/GDL
Maps by GDL / Toby Foord
All interior photographs © Peter McCart

The publisher gratefully acknowledges the support of
The Canada Council for the Arts and the Department of Canadian Heritage.

THE CANADA COUNCIL | LE CONSEIL DES ARTS
FOR THE ARTS | DU CANADA
SINCE 1957 | DEPUIS 1957

We acknowledge the financial support of the Government of Canada through the Book Publishing Industry Development Program for our publishing activities.

Printed in Canada.
00 01 02 03 04/ 5 4 3 2 1

Canadian Cataloguing in Publication Data

McCart, J. (Joyce), 1936-
   On the road with David Thompson

   Includes bibliographical references.
   ISBN 1-894004-50-7

   1. Thompson, David, 1770-1857. 2. Alberta—Guidebooks. 3. British Columbia—Guidebooks. 4. Northwest, Pacific—Guidebooks. 5. Northwest, Canadian. 6. Northwest, Pacific. I. McCart, P. J. (Peter James), 1937- II. Title.
FC3212.1.T46M32 2000   971.2   C00-911036-4
F1060.7.T48M32 2000

Published in Canada by
Fifth House Ltd.
A Fitzhenry & Whiteside Company
1511-1800 4 Street SW
Calgary, Alberta, Canada
T2S 2S5

Published in the U.S. by
Fitzhenry & Whiteside
121 Harvard Ave.
Suite 2
Allston, Massachusetts
01234

Contents

To Sue and Peter D.

List of Photographs

List of Maps

Introduction

Why David Thompson?

As long-term residents of Alberta, Canada, we've been aware of the name David Thompson for decades, but it wasn't until we ran across a mention of him down in Montana that our curiosity was piqued. What was the man who mapped Canada doing in the United States?

We read everything we could find on Thompson's explorations, and a few months later, knew why he was in Montana, when he was there, and something about the route he took to get there. On long drives, we amused ourselves by pointing out places where David Thompson had passed by. We wanted to trace him in more detail but failed to find a book connecting his trail to the roads we travel today.

On the Road is our attempt to make that connection. We've written it for travellers who tour the northwest by car, motorhome, bicycle, or even on foot, in the hope that they might enjoy the company of a man who walked, rode, and canoed the same routes two centuries ago. For the benefit of armchair travellers, we've included descriptions of the passing scene—both in Thompson's words and our own.

A Word about Conventions

Like other authors who deal with distances, we had to decide how to handle the miles/kilometres problem. Using one and bracketing the other we considered too distracting, and since Thompson's story is an international one, using kilometres in one country and miles in the other seemed too confusing.

In the end we opted for miles: first, and most important, because Thompson used miles; second, because American drivers favour miles; and third, because most Canadians are familiar with both systems, and we all have a handy "calculator" on our speedometers to convert from one to the other. For similar reasons, we've adopted imperial measure throughout.

On the other hand, we've used Canadian spellings (colour rather than color, for example), again, primarily because Thompson used them. When we quote him, we write the proper names of places as he wrote them (Kootanae, for example), but in the text, we use the modern spelling (Kootenay River in Canada; Kootenai in the United States). In the case of Thompson's names for Native peoples, we use his spelling if we quote him (Peegan, for one), but in the text, we use the Canadian spelling (Peigan).

In an effort to preserve the early nineteenth-century flavour of the North American frontier, we've included passages on the historical context, left the French terms used by the fur trade intact, and quoted freely from Thompson's journals.

A Bit of Background

Thompson's journals represent a detailed daily log spanning twenty-three years of work in the wilderness. Though most of this prodigious output has survived to this day, only selected journals have been edited and published. In 1950 a thesis by M. Catherine White covered Thompson's travels in the vicinity of the state of Montana; in 1994 a book by Barbara Belyea dealt with his journeys throughout western Canada and the northwestern United States.

Fifty years after he retired from the fur trade, Thompson wrote another work called the *Narrative*, which was later edited by Canadian geographer J. B. Tyrrell. Tyrrell's edition was published in 1916, long before the field journals started to appear in print. As a result, the *Narrative* was for many years the main source of information on Thompson's explorations.

In a way, this development was unfortunate. Thompson intended the *Narrative* as a popular work, and though it contains some of his finest ethnographic descriptions and a brilliant essay on the behaviour of rattlesnakes, it also tends to be more nostalgic, more dramatic, and more evasive than his journals. In other words, the *Narrative* sometimes takes a few liberties with the truth, a common enough practice in memoirs, but one that almost cost Thompson his reputation as an explorer.

Although we've used the *Narrative* for background, we've tried not to take it too literally. Unless otherwise noted, all Thompson's quotes have been taken from either the Belyea or White editions of the journals he wrote in the field.

A Word to the Wise

Much of the country Thompson travelled is still wilderness, and its back roads can be hazardous. Cougars and bears, moose and elk remain relatively abundant in the northwest and often threaten the safety of unwary photographers, hikers, and campers.

Some roads are so remote they shouldn't be driven without emergency supplies and equipment; in some places, cellular phones won't work. During the winter, even Canada's national park highways can be deceiving—easily accessible and beautifully paved, but lacking services of any kind for hundreds of miles.

The maps provided in the text are intended as a general guide to the routes Thompson followed but are best suppplemented by a larger-scale road-map. We've found the official maps produced by states and provinces both accurate and informative. They're usually given away or sold at tourist information centres. Even more detail is necessary whenever you venture off the beaten track. Forestry and county maps are ideal and are available in most areas at little or no cost.

And Finally
May you enjoy going on the road with David Thompson as much as we have.

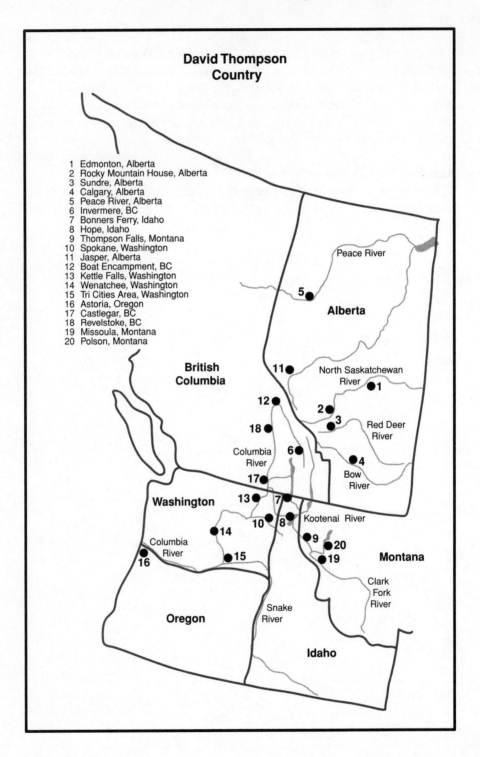

David Thompson Country

1 Edmonton, Alberta
2 Rocky Mountain House, Alberta
3 Sundre, Alberta
4 Calgary, Alberta
5 Peace River, Alberta
6 Invermere, BC
7 Bonners Ferry, Idaho
8 Hope, Idaho
9 Thompson Falls, Montana
10 Spokane, Washington
11 Jasper, Alberta
12 Boat Encampment, BC
13 Kettle Falls, Washington
14 Wenatchee, Washington
15 Tri Cities Area, Washington
16 Astoria, Oregon
17 Castlegar, BC
18 Revelstoke, BC
19 Missoula, Montana
20 Polson, Montana

Peace River

Alberta

British
Columbia

North Saskatchewan
River

Red Deer
River

Columbia
River

Bow
River

Washington

Kootenai River

Columbia
River

Montana

Clark
Fork
River

Oregon

Snake
River

Idaho

Prologue

David Flint Thompson was born in London, England, on April 30, 1770, the first-born child of David and Ann Thompson, a Welsh couple. In 1772, one month after young David's brother was born, his father died, leaving his mother to raise two infant sons on her own. As a result, the brothers were raised in poverty and David, at least, was educated by charity. While they were still in their early teens, both boys left England to work in the North American fur trade. John Thompson ended up as a sea captain, David Thompson as one of the great land geographers of his time.

When he was seven years old, David Thompson was accepted into the Grey Coat School at Westminster, London, a charitable institution that catered to the children of the poor. There, he acquired a Christian background and what we now call a technical education—a heavy concentration of mathematics and geography, coupled with studies of the ocean tides and marine navigation.

The late eighteenth century was a time of significant change in British education. Samuel Johnson had published the dictionary that would standardize English spelling, and the modern cast of Thompson's own spelling shows its influence. During the same period, John Harrison developed the chronometer, a seagoing watch that was about to revolutionize the field of celestial navigation. Thompson's schooling showed no sign of this latter development, however. Many of the textbooks he studied were even then a hundred years old.

In 1784 the Hudson's Bay Company canvassed the Grey Coat School for four boys of a mathematical bent to work in the North American fur trade. Only two boys qualified. One ran away; the other was David Thompson. He was barely fourteen when he was apprenticed to the Hudson's Bay Company for seven years, a privilege that cost his school five British pounds.

Thompson sailed on the *Prince Rupert* in May of 1784 and reached Fort Churchill on Hudson Bay in September of that year. After a frigid winter at Churchill, he walked 150 miles to take up a post at York Factory; the year after that, the Bay sent him west to winter with the Peigans on the Canadian Prairies. After two more years of trading furs at remote posts, he was transferred to Cumberland House on the Saskatchewan River, nursing a broken leg that had refused to set.

It was a lucky break for Thompson. He was able to spend that winter studying celestial navigation under Philip Turnor, the Bay's head surveyor, and he made the most of the opportunity. He devoted his nights to studying the stars, and his days to working out the position of Cumberland House, and he started keeping the journal that would form the basis of his cartography. He was nineteen years old at the time.

After thirteen years of service, Thompson tired of the Bay's indifference to his ambitions as a geographer. When he was twenty-seven, he quit amid acrimony on both sides, hiked seventy-five miles to the nearest North West Company post, and signed on with the competition.

Thompson's new employer had a very different history and corporate culture from his old one. The Hudson's Bay Company had been founded in 1670 as a joint-stock company (that is, its owners were shareholders). Its charter gave it exclusive trading rights to all the land drained by rivers flowing into Hudson Bay, an area called Rupert's Land. The company was headquartered in London and directed by an elected governor who made the policy decisions that guided operations in North America. The company's field representatives were salaried employees and had no share in the firm's profits.

The Hudson's Bay's early strategy was to establish forts near the mouths of rivers entering Hudson Bay and wait for the Natives to bring their furs to the trading posts. The largest of these establishments was at York Factory near the mouth of the Hayes and Nelson Rivers. Each year sailing ships from England delivered European goods to the forts and returned to England loaded with furs. This strategy was in place for over one hundred years.

The North West Company, in contrast, was owned and controlled by its partners, all of whom lived and worked in Canada. The name was first used by a group of Montreal fur traders who formed a partnership in 1776. The company, which throughout its history was dominated by Highland Scots, underwent a series of transformations and reorganizations but remained a partnership until it was eventually absorbed by the Hudson's Bay Company.

The Nor'Westers' approach to the fur trade was based on an earlier one developed by French fur traders from New France. Rather than waiting for the Indians to come to them, the North West traders pushed inland to where their customers lived. There they established local trading posts, intercepting many of the furs that would otherwise have gone to the Hudson's Bay Company. By the mid-1790s, the Nor'Westers controlled over two-thirds of the Canadian fur trade, much of it originating in areas within Rupert's Land, the rest in the fur-rich Athabasca country (part of the Mackenzie River drainage, and therefore outside the Bay's chartered territory).

The North West Company's approach involved much more elaborate logistics and much greater distances than the Bay's system. At ice break-up each spring, a brigade of large birchbark canoes loaded with trade goods would embark at Lachine (just outside Montreal, Quebec), bound for the western end of Lake Superior (Grande Portage in the early years, Fort William later). From there, goods were transferred to smaller canoes and distributed throughout the company's network of trading posts. In the west, the direction of the canoes was reversed as furs, pressed into ninety-pound packs, were transported to Montreal for export to Europe. The canoes were manned by French-speaking *voyageurs* and French was the working language of the company's traders.

The Hudson's Bay Company was soon aware of the incursions of the Nor'Westers and began to counter them. It started building forts of its own on rivers flowing from the west, the first at Cumberland House on the Saskatchewan River in 1774. By the 1790s, the Bay had developed brigades of wooden boats, most of them York boats powered by oars and sail, to compete with the Nor'Westers' canoes. By that time, both companies had an extensive, and largely overlapping, distribution of trading posts, often located side by side.

During this period, the younger company was the more aggressive and dynamic of the two. Its partners encouraged extensive exploration of new territory, sending Alexander Mackenzie down the Mackenzie River to the Arctic Ocean, Mackenzie again via a series of rivers to the Pacific Coast, Simon Fraser down the Fraser River, and David Thompson down the Columbia. These explorations were not government-sponsored, but financed by the North West partners in hopes of future gain.

Thompson's defection to the North West Company took place during these years of intense competition, and we can imagine that he was looked on as a traitor by some of the Bay men. It seems almost certain, however, that if he hadn't left his old employer, he would never have attained what he did. Instead of being recognized as one of the foremost explorers and geographers of western North America, he might be nothing more than a footnote to history, the factor of some forgotten fort.

Thompson's first job as a Nor'Wester was to survey the forty-ninth parallel from the Great Lakes to North Dakota, a project that took him ten months of travel by horse, dogsled, and canoe to complete and marked the beginning of his career as a surveyor. But once the survey ended, so did his new role. In 1798 the North West Company sent him north to the Athabasca to work as a clerk in the fur trade.

Thompson's education hadn't ended with his studies under Philip Turnor. What he couldn't learn from the Natives, he taught himself. His natural curiosity, his passion for accuracy, and his addiction to measuring everything in his path produced a master geographer. During his years in the wilderness, he packed a collection of books wherever he went, and not all of them had to do with astronomy. He identified waterfowl, fish, and wildlife; described trees, shrubs, and groundcovers; and speculated often and accurately on the geology, hydrology, and early ethnography of the inland northwest.

No portrait remains to show us what David Thompson looked like, though his habits indicate he was clean-shaven. In later years, J. J. Bigsby (author of *The Shoe and The Canoe*) noted that Thompson spoke with a trace of a Welsh accent, and went on to sketch a striking verbal picture of his colleague.

> He was plainly dressed, quiet and observant. His figure was short and compact, and his black hair was worn long all around, and cut square, as if by one stroke of the shears, just above the eyebrows. His complexion was of the gardener's ruddy brown, while the expression of deeply furrowed features was friendly and intelligent, but his cut-short nose gave him an odd look ...

> Never mind his Bunyan-like face and cropped hair; he has a very powerful mind, and a singular clarity for picture-making. He can create a wilderness and people it with warring savages, so clearly and palpably, that only shut your eyes and you hear the crack of the rifle, or feel the snow-flakes on your cheeks as he talks.[1]

The present story opens in 1800, the year David Thompson arrived at the North West Company's Rocky Mountain House in central Alberta. He was thirty years of age, recently married, and about to embark on an ambitious project to survey the entire length of the Columbia River. The undertaking occupied the next twelve years of his life.

The Red Deer River–1800[1]

In the year 1799, the North West Company ordered
the construction of a fur trade post called Rocky Mountain
House. The newest and most westerly of the company's
string of prairie forts, Rocky Mountain House went up
on the grass-covered flats above a bend in the North
Saskatchewan River. "Our establishment at this place,"
Nor'Wester Alexander Henry later wrote, "stands on
a high Bank on the North Side of the River; the
situation is well adapted for defense."[2]

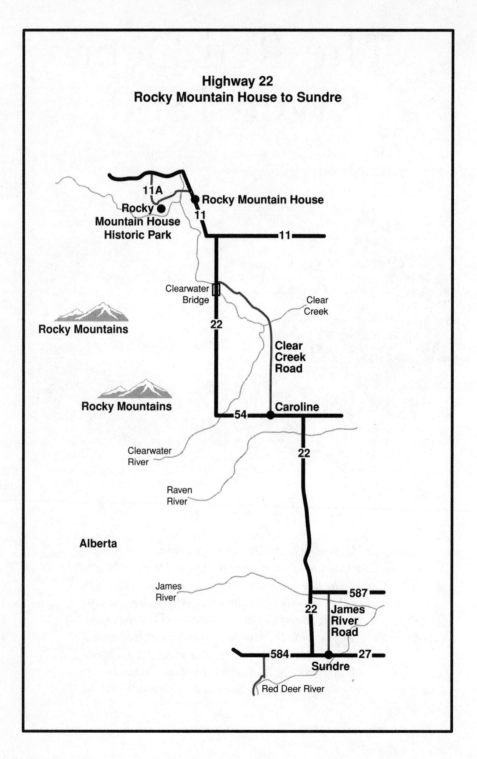

Highway 22
Rocky Mountain House to Sundre

ROCKY MOUNTAIN HOUSE WAS BUILT BY A MAN NAMED JOHN MCDONALD, one of the North West Company's youngest partners and one of three "John McDonalds" in its ranks. To distinguish one from the other, each man's origin was appended to his name, so this particular Nor'Wester was known as John McDonald of Garth. Though McDonald had a withered arm—the *voyageurs* called him *Le Bras Croche*—and was said to be a small man, he was noted for his feisty nature. He'd once astonished the Hudson's Bay Company's William Tomison by informing him that if he didn't share the available water with the Nor'Westers, one of them would pay a visit to the bottom of the well.

The name "Rocky Mountain House" reflected the high hopes of the North West Company and not, as might be expected, a fort with a mountain setting. The new post stood at the edge of the boreal forest, nearly one hundred miles from the main ranges of the Rockies. Although the Hudson's Bay Company immediately built Acton House at the same location, when the last post was abandoned in 1875, it closed under the name Rocky Mountain House. The buildings inevitably fell into ruins, but early settlers carried the old name into the new century. In 1926, when the remains of the trading posts were declared to be of national importance, the preserved site inherited the name of the original North West fort.

Today the Rocky Mountain House National Historic Park occupies the "high Bank on the North Side of the River." The park is located on Old Highway 11A, a four-mile drive west of the town of Rocky Mountain House, Alberta. Of the original forts, only two stone fireplaces and an archaeological excavation remain, but an interpretive centre on the site houses a comprehensive collection of artifacts, replicas, and reconstructions of the early Canadian fur trade. The park protects five hundred acres of historic landscape and is managed by Parks Canada.

In 1799 two Indian nations took a keen interest in the construction of Rocky Mountain House—the Kootenay and the Peigan. Although the Peigans were soon treating the post as their own, it was originally intended to attract the trade of the Kootenays who lived on the western side of the Rocky Mountains. That trade never did materialize, however, primarily because the Peigans so terrorized the Kootenays that they were reluctant to venture into Peigan country with their furs.

The Peigan people were part of the powerful Blackfoot Confederacy that dominated the eastern slopes of the Rockies from the Missouri River to the North Saskatchewan. Only a few years before, they'd used their superior firepower to drive the last of the Kootenays from the Prairies, and they were naturally opposed to the North West Company's

efforts to draw them back. The Peigans had two reasons for their thinking: first, they operated as middlemen between the traders and the tribes
west of the Rockies, a profitable business they had no intention of giving up; second, they knew that sooner or later, the traders would put
guns in the hands of the Kootenays. The year Rocky Mountain House
was built, the relationship between the two nations was ambivalent—
peaceful so long as the Kootenays remembered their place, close to war
when they edged onto Peigan turf.

Before Rocky Mountain House was a year old, the North West partners realized that the Kootenays were unwilling to risk their lives
travelling to the company's new fort. Rather than lose a potentially
lucrative source of furs, the Nor'Westers adopted the same strategy
they'd used to build an empire: if the customers wouldn't come to them,
they'd take the trade to the customers. By the fall of 1800, Rocky
Mountain House was playing a new role in the North West Company—
it was the jumping-off point for the first attempt to carry the fur trade
west of the Rocky Mountains.

David Thompson and his young wife, Charlotte, arrived at Rocky
Mountain House in September 1800, a little over a year after they were
married. Thompson was only thirty at the time, but he'd already logged
sixteen years in the fur trade, thirteen with the Hudson's Bay Company
and three with the North West Company. He'd traded furs across
Canada's northlands from Hudson Bay to the Athabasca Territory, used
his knowledge of the stars to chart the rivers he travelled, and, ever since
he'd turned nineteen, maintained a detailed journal. When he joined the
North West Company, his first job was to establish the position of the
company's eastern posts relative to the forty-ninth parallel, an ambitious survey that took him ten months and four thousand miles of travel
by dogsled, horse, and canoe to complete. Nevertheless, when he arrived
at Rocky Mountain House, it was in the humble capacity of company
clerk, a job for which he was arguably overqualified.

Thompson met Charlotte Small when the North West Company
sent him north to work in the Athabasca Division. The two were married in a Cree ceremony at *Île à la Crosse*, a trading post on the
Churchill River in northern Saskatchewan. Thompson was twenty-nine,
and Charlotte not quite fourteen—young by today's standards, but not
unusually so for a daughter of the fur trade. The day he married
Charlotte, Thompson's journal carried only the terse note, "This day
married Charlotte Small," though one draft of his *Narrative* added, "My
lovely wife is of the blood of these people, speaking their language and
well educated in the English language, which gives me a great advan-

tage." Thompson, so one story goes, spent his wedding night fixing the position of *Île à la Crosse* by making eight observations of the transit of Venus. Since Venus is the goddess of love, somebody decided to have a bit of fun at Thompson's expense. The transit occurs when Venus crosses the sun, one celestial event that's guaranteed to occur in the daytime.

Since the official clergy had yet to venture into the northwest, Charlotte's status as a married woman was that of a "country wife." Some traders (Charlotte's father among them) left their country wives behind when they retired from the northwest, leading an anonymous writer to brand such marriages "little better than concubinage." This view, however, tends to undervalue these unions, most of which were beneficial to both parties and some of which lasted a lifetime. The *voyageurs* often settled in the west with their wives and children, and some traders demanded that their marriages be recognized as legitimate and remembered their families in their wills. Still others took their wives and children back to eastern Canada and formalized their marriages there.

Not that all was sweetness and light in the forts of the North West Company. Wives unfortunate enough to be left behind were often "turned off," as the saying went, that is, given or sold to another man. Native women were sometimes obliged to return to their own people. Despite the possibility she might be abandoned as her mother had, Charlotte Small married into the fur trade.

When she was young, Charlotte regularly accompanied her husband on his travels, but it wasn't Thompson who said so. His brief note about their marriage represents one of the few occasions he ever mentioned his wife in his journals. During the years he worked in the fur trade, Thompson wrote reams of material—his journals represent a detailed accounting of twenty-three years in the wilderness—but his personal life is missing.

Because Thompson had been with the North West Company only three years, his associates at Rocky Mountain House all outranked him—John McDonald of Garth, who built the post; James Hughes, who took charge of the trade there; and Duncan McGillivray, who was planning to lead the company's expedition across the Rocky Mountains. All three were younger than Thompson and all three were more or less connected to him through his marriage to Charlotte. Charlotte's brother Patrick married James Hughes's daughter, her sister Nancy married John McDonald of Garth (himself a relative of the Smalls), and Nancy's sister-in-law, Magdelaine McDonald, married Duncan McGillivray's brother.

Thompson was to serve as McGillivray's second on the journey across the mountains, and the two men had planned to meet at Rocky Mountain House the third week in September. By early October, McGillivray was two weeks overdue, and Thompson was growing restless. When word came that the Kootenays were making their way across the mountains, he leaped at the chance to meet them. On the morning of October 5, 1800, he left Rocky Mountain House accompanied by six *voyageurs* and a Peigan guide.

> At 8 Am the Men crossed the River, La Gassé, Beauchamp, Morrin, Pierre Daniel, Boulard & myself, with the He Dog, a Cree, and the Old Bear, a Pekenow Indian, our Guide. We had an assortment of Goods, amounting to about 300 Skins, & each of us a light Horse, belonging to himself, and 3 Horses of the Company's to carry the Baggage.

Depending on what he was writing about, Thompson's style changed radically. His business writing was cryptic. Although the account of his departure from Rocky Mountain House would have made sense to a trader, an outsider might wonder which river the men crossed that morning (the North Saskatchewan); why He Dog had joined them (he'd probably been hired as a hunter); what went into the loads of "goods" (usually an assortment of British tools, textiles, trinkets, and tobacco); and what the reference to "skins" meant (the value of the goods expressed in beaver pelts).

At other times, Thompson seemed aware of a wider audience. His descriptive passages are graphic in their detail, and often provide the only clue to where he was and what he was looking at. He devoted space to describing the landscapes he rode through, the Indian bands he visited, the animals he encountered (or shot for meat), and the trees that lined his trail. He had a different term for the size of every stream he saw. A "river" meant a river navigable by canoe; a "rivulet" was navigable at high water; a "bold brook" was a sizeable stream or sometimes a swiftly flowing one; a "brook" was a small stream; a "rill" was a trickle that might be intermittent; and a "raveline" was a dry channel.

His surveys, in contrast, assumed an audience of one—himself. Thompson peppered his text with dates, times, distances, temperatures, compass headings, and intricate strings of geographical coordinates. These numbers convey masses of information, but occasionally they're misleading. In some entries, he effectively doubled his distance by including a point-to-point breakdown of his mileage as well as (without warning) his total mileage for the day. In other entries, he recorded only part of his mileage or no mileage at all. The result is a writer who usually knew where he was, but a reader who often doesn't.

His direction of travel is even more troublesome. As a rule, he looked ahead to record his direction, but sometimes he looked back. That is, he might write "northwest" (or something like N15W), though he was actually travelling southeast (or S15E). This habit often baffles his readers, but it's unlikely that was Thompson's intent. He recorded his direction for mapmaking, and a line on a map would run exactly the same way no matter which way he drew it.

From the day the expedition set off to search for the Kootenays, it was apparent Thompson was operating in Peigan territory. On the first day out, he met a party of Peigans coming in to Rocky Mountain House to trade. On the morning of the second day, he stopped for a brief smoke with a band of Peigans camped near the James River, and that evening, he put up with five tents of Peigans on the plains west of Sundre. On the days he went hunting, his partner was as often as not a Peigan, and, for the duration of the trip, his guide was the Peigan Chief, Old Bear. Although all the Peigans he came across seemed amiable enough, it wasn't long before they let Thompson know they disapproved of the reason for his journey.

> They are so jealous of the Kootanaes coming in to Trade, that they
> do all they can to persuade me to return, assuring me that it is
> impossible for me to find them, and that in endeavouring to search
> them out, our Horses will fall by Fatigue and Hunger, and perhaps
> also ourselves.

To find the Kootenay Indians, Thompson followed his guide from Rocky Mountain House to the interior of what is now Banff National Park—a distance of more than 120 miles. Today, Alberta Highway 22 dogs Thompson's trail southward for fifty-four miles, a mountain road then follows him westward for just over forty miles, and remote trails pursue his course over the last thirty miles into the park.

Between Rocky Mountain House and the town of Sundre, Highway 22 runs through the same country and crosses the same rivers as Thompson did, though it seldom follows the same course. Most of the highway has been cobbled together from existing roads, and every time it runs out of one piece of road, it takes a jog to follow another one. Over its entire length, however, Highway 22 consistently runs south and jogs east, and since Thompson was angling southeast, the road often intersects his route.

Highway 22's eccentric course takes it through an ever-changing scene. South of Rocky Mountain House, it skims the edge of the boreal forest, then runs through a countryside of mixed woods and farmland. Farther south, it crosses the open landscape of the parkland, winds through a broad band of wetland, and approaches Sundre through a corridor of thick woods. On the way, the highway passes a series of Thompson's landmarks, several of which have the same name now as they had then.

Thompson's Name	Modern Name
Rocky Mountain House	Rocky Mountain House National Historic Park
North Saskatchewan River	North Saskatchewan River
Clear Water River	Clearwater River
Brook Bridge	Clear Creek
A Bold Brook	Raven River
A Rivulet	James River
Red Deers River	Red Deer River
Another Bold Brook	Bearberry River
The Plain of the Grand View	Sundre, Alberta

Thompson and his men forded the North Saskatchewan River, then rode on for a few more miles before crossing the Clearwater River.

> After crossing that stream, we went on about SE 1/2 M to the parting of the Roads, where finding we had forgot to take a Kettle with us, I sent La Gassé back again to the House for one. Mean Time we went on to the Bridge, which is a few Sticks laid across a Brook—our Co[s] [courses] during this time thro' mostly thick Woods of Pine and Aspin may have been SEbS 1 1/2 M ... then SbW 10 1/2 M to the Brook Bridge: here we put up to wait La Gassé, who came in the Evening with 2 Kettles.

A forgotten kettle was a serious matter. No kettle meant no tea, no supper, and no peace in the ranks. When Thompson called a halt for the day, the expedition was less than fifteen miles from the fort. After crossing the Clearwater, he'd followed the course of the river southeast. Initially, he was on the west side of Highway 22, but by the time the highway approaches the Clearwater Bridge, he was on the east side and moving steadily away. (The "SbW" in this entry is a slip of the pen—south by west would have taken him back across the Clearwater again.) His camp by the Brook Bridge was at the easternmost bend of the Clearwater, four miles from Highway 22, on the banks of a stream known as Clear Creek.

Today the owner of the pasture where Clear Creek flows is Del Northcott, a rancher and well-known breeder of rodeo bulls. He told us that Alberta Fish and Game had done some work on Clear Creek, fencing his cattle away from the stream and restoring the banks to their natural state. In the process, the work party had removed the remains of a primitive bridge from the streambank, an indication that Thompson wasn't the only traveller who needed a bridge to cross Clear Creek. Even today, a massive concrete structure connects the Northcott corrals on one side of the stream with the pastures on the other.

Northcott called Thompson's visit "a new one on me," but he did know the reason for Clear Creek's history of bridges. That reason was mud. A thick coating of slippery blue clay lies four feet deep over the stream's gravel substrates, and its lazy flow leaves the mud undisturbed, the water clear, and the bottom of the stream deadly. Northcott himself had once lost a horse in the treacherous depths of Clear Creek.

Even though Thompson didn't think much of the Brook Bridge, he deliberately chose to cross it. A few miles farther east, another trail skirted the headwaters of the stream and avoided the bridge altogether. Thompson knew this but evidently preferred an argument with the horses to riding miles out of his way. At six in the morning, he and his men tackled the bridge. The horses balked at setting foot on the thing "which we found very bad," and his cursing men wasted half an hour muscling the animals across it. With the bridge safely behind them, the riders left the course of the Clearwater and continued their ride southeast.

Brook Bridge

~ If you leave Highway 22 and take a fourteen-mile detour along a country road, you can visit the site of Thompson's Brook Bridge.

~ Immediately north of the highway's Clearwater Bridge, the road sets off east along Thompson's trail. Farm fields line the road, and the Clearwater River is hidden behind a screen of trees. There are no guide posts to show the way.

~ The only landmark is a stop sign, about three miles east of the

---

> highway. Here, you turn right, and three miles down the road, at the point where gravel gives way to blacktop, Thompson's brook runs through a culvert under the road.
> ∾ Resist the temptation to visit the cattle—these are the cows that produce Mr. Northcott's rodeo bulls.
> ∾ The blacktop carries on for six miles before joining Highway 54 at the four-way stop in downtown Caroline.

We went on thro' a willow Plain about SE 4M, then we entered the Woods, then Co SE 4M south 3M very bad swampy Ground thick Woods of Pines. Co SbE 2M small Plains, saw Herd of [buffalo] Cows—end of Co stopped an Hour at 10 to a bold Brook—Co along it mostly SEbE 1M when we crossed it.

The "willow Plain" bordered the North Raven River, sometimes called Stauffer Creek, a stream known today for its brown trout fishing. As Thompson and his men rode south, they were east of Highway 22 and angling away from it, but when Highway 22 meets its T-junction with Highway 54, it makes an eight-mile leap to the east to close in on Thompson's route again. A few miles east of Caroline, Thompson crossed Highway 54. The "bold Brook" that he crossed a mile or two later is called the Raven River.

Raven Country is parkland, and here Highway 22 runs through a panorama of rolling fields and clusters of trees; the Rocky Mountains, much closer now, rise in the background. The view gives a sense of just how extended Thompson's ride to the mountains was, and calls up images of horses and riders trotting across the grassland, winding among the trees along the river, then disappearing over the ridge that lines the Raven River Valley.

Co SE 6M to a Plain in which we went ab' So 3M, at end of Co a Rill of Water—crossed it. Co SbE 4M when we came to 5 Tents of Pekenow Indians, with whom we staid to smoke about 1/4 H. We then went on SbE 1 1/4 M and crossed a Rivulet, which a small Distance below us falls into the Red Deers River.

Thompson didn't go into any detail about the first six miles of this ride, probably because the tortuous trail defeated even his powers of record-keeping. The country south of the Raven is a maze of sandhills,

swamps, pothole lakes, small ponds, and close-growing stands of tamarack and bog spruce. Even Highway 22, which tends to be straight, starts
to wind as it enters this six-mile band of wetland. No doubt the riders
were winding as well—avoiding the swamps and potholes, searching out
higher ground and solid footing for the horses. The "Rivulet" at the end
of this trail was the James River, and the "Rill of Water," a small tributary that still wanders there today.

When Highway 22 meets its junction with Highway 587, it continues south toward Sundre's western limits. But the original Highway 22
jumped a mile east along Highway 587, headed south down the James
River Road, and ended in Sundre's downtown. Just east of the James
River Store, Thompson's "Rill" trickles under Highway 587. When he
stopped to smoke with the Peigans, he was probably in one of the fields
to the east of the store and slightly north of Highway 587.

From the Peigan camp, Thompson and his men rode south, crossed
the James River, then cut southwest to follow the Red Deer River.

> Co SSW 2M to the Red Deers River, which we also crossed. We
> then went on up along the River, mostly on the Gravel Banks, which
> formerly in high Water were part of the Bed of the River. SWbS 2M
> SW 2M in these Co' several [times] crossed & recrossed the small
> Channels of the River, as they came in our Way, and at the end of
> Co recrossed the River altogether.

Once Thompson crossed the river for the last time, he followed it
upstream through a "tolerable fine Plain," until he came to the confluence of the Red Deer and Bearberry Rivers. Struck by the view of the
mountains, Thompson christened the future townsite of Sundre "The
Plain of the Grand View."

> Here we had a grand view of the Rocky Mountains, forming a con-
> cave segment of a Circle, and lying from one Point to another about
> SbE & NbW. All it's snowy cliffs to the Southward were bright with
> the Beams of the Sun, while the most northern were darkened by a
> Tempest ... which spent it's Force only on the Summits.

After Highway 22 crosses the James River Bridge, it parallels
Thompson's approach to Sundre, running over its final mile down a long
hill that overlooks the town. To the east, hidden behind a ribbon of trees,
is the Red Deer River; to the west, the Rocky Mountains. Halfway down

the hill, the mountains are suddenly close, revealing the vista that Thompson described when he reached "The Plain of the Grand View."

Today, the plain has been settled by a motley collection of ranches and acreages, gravel pits and lumber yards—only the view of the Rocky Mountains is unchanged. At Sundre, Thompson noted that the Red Deer Valley was five hundred yards across, and that the river's main channel occupied only a tenth of it. He paused to wonder why. His speculations (probably written the next day when he was snowbound) developed into a lengthy disquisition on climate change and ended with a description of the consequences.

> Whatever Opinion we may form, the Fact is certain, that at present
> and for several Years past the Mountains do not send forth above
> two thirds of the Water they did formerly, for we see upon the
> Banks of all the Rivers large Trees that have been carried down by
> the Stream and left ... far above the greatest known Level of the
> present Times. These Trees are not only to be found singly, but in
> vast Numbers, piled so intricately together that it is next to impossi-
> ble to disentangle them.

During the emergency of the forgotten kettle, Thompson had toler-ated a mere fifteen miles of progress, but on the second day, his drive to cover ground reasserted itself. Instead of the usual march of twenty-three miles, he pushed on for a punishing forty (neatly maintaining his average). That evening, the weary men rode the last six miles across the plain west of Sundre and camped with a band of Peigans at the foot of a "high woody Hill." That hill marked the beginning of a trail to the head-waters of the Red Deer River.

During the night it rained heavily, and by morning it was snowing. Snow fell the rest of the day, and by evening lay a foot deep over the Peigan campsite. Since Thompson didn't record any mileage, he proba-bly stayed where he was. This was routine. He rarely broke camp when the weather was bad. The next day was October 8, and again, Thompson didn't record any travel. His journal says only that he went hunting, that he and his Peigan companion killed two deer, and that the nature of the river had changed. Although he reported bringing the deer meat back to the tents, he said nothing about his men moving the camp west. Over the next two days, he repeated the same pattern: one day a note about waiting for Chief Old Bear, the next day an account of killing a buffalo bull and bringing two horseloads of meat into camp. But, again, no record of travel. Since Thompson didn't record any distances for four days, it's natural to assume he was still camped by the "high woody Hill" west of Sundre.

On October 11 Thompson started keeping track of his mileage again—six miles that day, and eight and a half miles the next—ostensibly a move to the west of fourteen and a half miles. The following day, he climbed "a very high knowl" and described the landscape around him.

I had a very extensive View of the Country: from the southward extending by the westward to the North, it was every where Ranges of woody Hills lying nearly parallel to the Mountain, and rising one behind another higher and higher to the snowy Summits of the Mountain.

This is the view from Ya Ha Tinda Ranch, an outlying expanse of prairie perched in the lap of the Rocky Mountains. Today Parks Canada winters its horses on this pocket of grassland, and hunters haul their stock trailers up there to hunt on horseback.

In her notes, Barbara Belyea, who edited Thompson's Columbia journals, used the fourteen and a half miles that Thompson recorded to fix his position at a landform called Parker Ridge.[3] Thompson's "extensive view," however, doesn't fit the country around Parker Ridge, and from his position down on the riverside, he couldn't possibly have seen the "snowy Summits of the Mountain." Still, his description of the view from Ya Ha Tinda is unmistakable, even though the ranch isn't fourteen and a half miles west of the "high woody Hill." It's well over forty. Evidently Thompson covered more miles than he recorded, but there's a reason for the gaps in his record. They occurred on the days he was hunting. Since chasing deer through the bush was irrelevant to the business of mapmaking, he didn't bother to keep track of his mileage.

On the first day he was hunting, Thompson described the Red Deer River as running in a single channel, about forty yards wide, "and very strong current with Banks of Rock." Along the Coal Camp Road, between Cartier Creek and Deer Creek, a reach of the Red Deer matches Thompson's description. The rocky sills and a narrower, more turbulent river indicate that he'd already moved ten or twelve miles west. And it's a safe bet that his men had moved the camp as well.

Even at the relatively slow rate of ten to twelve miles a day, Thompson would have reached the Ya Ha Tinda Ranch by October 12, and an incident noted in his journal suggests that he did. On that date, he reported that two tents of Peigan Indians had killed eight eagles in a single day. The chances of a small group of men capturing eight eagles in such a short period of time seem pretty slim—either the Peigans had an uncanny ability to bring down this solitary bird, or there must have been a phenomenal number of eagles around.

We had once listened to a CBC Radio interview with a naturalist who described the massive migration of golden eagles that occurs along the eastern slopes of the Rocky Mountains. Recalling the program, we wondered whether the Peigans might have been hunting during a migration. The readiest source of information proved to be the Internet, where interested groups contribute information on the flight of the golden eagles, including timing, numbers, and the events associated with the migration.

Eagles on the 'Net

~ Each year, the town of Canmore, Alberta, holds an Eagle Festival during the third week of October.

~ Spring and fall, an Eagle Watch is held on Mount Lorette in Kananaskis Provincial Park.

~ The count during the spring of 1996 was 3,664 golden eagles, and some years approaches 5,000.

~ The fall migration lasts for about six weeks, from late September to early November.

In 1977 a more recent CBC broadcast gave the eagle count for October 14 (197 years and two days after the Peigan hunt). For that one day, the count was 531 golden eagles.

Although we'd found out that both Kananaskis and Canmore lie on the route of the golden eagles, and that the eagles would have been in mid-migration the day the Peigans were hunting, one question remained: Do the eagles fly over Ya Ha Tinda Ranch? None of the people we asked was quite sure; all of them suggested we get in touch with a man named Peter Sherrington.

Peter Sherrington is the naturalist who was interviewed by the CBC. He's familiar with Thompson's account of the eagle hunt and believes it was the first recorded instance of the flyover. He confirmed that the golden eagles' route would have taken them over Ya Ha Tinda, probably on its western side, and pointed out that the ranch was far richer in meat then than it is now, one explanation of why the eagles might have been attracted to the area. Sherrington seemed to be something of a Thompson fan, considered the man much underrated, and expressed himself sorry for any Welshman who had to work with a crowd of Scots.

Five miles west of Sundre on Highway 584, a country road leads south toward the Red Deer River, then turns to follow it into the front ranges of the Rocky Mountains. This is the Coal Camp Road, which begins as a much-patched strip of blacktop and continues as reasonably smooth gravel. The road winds along the course of the Red Deer, but it doesn't climb high. It comes to an end at its junction with the Forestry Trunk Road, not far from a seasonal hunting lodge called the Mountain Aire.

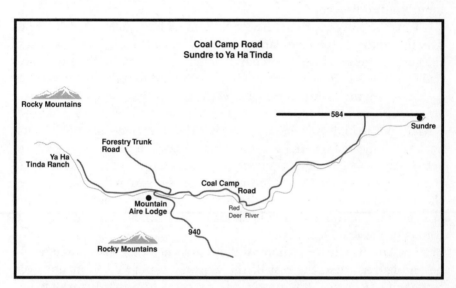

Just north of Mountain Aire Lodge, another gravel road picks up Thompson's trail and tracks it for eighteen miles to the gates of Ya Ha Tinda Ranch. The ranch is open to the public, but not to the public's vehicles. Ya Ha Tinda is an ecological preserve that borders Banff National Park, and explorers who want to follow Thompson into the mountains have to set out on foot or visit a local outfitter and equip themselves with a horse.

On the morning of October 14, 1800, Thompson and his party rode west for another twenty-two miles, and by early afternoon were threading their way among the headwater streams of the Red Deer.

> Our Road to day has been mostly along small Brooks—the Scources of the Red Deer River—which every where intersect the Hills ... crossing & recrossing [the streams] we gained the heights of the Mountain. A very clear, cold Night obliged to tye our Horses as there was little or no Grass for them.

Belyea used Thompson's record of these twenty-two miles to place him at the junction of the Red Deer and Panther Rivers, just west of Mountain Aire Lodge.[4] Thompson's description, however, is clearly that of the headwater streams of the Red Deer, and he also mentioned a line of high cliffs that were "inaccessible to human Feet." There are hills at the Red Deer's junction with the Panther, but none that Thompson would have described as "inaccessible." He was an active man and would have thought nothing of scrambling up the slopes above the mouth of the Panther River.

Travelling twenty-two miles west from Ya Ha Tinda would have put Thompson inside the boundaries of Banff National Park, and it was here that he encountered the Kootenay Indians. At that time, the Kootenays had so many routes over the mountains, it's hard to tell which pass they used to cross the Continental Divide. (A map by Scott and Hanic shows twenty-one mountain passes on the Canadian side alone.[5]) Author Edward Nuffield, however, suggests that the Kootenays used Vermilion Pass,[6] now located on Highway 93. This suggestion makes quite a bit of sense. Highway 93 originates in country where the Kootenays lived and follows the Kootenay River through Kootenay National Park. It passes the Vermilion Paintpots that the Kootenays were known to visit and crosses the Continental Divide about twenty miles south of the headwaters of the Red Deer River.

Early in his journey, Thompson had assumed that their guide would be "no better" than the rest of the Peigans. Chief Old Bear, however, turned out to be on Thompson's side, assuring him that his people had their own reasons for "misrepresenting" the country. Thompson already knew that. He'd wintered with the Peigans as a boy of seventeen and was perfectly aware they'd say anything to discourage trade with "strangers." He'd taken none of their warnings about "fatigue and hunger" seriously.

Despite the young braves' efforts to get Thompson to turn back, the appearance of friendship between them was preserved until the day he met the Kootenays. Not only did he smoke and hunt and camp with the Peigans, he joined them at the feast held in celebration of their eagle hunt.

> In the evening the Indians, having finished their Eagle Hunt and
> having killed 8 this Day, they made a Feast. A clear Place being
> made within the Tent, at the back Part, the Eagles were all laid there
> upon clean Grasses with their Heads towards the Fire—very little
> Ceremony of any kind was used, except in smoking when the Eagles

had, each separately, the pipe presented to it. As the Pipe went round, the People who were seated on each Side of the Tent and of the Eagles, sung & took the Rattle alternately—this lasted about 3 Hours when the Company broke up.

The day after the feast was spent waiting. That evening, two young Peigans returned from a scouting trip, bringing the news that the Kootenays would reach the heights of the mountain the next day. As evidence their sources were reliable, the braves produced a pair of "fine Mares" they'd stolen from the Kootenays. Thompson didn't wait for the Kootenays to find him. Possibly with the idea of sparing them any more harassment, he decided to ride west to meet them. Early in the morning, he saddled his horse and set out with three of his men, Chief Old Bear, and several Peigans "who came with us from Hopes of Plunder." Two men stayed at Ya Ha Tinda to guard the baggage left at the camp.

Thompson had no trouble finding the Kootenays, encountering them that afternoon at the foot of a line of high cliffs. The Kootenay chief had twenty-six men and seven women with him, most of them on foot, as the Kootenays had only eleven horses among them. The chief presented Thompson with a bow and a quiver of arrows, a red fox skin, and a yellow horse.

> We then all sat down & smoked together. I cut a fathom of Tobacco which I had brought with me among them—after having sat about ½ Hour, I proposed going to some Place where we could Camp, which we instantly did, returning back about 1 Mile. These poor Fellows are but poorly clothed notwithstanding the rigour of the Cold in these Mountains; they give me to understand that the Pekenow Indians have stolen most of their Horses.

When Thompson found himself within reach of the western side of the Rockies for the first time, he was eager to climb to the "Height of Land" and have a look, but his attention was soon diverted elsewhere.

> The poor Kootanaes were hardly arrived when one of the Pekenow Scoundrels took a Fancy to a Black Horse belonging to them, & wanted to take him by Force—but the Kootanaes bravely springing upon their Arms, he was obliged to relinquish his Prize but it raised a small Tumult in which our Guide, a Chief & distinguished warrior of the Pekenows, went out & made a Speech suitable to the

Occasion, bidding the young men remember his Example: that
when he wanted Horses, he went & took them from his Enemies
bravely, and that it was an Act neither brave nor manly to rob a few
Strangers, their Allies, of their poor starved Horses.

Neither the Kootenays' bravery nor Old Bear's speech had the slightest effect on the behaviour of the young Peigans. All the way back to Rocky Mountain House, they remained much in evidence, hanging around Thompson's camp, tagging along whenever the party made a move, and amusing themselves by pestering the Kootenays and picking off their horses one by one.

The Peigan Indians were known to be inveterate horse thieves (once stealing 650 horses from Fort Edmonton in a single year), and when the Peigans were around, as Alexander Henry could have told the long-suffering Kootenays, the only time you were sure of your horse was when you were on its back. And sometimes not even then. In a last attempt to shake off the young braves, Thompson gave his men orders to ride on by when the Peigans stopped to put up for the night.

They did so, but no sooner did the Pekenows see them pass, than 3
young Men took hold of the foremost of the Kootanae Horses, to
make them turn round—I rode up & with the assistance of Boulard
made them relinquish the Horses & get out of the Road. This done
I instantly went to where our Guide was about pitching his Tent &
told him to come on if he had any Friendship for us, and wished to
avoid the spilling of Blood.

Understandably fed up, the Kootenays wanted to get out of Peigan territory and head back to their own country, but Thompson "by Entreaties & encouraging Conversation brought them from their Fears & prevailed on them all to come in to the House." In the end, the Kootenays agreed to carry on. That night, the Peigans stole five more of their horses.

The next day Thompson rode in company with the Kootenays, listening with sympathy as they bitterly complained about the thieving Peigans. Although they vowed never to forgive them, and swore to have their revenge, only once did the Kootenays have a chance to get even with their tormenters. That was the evening the Peigans challenged them to a gambling match, and the Kootenays readily agreed to take them on. "They assembled round our Fires," wrote Thompson, "but the

Pekenows were by no means a Match for these Strangers—they lost every Game." It was midnight before the Peigans gave up the match. The next day, they recouped some of their losses by stealing another horse.

By that time, the Kootenays had hardly a horse left, and Thompson was finally forced to act. Taking one man with him, he hurried ahead to Rocky Mountain House. The next morning he headed back with three men and two extra horses. At the Brook Bridge, he rode on alone to meet the Kootenays, finding them a short distance away, staggering along under a burden of the meat of two buffalo cows they'd killed while he was gone. Two horses weren't much help to thirty-four footsore travellers, but at least the extra mounts relieved them of the chore of carrying the meat.

By the time Thompson and the Kootenays reached Rocky Mountain House "with much Trouble and Dispute with the Pekenows, even to drawing of Arms," the visitors had only two horses left. All the rest (including the yellow horse the Kootenay chief had given to Thompson) had been stolen by the Peigans. Thompson delivered his charges to the gates of Rocky Mountain House with a fervent "Thank God." He presented the Kootenays with half a keg of rum, and gave three gallons to Chief Old Bear to share with the three braves he had with him.

The next morning, Thompson paid Old Bear and his men for their services, then spent the afternoon trading the skins of 2 wolverines, 5 fishers, 10 bears, and 110½ beavers with the Kootenays. He listened closely as Boulard translated valuable information about the mountains and rivers and lakes of Kootenay country and decided to outfit Charles La Gassé and Pierre Le Blanc to go with the Kootenays for the winter.

Since the Kootenay chief had no horse, Thompson arranged to lend him one, and as the visitors prepared to set out on their return journey, he reminded them of their promise to come back in the spring and show him the way across the mountains.

The Bow River–1800[1]

On the same day the Kootenays left, North West partner
Duncan McGillivray arrived at Rocky Mountain House, and at
McGillivray's request, Thompson took him on a short trip south.
The two men visited the Peigan camps along the Highwood River,
explored the Bow Valley to the foot of the Rocky Mountains, hunted
along the way for buffalo, deer, and moose, and were back at
Rocky Mountain House in a little over two weeks. The trip
represented one of the few times Thompson was able to
travel light and, of all the journeys he made in his
career, came closest to being a pleasure jaunt.

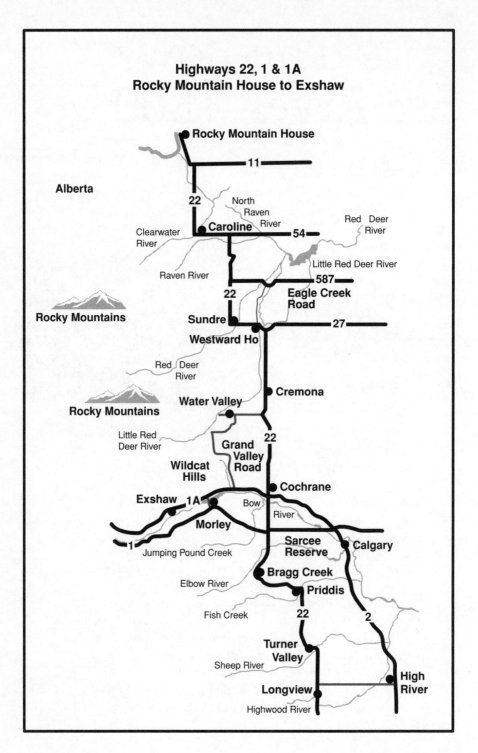

Highways 22, 1 & 1A
Rocky Mountain House to Exshaw

Rocky Mountain House

11

Alberta

22

North Raven River

Caroline

54

Red Deer River

Clearwater River

Little Red Deer River

Raven River

587

22

Eagle Creek Road

Rocky Mountains

Sundre

Westward Ho

27

Red Deer River

Rocky Mountains

Cremona

Water Valley

22

Little Red Deer River

Grand Valley Road

Wildcat Hills

Cochrane

Exshaw 1A

Bow

Morley

River

Sarcee Reserve

Calgary

1

Jumping Pound Creek

Bragg Creek

Elbow River

Priddis

22

2

Fish Creek

Turner Valley

Sheep River

Longview

High River

Highwood River

BY NOON OF OCTOBER 22, 1800, MOST OF THE KOOTENAYS HAD SET OFF ON their return journey; the rest were waiting for La Gassé and Le Blanc, who couldn't find their horses. Toward evening, alarmed by the sudden appearance of a band of mounted Peigans on the far side of the river, Thompson ordered the rest of the Kootenays off, urging them not to stop until they'd caught up to the others. Although the Peigans' intentions turned out to be innocuous (they'd merely come in to trade), in the scramble that followed, La Gassé and Le Blanc, still horseless, were left behind.

It wasn't unusual for the company's horses to be missing. Since they had to be turned loose to scuffle for grass, they often wandered away, and delays caused by their wanderings were routine. Thompson's daily record regularly began with "difficulty finding the horses," and from time to time an entire expedition would go on hold while the men searched for their mounts and rounded them up. By seven o'clock the next morning, La Gassé and Le Blanc had found their horses and ridden off in pursuit of the Kootenays. Thompson, always on the lookout for a route to the Rockies, saddled up and rode part of the way with them.

On his return to Rocky Mountain House ten hours later, he noticed a group of horsemen preparing to cross the river: three Indians, two *voyageurs*, a man he recognized as James Bird of the Hudson's Bay Company, and the North West partner whose arrival he'd been waiting for—Duncan McGillivray.

> ... saw Mr Duncan McGillivray on the other side the River just
> arrived from Fort William a Month later than he intended. Crossed
> to him. He was very anxious to see the Kootanae Indians, but they
> were too far advanced. Mr D. McGillivray remained quiet, when
> from my account of the Country to the Southward he wished to
> see it.

McGillivray's arrival heralded the first step toward a North West expedition across the Rocky Mountains, an expedition he was to lead the following spring. But since there were six months of a prairie winter to get through first, there was plenty of time for Thompson to grant McGillivray's wish.

The two men decided to pay a visit to the Peigans' winter camps along the Highwood River. At the time, the North West Company was considering introducing a group of Iroquois and Ojibwa trappers to Peigan territory. The trappers wanted to leave eastern Canada, where iron axes and steel traps had rendered the beaver commercially extinct and reduced the Indians to poverty. The North West Company would have welcomed their services, primarily because the buffalo-hunting Peigans had little interest in trapping beaver. Or, as John Jackson phrased it, their "equestrian pride precluded dismounting to dig rodents from the cutbanks of prairie rivers."[2] Although the newcomers were unlikely to cause any conflict, no one knew what the Peigans would think of the proposal. McGillivray and Thompson planned to find out.

On November 17, 1800, six men mounted their horses and set out from Rocky Mountain House.

> A cold cloudy Day with light Snow at Times. We could not cross the River for driving ice 'till 11½ Am, when we set off—Mr Duncan McGillivray, Boulard, Charron, Dumond, Baptiste Regnie & myself. At 3½ Pm we came to the Bridge, where we warmed ourselves a few Minutes and then came off with a Pekenow young Man, whom we have engaged to guide us ...

The bridge, of course, was the infamous crossing at Clear Creek, but on this trip, they didn't have to deal with it. Their Peigan guide led them instead across a slight divide to the headwaters of the North Raven River, then along its course to the southeast. Thompson is always harder to follow when he's riding cross country, and his journal isn't sufficiently precise to track him exactly. But his general direction, the streams he crossed, and the lay of the land all suggest that the Peigan trail lay within a series of south-tending valleys, probably those of the Raven River, Eagle Creek, Little Red Deer River, and Grand Valley Creek.

When Thompson and his party started their ride down the North Raven River, they were five miles east of Highway 22, and their course down the stream progressively widened the distance. They rode along the North Raven River to its junction with the Raven River (now the site of a small wooded recreation area on Highway 54), then followed the Raven downstream to its confluence with the Red Deer River. Once they'd crossed the Red Deer, they probably headed up the surprisingly broad valley of a very small tributary known as Eagle Creek.

Eagle Creek Road

~ Today you can drive the road that runs through the Eagle Creek Valley. At the junction of Highways 22 and 587, head east for eight miles. Here the Garrington Bridge crosses the Red Deer River at approximately the same place Thompson did.

~ Just across the bridge, a road on the right sets off to wind south through the valley. The road is hard-surfaced and offers a pretty drive through a pastoral scene of farm fields enclosed by low hills.

~ Eleven miles later, the Eagle Creek Road comes to an end at Highway 27. At this point, Thompson and his riders were five miles east of Sundre, and only one mile west of the next section of Highway 22.

As Eagle Creek neared its headwaters, the riders crossed over into the valley of the Little Red Deer River. Here the countryside suddenly opens up. The prairie rolls away westward to meet the foothills, high lands that mark the end of the grasslands and signal the beginning of the mountains. Beyond the foothills, the Rocky Mountains lift skyward, a line of towering stone peaks that early explorers described as a "wall." With the rolling meadows on their left, and the mountains widely visible on their right, Thompson's party rode to the banks of the Little Red Deer, forded it, and followed its course south.

Thompson was now close to the route of Highway 22 again, riding through the expansive view to the west of the road. Although we'd driven this section of the highway many times, apart from agreeing that the view was admirable, we knew very little about it. We did know that years ago it was gravel and potholes, and that now it's a ribbon of pavement. We also knew that it jogged along Highway 27 to resume its southward run about six miles east of Sundre. What we didn't know was that Thompson had marched along the highway's western side, passing near the communities of Westward Ho, Cremona, and Water Valley. Apparently, the local townspeople don't know either. Like most Albertans, they're aware of David Thompson, but they seem unaware that his travels might have taken him past their own doorsteps.

On the third day out, the travellers put up at three o'clock in the afternoon, ostensibly because the weather had turned "very bad." Since Thompson and McGillivray promptly went hunting, there's grounds for suspicion that the presence of "plenty of small Deer" had more to do with the early halt than the weather did. For the North West partners loved to hunt. On river journeys, they preferred riding with their Indian hunters to sitting in a canoe, and on cross-country trips, they often left packhorses, women, and children in the care of their *voyageurs* and went chasing after game. Like most Nor'Westers, Thompson enjoyed hunting, but it was McGillivray who best expressed (and hastened to jus-tify) why.

> Hunting is the only amusement which this country affords ... In our vacations from business we fly to it with impatience to pass a few agreable hours and when we are successful it gives us satisfaction, to think that we have united pleasure and profit together ... besides from the nature of the country & quantity of animal food we devour, I am persuaded that violent exercise is very necessary for the preservation of the constitution.[3]

November is one month when Albertans can expect to be handling the wrong end of a shovel, but some years it snows very little and the province enjoys what is called an "open winter." Since Thompson's party encountered so little snow on this journey, 1800 was probably one of those years. That November, the only heavy going the riders encoun-tered was caused, not by snowcover, but by the lack of it.

> Most of this open Meadow Ground, upon our Right a bow of strag-gling Woods but the left seems to be boundless Meadow—bad footing for the Horses from the uneven Surface, called by the French Tate des Femmes.

The country along the Little Red Deer River was well endowed with *têtes des femmes*, which still plague almost every pasture lining the route of Highway 22. The phrase translates as "women's heads" and is as good a description as any of these tussocks of grass. Typical of low-lying land, tussocks form hard, uneven lumps that render every step unpredictable—very hard on the fetlocks of horses, to say nothing of the ankles of humans.

The next morning, the riders left the valley of the Little Red Deer and "held on" to the south until they reached a thick grove of trees. "The Indian informing us that we should find no Woods in our Road fit for Tent Poles, we cut Poles sufficient for that Purpose, & took them with us." A few hours later, they emerged into open country again.

... all fine open Meadow with chance patches of Willow. We go in a
Line parallel to the Mountain which every where is covered with
Snow & seems to present an impenetrable Bank. The view is grand
in a high Degree: on our right we have the Bow Hills, lofty in themselves and Brown with Woods, above them stately rises the Rocky
Mountain vast and abrupt whose tops pierce the clouds—on our
left, before & behind us a verdant Ocean.

Today the Grand Valley Road runs through this view. The Bow Hills,
now called the Wildcat Hills, originate opposite Devil's Head Mountain,
a nine-thousand-foot knob in the Rocky Mountains, and range south as
far as the Bow River. At the base of the hills flows Grand Valley Creek,
a minor tributary of the Bow River.

Grand Valley Road

~ Grand Valley Road begins as Range Road 5.03, one mile west of
Water Valley and six miles west of Highway 22. For thirteen
miles, a gravel road winds among spindly trees that could still
do duty as tent poles; for the next twelve miles, a paved road
swings down a broad valley.

~ Grand Valley has changed little since Thompson's day.
The meadows are preserved as hayfields and pastures, and the
surrounding view is still "grand in a high Degree."

~ The road ends at its junction with Highway 1A, just over four
miles west of Cochrane.

The riders followed Grand Valley Creek to the Bow River. Snow
dusted the ground, but except along its margins, the Bow was remarkably free of ice. They camped for the night near Cochrane, where
Thompson noted: "Marks of Indians having gone from here to Day, as
their Fire was still alight." The next morning, the riders set out once
more along the Bow, following its course east to reach today's city of
Calgary.

We then descended the Banks of the Bow River and crossed it—it
may be here ab^t 200 Y^{ds} wide and 2½ feet at 2M an Hour, with a
Bottom of Gravel and Pebbles ... we staid there smoking about ¼ H
when we resumed our Journey. Our Course to the Spitchee River
S25E 5M which we crossed & came to a Camp of 7 Lodges of
Pekenows, with whom we put up at 2 Pm.

The Spitchee, now called the Highwood River, is a southern tributary of the Bow. Even with the time they'd taken off to hunt, Thompson and his party had ridden the 170 miles to the Highwood River in only six days—one advantage of travelling light through open country. By today's standards, however, even a light load was heavy baggage. The travellers still had to carry virtually everything they needed to exist: clothes, tents, bedding, tools, packs of meat and flour and sugar, guns and ammunition, the ubiquitous kettle, and (though it's hard to picture how) the bundle of freshly-cut tent poles. But for once—except for a keg of rum and some ropes of tobacco—they'd been able to dispense with the burdensome loads of trade goods.

The expedition reached the Peigan Camp on the afternoon of November 22. That evening, Chief Sac o tow wow and a group of his men entered Thompson and McGillivray's tent, and the Peigan chief immediately tackled Thompson about his recent dealings with the Kootenays.

> ... he complained of our having armed them by which means the
> Flat Heads would also acquire Arms to their great Hurt. To this I
> replied that they themselves, the Pekenows, had first & principally
> armed the Kootanaes in exchange for Horses &c, & replied to all
> the other Parts of his argument.

The Flatheads were a Salish-speaking people from western Montana, close friends of the Kootenays and sworn enemies of the Peigans. Chief Sac o tow wow's greatest fear was that the Kootenays would arm the Flatheads, and his harangue on the subject threatened to go on all night. When they could get a word in edgewise, Thompson and McGillivray brought up the proposal to establish the Iroquois and Ojibwa trappers in Peigan territory.

They explained to Sac o tow wow and his men that the newcomers would live quietly in the hills at the foot of the mountains, and pointed out that their presence would serve as a barrier between the Peigans and their enemies. Despite their indignation over the Nor'Westers' trade in guns, the Peigans gave their consent, and Thompson cut a pipe of tobacco for each man and passed out a few pints of rum. The next morning, Thompson's party left Sac o tow wow's camp and rode south toward a larger Peigan encampment located near today's town of High River.

Here they were warmly welcomed by Chief Old Bear—Thompson's guide on the journey to meet the Kootenays—and soon made themselves at home. McGillivray and two men disappeared into Old Bear's tent, and

Thompson and two others into Foxe's Head's tent. "We were all very well received," wrote Thompson. They again brought up the subject of the Iroquois and Ojibwa, but found they didn't have to argue the proposition—"indeed they were all well pleased with it."

> We mentioned our Intention of going close to the Mountain, & if possible into it, when they warned us in a friendly manner to beware of the Flat Heads, who were constantly hovering about there to steal Horses, or to dispatch any small weak Party they might chance to fall in with. After ... getting information on all the Brooks & Rivulets which fall into the Bow River from the Mountain southward of its Scource, we parted & went to Bed.

The formal business of the trip dispensed with, Thompson and McGillivray were free to devote the next six days to hunting. Sometimes they hunted for food but, as is evident from Thompson's vocabulary, just as often for pleasure.

> We amused ourselves with running Buffalo, of which there were vast numbers—we killed 2 Cows 1 Calf & 1 Bull.

> A very fine Day. We had the pleasure of running a few Cows—I assisted at the Death of Two…

> We came to large Herds of Cows: twice we attempted to approach them, but the wind was too calm & unsteady—I run a tolerable good Cow, and another old Cow—also assisted Dumond in Killing a Calf.

> Saw many small Deer to Day—where we put up our Guide fired at a Buck Moose, but missed him—saw plenty of Cattle all Day.

> Saw many Herds of Cows in the Morning ... we stopped 20' to wait the Indian, who was running after small Deer, which are very Plenty about here ... Saw many large herds of Bulls, but few [or] no Cows.

Thompson's "cattle" were buffalo, as were all the bulls, cows, and calves he went after. Buffalo are properly called bison, but Thompson called them buffalo and (apart from A.A. Milne's "Biffalo-Buffalo-Bison"[4]) most of us still do. The "small deer" were probably white-tailed Virginia deer, since Thompson called black-tailed mule deer "jumping deer." Jumping was his term for "stotting," the stiff, four-legged bound that characterizes the gait of the mulie. In later years, he would encounter the small Columbia deer, which he called *chevreuil*, the French term for the European roe deer. He discriminated between these species and what he called "Red Deer" (a term he imported from England). In Canada red deer are known as wapiti, or elk. We sometimes wonder whether residents of Red Deer, Alberta, realize that their city is named, not for the leaping deer pictured on their logo, but for the more stately elk that still graze in huge herds in Canada's mountain parks.

The Nor'Westers hunted with guns that had to be loaded with black powder and a lead ball, an awkward system that required the guns to be laboriously reloaded after every shot, with the added disadvantage of a range of only about fifty yards. Even so, flintlock hobbyist Brian Cargill considers the cumbersome weapons to be as deadly as a modern rifle with telescopic sights, "if you get close enough." But the effects of weather, Cargill admits, are "something fierce ... And differences in temperature can throw the weapon's sights off by several centimetres."[5]

The awkwardness of ball and powder, the scarcity of guns and ammunition, and the unreliability of the guns themselves (they sometimes failed to fire in cold weather) may be why the Peigans seemed reluctant to adopt them for hunting. Although they'd quickly taken up guns for making war, as late as 1793, Peter Fidler of the Hudson's Bay Company had watched some young Peigan braves, armed only with bows and arrows, running buffalo.

> ... they are so expert at this business, that they will ride along side of the Cow they mean to kill & while at full gallop will shoot an arrow into her heart & kill her upon the spot—sometimes when they happen to miss their proper aim (which is very seldom) they will ride close up to the Buffalo while at full Gallop & draw the arrow out & again shoot with it.[6]

In the early 1800s, buffalo roamed the Prairies by the millions, but before the century was out, they were virtually extinct. Starting in 1830, the herds were subjected to decades of overhunting. Indian subsistence hunters, fur traders, early settlers, Métis buffalo runners, and European sportsmen all contributed to the decline of the buffalo, and the increasing commercialization of the robe trade accelerated it. Buffalo robes were used to make belting for the machinery of the industrialized east and, by the 1840s, the American Indians alone "were annually bringing to the steamboats over 100,000 bison robes."[7]

The U.S. government did nothing to stop the slaughter, apparently in the hope that the loss of the buffalo would force the Indians onto the reservations, where they were expected to turn themselves into farmers. By 1900 fewer than a thousand buffalo remained, and the era of settlement that followed ensured that the disappearance of the massive herds would be permanent. With them went a way of life. Not only did the Plains Indians depend on the buffalo for food, but also on its hide for clothing and shelter, its sinews for thread and ropes, its hooves and bones for glue and tools, and its "chips" for fuel.

Of the buffalo that remain in Alberta, most enjoy protected status in national parks (Jasper, Elk Island, and Waterton Lakes), one herd ranges free in Wood Buffalo National Park, part of which lies in northern Alberta, and a small herd occupies a paddock on the Rocky Mountain House Historic Park. Others are raised domestically to make an occasional appearance on restaurant menus as buffalo burgers or (incongruous as it may seem) buffalo stew in puff pastry.

Deer, however, are probably as abundant as ever, and though most of the countryside is now under cultivation and some of it is fenced, these animals live pretty well where they want. Deer populate the edge lands between field and forest and make their living along river valleys and on well-treed farmsteads. In Alberta the ranges of the mule deer and white-tails overlap, and both species regularly appear along roadsides. During the winter, large groups of up to twenty mule deer, and smaller groups of white-tails, are often seen nibbling along hedgerows or grazing in farmers' fields.

Aside from their inevitable collisions with vehicles (usually at dawn or dusk), deer seem undisturbed by agricultural settlement. They jump fences without effort, raise their young in woodlots and shelterbelts, and prefer expensive second-cut alfalfa to coarser varieties of hay. There are fewer hunters now than there were twenty years ago, but deer, moose, and elk are still hunted by anyone sufficiently determined to plough through the complex regulations that govern hunting in Alberta today.

By November 26, Thompson and McGillivray had taken their leave of Chief Old Bear and set off on their excursion to the Rocky Mountains. Over the next four days, they rode northwest over the plains they'd found so rich in game, crossing on the way the Sheep River, Fish Creek, and the Elbow River. Mindful of the Peigans' warning about marauding Flatheads, they took turns mounting guard over the horses, and "lay under Arms" all night. At noon on the fourth day, they reached Jumping Pound Creek, a stream named for the high banks near its mouth that early Natives used as a buffalo jump.

Thompson's party crossed Jumping Pound Creek, then rode northwest for three and a half miles. "When seeing only high Ridges or Hills before us, we struck off N35W 9M to a Gully with a Spring of water near the Bow River—where we put up ... within 1¼ M of the Bow River."

Between Longview and Priddis, Highway 22 now runs through a countryside evocative of the Nor'Westers' ride to the Bow. Although Highway 22 tends to head north rather than northwest as Thompson did, it cuts through an expanse of open ranchland little changed from the days of the buffalo and crosses the same series of streams that Thompson crossed. South of Bragg Creek, however, where the highway detours into the forest, Thompson would have continued on through the grasslands of today's Sarcee Reserve, though he probably reached the present route of the TransCanada Highway at much the same point as Highway 22 does.

The TransCanada now snakes across Thompson's "ridges," and, as the riders drew near them, they turned northward to do the same. Once across the ridge, they descended its western slope into the "Gully" on the Bow River. Judging by the description of his route, the gully could well have been associated with Chiniki Creek (pronounced CHIN-i-kah), a spring-fed stream that flows under the TransCanada to empty into the Ghost Reservoir. Named after the first chief of the Morley Indian Reserve, Chiniki Creek is on land that belongs to the Stoney people.

The next morning, having left Boulard in charge of the pack horses and baggage, Thompson, McGillivray, three of their men, and their Peigan guide rode west to follow the Bow River to the Rocky Mountains.

> Our Road lies along the Bow River, which all along to the very
> Mountains has beautiful Meadows along its Banks: those on the
> South Side the River tho' the most extensive are so frequently cut by
> Brooks, whose Banks here are always high & often very steep, and
> Ravelines, the remains of old Streams whose waters have failed; on
> the North Side the Meadows are not extensive, but they are the best
> Road, as they are not so often intersected by the small Streams
> which come pouring from the Hills.

About three miles upstream of their camp in the gully, the party crossed the Bow River, probably close to where the Morley Bridge crosses it now. This bridge connects the north and south parts of the Morley Reserve, as well as serving as a link between the TransCanada (Highway 1) and the Bow Valley Trail (Highway 1A). Once they'd reached the north side of the river, Thompson's party continued to ride west, following the same general route that the Bow Valley Trail follows today, past the gates of Stoney Indian Park, through scenery that movie-goers might recognize as the setting for the Brad Pitt film *Legends of the Fall.*

> The Bow River for the last 3 Miles has many strong Rapids with several Falls but none of these above 8 or 10 feet perpend height ... the most considerable of these Falls are Three which all lie in the same bend of the River, and may be avoided by one Portage across the Point of ab.ᵗ 300 Y.ᵈˢ.

Although Thompson was interested in the navigability of the river and not its potential for power production, the three falls were probably the Horseshoe Falls, now the site of TransAlta's run-of-the-river hydro dam at Seebe. Along this stretch of the Bow, the river runs between steep cliffs that Thompson judged to be two hundred feet high. It was here, near Seebe, that he caught sight of bighorn sheep for the first time. On first acquaintance, Thompson misnamed them, but in his later journals, he recognized the difference and made a point of separating the sheep from the goats.

> ... we put up at 4 Pm having amused ourselves the whole Afternoon with running after the Goats ... steep as these Banks are, the Mountain Goats are seen to take to them ... and seemingly run along the steeps as securely as on the Plains. Indeed this Animal is remarkably agile, and jumps both well and sure; his make is strong, at the same time light, his Hoofs pointed, & somewhat soft in the hind Part enables him to climb with Ease. The She Goats have a simple mild Look, and are curious to approach and examine with their Eyes whatever they see moving ... the Bucks divested of their Horns would have nearly the same Appearance, but their large weighty Horns superior size & Strength and more ardent curiosity, which makes them advance before the Herd, give them an Air of daring with a Dash of the Formidable.

In contrast to Thompson's observations, one of his contemporaries, William Guthrie, seems to have drawn freely on his imagination to document the habits of wildlife. Guthrie's description of wolves, which appeared in his 1807 reference book, *Guthrie's Geographical Grammar*, was reproduced, with humorous intent, in the *Globe and Mail* newspaper: "Wolves are scarce in Canada, but they afford the finest furs in all the country. Their flesh is white, and good to eat; they pursue their prey to the tops of the tallest trees."

The Bighorn

~ Thompson's description of bighorn sheep is typical of his accuracy when he had enough leisure to write a detailed account. His 1800 description compares favourably with that given in the 1980 edition of *The Audubon Society Field Guide to North American Mammals:*

~ "Rams have massive brown horns that curve up and back over the ears ... Ewes much smaller than rams ... an excellent rock climber and jumper, the Bighorn has hooves hard at the outer edge and spongy in the center, providing good traction even on sheer rock ...

~ "As the fall rutting season approaches, rams have butting contests ... They charge each other at speeds of more than 20 mph, their foreheads crashing with a crack that can be heard for more than a mile."[8]

Thompson's aesthetic appreciation of the bighorns, however, didn't rule out shooting several of them that afternoon and dining on them that evening. "[W]e found their Meat to be exceeding sweet & tender and moderately fat." Coming from Thompson, "moderately fat" represented a mild culinary compliment. In his view, the more fat an animal carried the better. He had a rating system for the animals he hunted—very good, tolerable good, fair, poor, etc.—where poor meant "thin," and good meant "fat." He rated them not because of the flavour and tenderness that fat lends to the meat, but because of the nutritional value of the fat itself.

When he favoured fat animals, Thompson was following a practice of the Natives who, like hunting cultures everywhere, had done so for thousands of years. As is often the case, scientific knowledge eventually overtook the lessons of practical experience. In his book on bison kills, archaeologist John Speth summarized the biological importance of fat, then went on to point out that a consistent diet of lean meat led to a condition known as "rabbit starvation." Speth quoted several examples describing the condition, the most graphic of these penned by Arctic explorer Viljalmur Stefansson.

If you are transferred suddenly from a diet normal in fat to one consisting wholly of rabbit you eat bigger and bigger meals for the first few days until at the end of about a week you are eating in pounds three or four times as much as you were at the beginning of the week. By that time you are showing both signs of starvation and of protein poisoning [ketosis]. You eat numerous meals; you feel hungry at the end of each; you are in discomfort through distention of the stomach with much food and you begin to feel a vague restlessness. Diarrhoea will start in from a week to 10 days and will not be relieved unless you secure fat. Death will result after several weeks.[9]

At the turn of the last century, as settlement increased, hunters began to appear on the Bow, and the bighorn's escape terrain along the river's cliffs made it an easy target for a bullet. Nowadays, shooting game from a boat is illegal, but in Alberta's early years, it was common, and the practice drove the bighorns from their traditional territory on the Bow River's cliffs. Today they live along the steep mountainsides farther west, where they can easily bound out of reach of most of their predators, including those of the two-legged variety. But the bighorns seem to have no fear of the residents of Exshaw, and despite valiant attempts to fence them out, they're often seen in the hamlet's gardens, helping themselves to a few fresh vegetables.

Exshaw marked the end of the journey to "the Mountain," as Thompson called the Rockies. (He often referred to ranges of mountains as one mountain, a habit that baffled us early on, when "Nelson's Mountain" kept turning up in both Canada and the United States.) Once the riders reached Exshaw, Thompson, McGillivray, and Dumont decided to climb one of the peaks to have a look around.

Our View from the Heights to the Eastward was vast &
unbounded—the Eye had not Strength to discriminate its
Termination: to the Westward Hills & Rocks rose to our View covered with Snow, here rising, there subsiding, but their Tops nearly of an equal Height every where. Never before did I behold so just, so perfect a Resemblance to the Waves of the Ocean in the wintry Storm.

Thompson's view to the east was the open prairie, and to the west the Rocky Mountains. The "waves" he described were the strata of the rocks outlined in white, an effect that can be seen whenever the mountains have a light dusting of snow. Judging by Thompson's description of the view, it's possible he climbed Exshaw Mountain, the rounded hump that looms over the hamlet of Exshaw. He'd rejected the "inaccessible Steep" at the entrance to the Rockies—the jagged teeth of Yamnuska Mountain—in favour of something more "practicable." Exshaw Mountain isn't very high, but it's visible from forty miles out on the prairie and would have offered Thompson his "unbounded" view to the east. To the west, the mountain overlooks *Lac des Arcs*, a widening in the Bow River he noted in his journal.

Still, Exshaw Mountain doesn't quite fit Thompson's description of the slope he climbed. He didn't mention any trees, and Exshaw is tree-covered now and probably was then. Another possibility is Door Jamb Mountain, just east of Exshaw. If Thompson attacked its western side, he could have reached the top with little more than a stiff climb. On a second visit to Exshaw, we reread Thompson's description more carefully.

> ... we found it very steep with much loose small stones very sharp, but as we got higher & higher the loose Stones became less frequent; when the Rock was solid, it was extremely rough and full of small sharp Points like an enormous Rasp—this enabled us to mount Places very steep, as the footing was good & sure, but it cut our Shoes, Socks &c all to pieces in a Trice. The Rock of the Mountain all the way to the Top is one and the same, of a dark Grey, with few or no Veins, very hard & Glassy, and upon rubbing Two Pieces of it together for a Moment produces when held near the Nose a strong disagreeable Smell, somewhat Sulphurous.

This could be a description of Door Jamb Mountain. The difficulty of the climb indicates a peak more challenging than Exshaw Mountain, and Door Jamb Mountain is faced in a grey, hard, glassy rock resembling the footing that Thompson encountered. In his book on the Canadian Rockies, Ben Gadd mentions that a formation originating in the Exshaw area is oil-bearing,[10] which provides a possible explanation for the "disagreeable Smell" of the rocks Thompson examined. In the end, we were left with a guess—Exshaw Mountain's relatively easy climb or Door Jamb Mountain's tough hike to the top. We leave the final decision to those whose "figures are more suited," as one early explorer put it, "to climbing mountains."

The three men spent four hours on top of the mountain. Immediately across the Bow River, they had a view of the imposing peak now known as Mount McGillivray, and at its foot, McGillivray's Pond, one of several small lakes bordering *Lac des Arcs*. If, as is likely, it was Thompson who named these two landmarks after McGillivray, they stand among the few names he assigned that managed to make it onto the maps of the twentieth century.

That afternoon, they descended the mountainside, remounted their horses, and rode back to their camp in the gully. On their arrival, Thompson noted "all well, thank God"—a relief inspired, no doubt, by the discovery that Boulard and the horses had escaped the attention of the Flatheads. On December 1, they set off on the return journey to Rocky Mountain House, this time crossing the Bow, the Ghost River, and the Wildcat Hills to regain their road through Grand Valley.

Two days later, Thompson and McGillivray reached Rocky Mountain House, where a different sort of business awaited their attention. That winter, they would plan a journey both more important and more formidable than their light-hearted trip to the Bow—the North West Company's first attempt to carry the fur trade across the Rocky Mountains.

The North Ram River–1801[1]

*If nothing else, the North West Company's initial
attempt to cross the Rocky Mountains proved that
bad luck really does come in threes. The first blow was the
crippling illness of Duncan McGillivray, the second was
the murder of the expedition's guide, and the third was hiring
The Rook as his replacement. Thompson, who recorded the
events of this ill-starred journey, had several terms for
The Rook, chief among them "Dastard," "Scoundrel,"
and "our worthless Guide."*

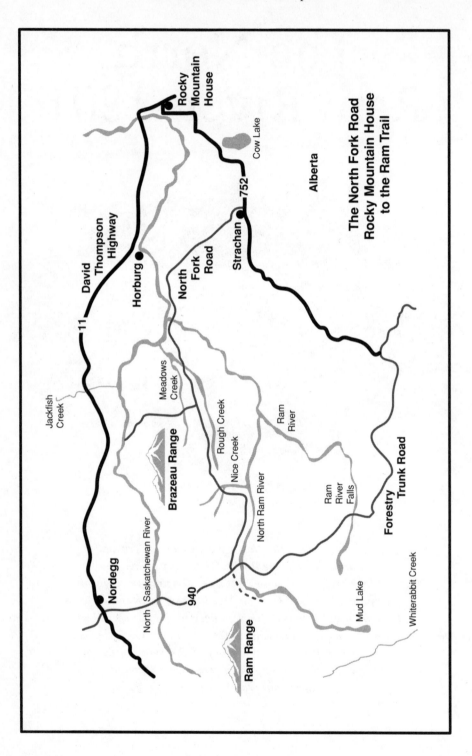

The North Fork Road
Rocky Mountain House
to the Ram Trail

Alberta

Rocky Mountain House

Cow Lake

752

Strachan

David
Thompson
Highway

North
Fork
Road

Horburg

11

Jackfish
Creek

Meadows
Creek

Rough Creek

Nice Creek

Ram
River

Brazeau Range

North Ram River

Ram
River
Falls

Forestry
Trunk Road

Nordegg

North Saskatchewan River

940

Mud Lake

Whiterabbit Creek

Ram Range

DUNCAN MCGILLIVRAY WAS ONE NOR'WESTER WHO STAUNCHLY BELIEVED that the future of the company lay on the western side of the Rockies. Another was explorer Alexander Mackenzie, who had come up with a similar notion, envisaging a fur empire that spanned the continent from Hudson Bay to the Pacific Ocean. But Mackenzie's vision would have required amalgamation with the Hudson's Bay Company, a move the Montreal partners refused to contemplate. In the uproar that followed, Mackenzie resigned from the company and went off to England to work on a book about his explorations.

Unlike Mackenzie's plan, McGillivray's didn't require any dealings with the Hudson's Bay Company. He just wanted to find a route over the Rocky Mountains to the Pacific Ocean—a last-ditch attempt to fulfill the centuries-old dream of a Northwest Passage across North America. The Montreal partners approved McGillivray's plan, possibly because his proposal was relatively modest, but more likely because his uncle was immensely powerful.

McGillivray's uncle was Simon McTavish, founding partner and chief director of the North West Company, and a man noted for boosting the fortunes of his own clan. McTavish had financed the young Duncan's education, started him on his career in the fur trade, and later coached him toward a partnership in the firm. Now that McGillivray was a fully qualified wintering partner, it would have been unlike McTavish to withhold support for his nephew's most recent venture. Whatever the reason, Duncan McGillivray had better luck with the partners than Alexander Mackenzie did and was given the go-ahead for his expedition.

McGillivray had brought along Captain George Vancouver's *Voyages of Discovery*, and Thompson was soon copying the passages that interested him into his journal. What interested him most was the British sea captain's description of his trip to the mouth of the Columbia River, particularly his account of Lieutenant Broughton's exploration of the river's lower one hundred miles. We can picture Thompson and McGillivray during their long winter evenings together, poring over Vancouver's journal by candlelight, absorbed in their own plans for a momentous journey across the mountains to the shores of the Pacific Ocean.

Not that Thompson's journal ever hinted that their journey was momentous. He seemed unconcerned about either the difficulty or the duration of the undertaking, even though he knew that sixteen-year-old Charlotte was due to give birth to their first child any day. His references to the coming trip were invariably casual, tossed off in phrases like "cross the Rocky Mountain" and "penetrate to the Pacific Ocean." Reading Thompson's journal, you'd think the Pacific Ocean was a mere hop-skip-and-jump to the west, and that he and McGillivray would be back in a day or two.

McGillivray, however, wasn't destined to lead the expedition across the mountains. As a chronic sufferer of what he called "rheumatism or some other vile disorder of that nature," he was put out of action in February, months before the expedition could be launched. Thompson blamed the illness on McGillivray's winter explorations of the headwaters of the Brazeau River, claiming that he "...took no precautions against the effect of exposure to the weather, wet feet, etc. [and] began to feel attacks of acute rheumatism, which became so violent as to oblige him to keep his bed." It's likely McGillivray suffered from rheumatoid arthritis, which would have allowed him an active life when it was in remission, but could disable him completely when it flared up.

Still barely convalescent by the time spring arrived, McGillivray reluctantly appointed James Hughes, the trader then in charge of Rocky Mountain House, to carry on in his place. In retrospect, it seems odd that he didn't delegate this job to Thompson, who certainly had enough field experience to carry it out. But Thompson had yet to be promoted to a partnership in the North West Company, and Hughes's rank apparently took precedence over Thompson's experience as a navigator.

Although McGillivray now had a leader for his expedition, it wasn't long before more bad news arrived to upset his plans. The Kootenays had kept their promise and sent Thompson a man to guide the traders across the mountains, but word now came that the guide had been killed by the Stoney Assiniboine, "murdered," as Thompson put it, "within a few Miles of the Fort." By then it was almost June, and to avoid any more delay, McGillivray hastily started looking for a replacement. He came up with a Cree Indian named The Rook.

McGillivray knew the Kootenays had crossed the Rockies on horseback, so he was looking for a guide who could show them how to do the same. On the face of it, The Rook seemed the ideal guide for such a journey. He knew a horse trail across the mountains, he told them. Oh yes, he'd crossed them himself on horseback, with a good road all the way. If he'd been with us today, he'd probably have added, "No problem." The Rook seems to have been a man given to telling his listeners whatever they wanted to hear, and both McGillivray and Thompson had doubts about his claims. To Thompson, The Rook was "a Man so Timourous by Nature, of so wavering a Disposition, & withal so addicted to flattering & lying, as to make every Thing he said or did equivocal and doubtful." Unfortunately, The Rook was their only hope. There was no time to find anyone else.

Because McGillivray was aware of the guide's character, he did everything in his power to make sure The Rook didn't mess up the expedition. McGillivray promised him generous compensation if he performed well, and threatened him with serious repercussions if he didn't. "[He] added to these," Thompson reported, "the awful act of making him smoke & imprecate the Wrath of the Great Spirit on himself, his Wife & Children, if he did not fully perform his Promise of guiding us across the Mountains."

This was one journey that Charlotte Thompson didn't make. On the eve of the departure for the mountains, she was only four days away from giving birth to her first child. Thompson would have left Charlotte in the care of other women: James Hughes's wife (mother-in-law of Charlotte's brother), the wives of the *voyageurs* based at Rocky Mountain House, and possibly Charlotte's sister Nancy, who might have been visiting at the time.

Although five of Thompson's children were born in the northwest, he wasn't present for any of their births. He was away when his first child was born and when his fifth child was born ten years later. In neither case did he have much choice—the fur trade dictated his movements. He was also away, however, when his second, third, and fourth children appeared on the scene, a meeting or an errand invariably demanding his attention just at the propitious moment. Still, Charlotte was never left on her own. A friend told us that the only thing she knew about Thompson's wife was what it said in a schoolbook—that Thompson had marched on ahead with his men, leaving Charlotte to give birth by the trail. It makes a good story, but it didn't happen. All Charlotte's country children were born in a company fort.

Several of the traders who kept a journal remarked on the ease with which Indian women had their babies. Alexander Henry's comment is typical: "The wife of François Deschamps, Jr., was delivered of a boy, and an hour afterward was running about the fort. How happy it is for the Indian women that childbirth has so little effect on them."[2] John Jackson, writing in 1996, took exception to these remarks and complained about them in his book on the Métis.

Observers like to draw the comparison between the hardy woman who stepped down along the trail for a casual delivery and the delicate flower of society who birthed her baby in bed. Was that a backhanded way of showing the difference between insensitive savages, or half-savages, and truly refined ladies of quality?[3]

The traders' observations could quite easily have been accurate. At the turn of the nineteenth century, a British young lady graduated from the care of her governess to life in the drawing-room, where she occupied herself reading poetry, playing the harpsichord, and indulging in the latest gossip while she awaited the attentions of the gentlemen. "'Ladies,'" pointed out British historian G. M. Trevelyan, "were not encouraged to exercise their bodies except in dancing. Very few women of this period hunted ... it became the hallmark of the lady to be idle."[4] A greater contrast to the energetic life of women in the fur trade is hard to imagine. They were horsewomen, accustomed to spending long days on the western trails with their husbands and riding about their own business of stripping bark, digging roots, and gathering firewood and berries. They rode like the men, astride, and would undoubtedly have been amused by the sight of their city-bred sisters seated sidesaddle. The "savages" probably gave birth more easily than the "ladies" because the former were in better shape. In any case, it's doubtful the traders meant their remarks to be offensive—their tone was more admiring than otherwise.

By the time the expedition to the mountains was organized and ready to leave, Thompson seems to have laid his worries about The Rook's competence aside. The guide gets scarcely a mention for the first leg of the journey, which began on June 6, 1801. Thompson recorded their departure with no mention of The Rook (or The Rook's wife) at all.

> ... every Thing being ready for our Journey to the Rocky
> Mountains, being in number Eleven Persons—Mr Hughes, nine
> Men & myself: we had thirteen Horses belonging to the NW^t
> Company of which ten were loaded either with trading Goods,
> Provisions or other Necessaries, each Horse had a burthen of from
> 120 to 130 lbs ... We also had with us an old Kootanae Woman who
> many years ago had been taken prisoner & had since mostly resided
> with the Canadians in the Company's Settlements ... Thus arranged,
> & carrying with us Birch Rind sufficient to make a Canoe, in the
> morning we loaded our Horses and set out.

Over the next two days, the expedition followed the same trail that the Kootenays had followed six months before, west along the high cliffs above the North Saskatchewan River, through a mixed landscape of sodden meadows and fallen trees. Seventeen miles west of Rocky Mountain House, they came to Horburg, now the terminus of a gravel road leading to a small park and canoe access to the river. Here the travellers left the banks of the North Saskatchewan to negotiate a series of swamps that lay in a bend of the river. They rode on for three more miles, then camped for the night in a wet meadow.

> We put up on the Banks of a Brook which traverses the Meadow.
> About 1 Mile SbW of us flows the Saskatchewan River. The whole
> of our Road to day, considering the Country, would have been toler-
> able had it not been for the late heavy Rains, which have so soaked
> & over flowed the Ground as to occasion the Horses often to sink to
> the mid Leg.

They set out again at 4:30 the next morning. A mile or so to the west of their camp, on the opposite side of the river, the Ram River joins the North Saskatchewan. The expedition must have passed this junction, though Thompson didn't mention it, possibly because he was too far away from the river to see it. On this second day of the journey, he reported only that they had moved another nine miles northwest and were again approaching the North Saskatchewan. The rest of the record is a litany of disasters.

> We now came to the Banks of the River, which were very high and
> steep, & cut in a perpendicular Direction by the craggy Sides of a
> Brook—which obliged us to descend and gain the River Beach; in
> doing this, one of our loaded Horses fell, & rolled down close to the
> edge of a Precipice at least three Hundred Feet high, but by good
> Fortune he brought up against a Pine Tree & recovered his feet.

Thompson's craggy brook was probably Jackfish Creek, the only stream along this stretch of the North Saskatchewan that's in any way remarkable for its canyon. The descent to the beach brought on a string of problems, and the day's progress came to a premature end. Shortly after the first horse tumbled down the cliff, another one lost its footing, fell "actually into the river," and only managed to save itself by swimming to the opposite bank.

> ... but how to recover the Horse & his Load was the Difficulty: we
> had no Canoe, & the Current was too deep & rapid to be crossed on
> a Raft. La Ramme, one of our Men, attempted to cross on
> Horseback—this he effected 'till about the middle of the Stream
> when, the Waves washing over the Head of the Horse, he reared up

& threw his Rider. Fortunately La Ramme could swim; he strongly
exerted himself & gained the Shore, where he secured the loaded
Horse.

Fortunately, too, the hunters had killed two buffalo earlier in the
day, and the men were able to use the hides to make a skin canoe. They
spent the next several hours ferrying La Ramme and the goods back
across the river (the two horses apparently being left to fend for themselves), then called it a day. They camped for the night beside the North
Saskatchewan River—still only nine miles from where they'd set out
that morning.

The next day, the expedition crossed the North Saskatchewan, then
wasted half the morning trying to get the horses up the bank on the
other side. Two more animals took a tumble, and "received such violent
Shocks ... as to deprive them for a Time of Motion." Three days later, the
horses went into their tumbling act again. As they traversed an icy slope
high above the North Ram River, another one slipped and plunged into
the current, soaking its load, nearly drowning itself, and emerging on the
wrong side of the stream. The men staged a rescue, but a second horse
soon followed the first; this one rolled down from such a height that
Thompson thought it had been killed. The horse survived, but the same
couldn't be said for its cargo. The horse had been loaded with the expedition's supply of salt and sugar, all of it "totally lost."

Once the expedition crossed the North Saskatchewan River,
Thompson elected to describe the next part of their route "without too
much detail." This lack of detail has led to a flurry of speculation about
exactly where Thompson was after he crossed the North Saskatchewan
River and a mild academic dispute about whether it was the Ram River
or its tributary, the North Ram, that he followed to its headwaters.
Because Thompson didn't name Jackfish Creek or any of the three
streams he followed after he crossed the river, it's sometimes assumed
that he travelled along the Ram River itself. J.B. Tyrrell, editor of
Thompson's *Narrative*, thought so, but placing the expedition on the
Ram River ultimately makes nonsense of Thompson's description of his
route.

Barbara Belyea pointed out that if Thompson were on the Ram, the
Ram River Falls would have blocked his way (which is true), and that it's
more likely that he followed the North Ram River to its headwater lake
(also true).[5] Unfortunately, Belyea backed off and awarded the last word
to F.W. Howay, a historian writing in the 1940s. Howay claimed that
Thompson followed the Ram River to its source in Onion Lake,

although he concluded that: "It is difficult if not impossible to trace exactly the route followed by Thompson under the blind direction of his ignorant and craven guide."[6] Difficult, maybe, but not impossible.

For a day or so after the riders crossed the North Saskatchewan River, Thompson's elliptical account of their course is admittedly difficult to figure out. A little later, however, his account of their route to the mountains is remarkably easy to follow. This is because, after they'd pursued a tangled path along the three unnamed streams (our guesses are Trout Creek, Lundine Creek, and Meadows Creek), they came to a trail that followed the same route as today's North Fork Road.

The North Fork Road is a back-country road that's dusty in dry weather, muddy in wet weather, and completely closed to traffic in the winter. It originates near the Strachan Campground (located on Highway 752 southwest of Rocky Mountain House) and runs westward for just under fifty miles. Dust and mud notwithstanding, the North Fork Road winds through some extremely pretty country—bubbling streams bordered by marshy willow flats, high hills cloaked in pine and spruce and poplar—a natural landscape that looks much the same today as it did in Thompson's time.

The North Fork Road sets off northwest, crosses the Ram River, swings southwest to cross Rough Creek, parallels the stream for a mile or two, then follows it west around the toe of the Brazeau Range. Near the headwaters of Rough Creek, the road turns abruptly south to run alongside Nice Creek (one of a pair of streams some humorist has named "Nice" and "Easy"). At Nice Creek's confluence with the North Ram, the road turns west to follow the river as far as the Forestry Trunk Road. Straight ahead, an abandoned track called the Ram Trail continues west along the North Ram River, following Thompson's route into the Ram Range.

A comparison of Thompson's route with that of the western end of the North Fork Road illustrates how closely he paralleled it. He seems to have joined the road a mile or two west of the bridge over Rough Creek. Just before he reached the stream, he described coming to "several fine little Meadows," then heading south for two miles to reach a "rapid Brook, whose banks we followed WSW 6 Miles." Today these meadows are still found a few miles north of the North Fork Road (a small sign marks the turnoff to the Meadows Historical Patrol Cabin), and Rough Creek is the "rapid Brook" coming from the west. Although Thompson's route lay along the stream's banks and the North Fork Road goes up and over, road and stream run parallel for six miles as they make their way past the Brazeau Range of mountains.

We are now behind the first Chain of Mountains, which from the Valley where we are camped, appears to be as firm, as compact & as high, tho' not so abrupt on this Western side as on the Eastern. The Tops of them are everywhere covered with Snow ... Saw the Tracks of several Grizled Bears & a small Herd of Bulls—one of the latter we killed; we also saw several mountain Goats, but they were far enough above our reach.

After following Rough Creek west to its headwaters, Thompson turned south to follow another stream. (This would have been Nice Creek, flowing in its turn parallel to the North Fork Road.) A few miles later, he reached the banks of "a bold & very rapid Stream of about Thirty Yards Wide," a stream he called the "South Branch of the Saskatchewan." Today it's called the North Ram River.

The most baffling question about Thompson's journey to the mountains, however, isn't which river he followed to get there, but why he allowed the expedition to cross the North Saskatchewan River in the first place. He knew that the murdered Kootenay guide would have taken a trail that followed the North Saskatchewan west; he knew where the Brazeau Range was and that the Kootenay Plains lay beyond; and he knew there was a pass in the mountains at the end of the trail. He'd learned all this from the Kootenays, and years later, he would pass it on to Jaco Finlay, the North West clerk who first marked the trail over Howse Pass. Why then did Thompson let The Rook lead the expedition on a fool's errand up the North Ram River? We don't know. Maybe McGillivray, Hughes, and The Rook outranked, overruled, and outvoted him. Or maybe he reacted as he occasionally did when his opinions were ignored—just did as he was told and let the chips fall where they may.

Once they'd reached the North Ram, the riders headed west along its north bank for three miles, where they found they would have to cross one of the channels of the river. The North Ram was flowing fast, its waters swollen with rain and runoff from the mountains. Since the channel was only twelve yards wide, the men attempted to make a bridge, but the current swept it away. For the next hour, they struggled in the stream, trying to get the horses and baggage across. It started to rain, and by the time they'd made it to the other side, it was pouring. They threw up the tents and took shelter, but the downpour turned into a tempest, demoralizing the men, scattering the horses, and soaking the tents and everything in them.

... the Water descended in Sheets from the Hills & flooded the
Country; the River, at all times Rapid, was now an over flowing
Torrent that bore down every Thing that opposed it's Course; the
Thunder rolled along the Hills ... we wished for the morning Light.

The Rook, whose spirits had been drooping ever since they'd
entered the mountains, was the most demoralized of all. "To keep him
hearty in the cause," James Hughes presented the guide with some rum.
It must have been a fair amount, enough to get The Rook royally drunk
and leave him with a monumental hangover. The next morning, he
arrived at the fire where the men were drying their gear, complaining
that his head and stomach were "out of order" and asking for some
medicine.

... finding [the medicine] did him neither good nor Harm, he called
his Wife to him where he was sitting amidst us ... She readily came:
he asked her if she had a sharp Flint, & upon her replying she had
not, he broke one & made a Lancet of it, with which he opened a
Vein in her Arm, she assisting him with great good Will; having
drawn about 3/4 pint of Blood from her into a wooden Bowl, to our
Astonishment he applied it to his Lips quite warm, & drank it off ...

Pausing only to wonder "whence so savage an Action could arise,"
Thompson goes on to record (at some length) the indignation of his men
at the act and the surprise of The Rook that they should be offended
by it.

But looking round on us all, & perceiving in our Countenances
marks of an utter Abhorrence of what he had done, he said no
more, for however it might be the Custom of his Nation, he saw
plainly he had done wrong to transact it before us.

Apparently fully recovered, The Rook smoked his pipe "with great
Tranquillity," and the journey up the North Ram continued, the river
growing narrower, the trail steeper, and The Rook increasingly fearful.
They were now well into the Ram Range, following the course of the
North Ram as it makes its final curve to the south.

Every Thing about us wore the Face of Winter: the Willows yet had
not budded, nor the Ground brought forth the least Verdure. We

staid 2½ Hours to give time to our Horses to pick up the miserable
remains of the Herbage of last Summer ... we still held on S10E
4½ Miles in a very narrow bottom between two stupendous Ridges
of rugged Rock. For the last two Miles we walked on small, sharp,
broken Pieces of Rock, which cut our Shoes to pieces & crippled
our Horses.

From this point, one week into the journey, Thompson's journal
starts to undergo a change in format. His record of the journey almost
disappears as he substitutes long disquisitions on their troubles with
The Rook.

Late in the Evening our Guide came to us with a woful
Countenance, desiring Permission to return, that he might still live
& see his Children. Mr Hughes asked him what he had to appre-
hend, that for his Part he saw nothing more formidable than the
Mountain Goat, from which he promised to defend him if ever they
became daring enough to attack him.

The Rook wasn't impressed by Hughes's sense of humour. "That is
the way of all you white Men—you joke at every Thing 'till you are
fairly killed." The guide argued that he dreamed constantly of strange
Indians who would murder them all, that some of the horses were fee-
ble and the rest were crippled, that the worst of the mountain was yet
to come, and that he wasn't going to stay around to be killed.

Thompson and Hughes refused to listen to any of this, arguing in
their turn that they were too far on to think of turning back, that they'd
go on while they had a horse left, and that, right or wrong, the guide had
to accompany them. The Rook finally gave up and went away, mutter-
ing, "You will see if we go much farther." Hughes suggested keeping an
eye on him overnight, but Thompson thought the precaution unnecessary, "for I knew the Dastard was more afraid to return all alone, than
even to remain where he was."

The morning heralded another difficult day. The riders hadn't
climbed a quarter of a mile higher before they ran into snow—three feet
of it that had the horses plunging through a weak crust. To spare the
horses, the men rode in the river, by then no bigger than a brook. But
relief from the crusted snow was temporary. Again and again, the riders
were forced back into it by avalanches that had come "shelving down"
and buried the stream under twenty feet of snow. Soon they couldn't

ride in the stream at all. Nothing was left of the North Ram River but a few rills running down the rocks.

We described to a neighbour how Thompson and Hughes followed the North Ram River to its headwaters. He listened and shook his head. "If they went that way, they had to turn back. They'd have run into a wall." They did run into a wall, and Hughes and Thompson finally understood what The Rook's fears were really about.

> For the last ¼ of a Mile we were on a bare Spot tolerably exposed
> to the Action of the Sun—here we were obliged to stop, for at the
> end of this was a deep Lake lying South one Mile by a quarter of a
> Mile wide, whose eastern Side rose abrupt & hid it's Head in the
> Clouds, accessible to the Eagle only, & it's western Side, equally
> lofty but broken, denied us a farther Road with the Horses.

Thompson was describing the headwaters of the North Ram River—Mud Lake. Sometimes called Farley Lake (after John Farley, who led many groups of hikers to its shores), Mud Lake earned its name by shrinking to half its size by late summer, exposing broad stretches of mud along its margins. In the spring, rain and runoff combine to fill the lake again, so that by the time Thompson reached it on June 13, Mud Lake would have been brimming.

Thompson looked at the men and saw by their pleased expressions that The Rook hadn't been the only one in the party who'd wanted to turn back. But it was The Rook who took the heat. Hughes and Thompson both turned on him, demanding to know if this was the road he'd followed across the mountains. The Rook assured them that it was.

> Pray, said we, in what Manner did you get your Horses to the other
> end of the Lake?

> Oh, replied he, we had no Horses with us—we left them with our
> Families, at the Entrance into the Mountains.

> Why you Scoundrel, we said, did you not tell us at the Fort that you
> had Horses with you the whole of the Road across the Mountains,
> & was it not upon the Supposition that you knew a good Road for
> Horses across them, that we engaged you for our Guide? Otherwise
> we would have followed, the best Way we could, the Banks of the
> Saskatchewan River.

All this is true, said our worthless Guide, but I thought where we
had gone on Foot, Horses might possibly go—but I forgot this Part
of the Mountain: you see plainly as well as me that if we go farther,
we must leave our Baggage & Horses.

Discouraged, Hughes and Thompson had the horses unloaded and
started considering what to do.

Mr Hughes now saw plainly as well as me that we had too many
Men: they had began the Journey with the greatest Reluctance as
Mr Duncan McGillivray well knows, & they had all along hoped
for, & now found, a fine Occasion of getting off.

Hughes soon came to a decision. He proposed that he and
Thompson explore the western side of the lake to see whether they
should swim the horses across. When the men heard this proposal, they
pronounced it "a Fatigue utterly unnecessary." But Hughes insisted, and
ordered two of the *voyageurs*, an unwilling Meillet and Gladu, to
accompany them.

We now set off & after going about 1/4 Mile, up to our middles in
Snow, we went along the lower Bank of the Lake, but it was so steep
that, however necessary it was to be well armed in such a Country,
we were all of us soon obliged to leave our Arms, & get along the
best we could on all Fours—our Situation was often dangerous, as
the least Slip would have precipitated us into the Lake, from a
height of above 100 feet.

As they neared the southern end of Mud Lake, the four men crossed
a piece of level ground, then started a tricky descent down a narrow
channel choked with broken rock. Within two hundred yards, they were
walking in water, struggling to keep from slipping on the rocky substrates of a streambed. Two and a quarter miles to the southwest, they
reached the bottom of the slope and were standing on the eastern side
of Whiterabbit Creek, a swift-flowing tributary of the North
Saskatchewan River. Thompson knew where he was. He estimated that
the North Saskatchewan and the Kootenay Plains were only ten or fifteen miles to the southwest, overestimating the distance by only a few
miles. By that time, however, he'd had to admit that bringing a horse
the way they'd come was impossible; they'd have to find another way to
get the goods down the mountain.

Hughes's notion was to send The Rook back to Rocky Mountain

House with the horses, ferry the goods across the lake, and have the men carry them down the mountain on their backs. But when Hughes and Thompson arrived back in camp several hours later, they found the *voyageurs* on the verge of mutiny and, not surprisingly, even more vigorously opposed to this plan than the first. Even the assurance that Hughes and Thompson would carry their share of the load failed to change their minds.

> ... for our Guide, while we were gone, had insinuated to them that he no longer knew the Road with certainty, & that the Saskatchewan was a long way off, beyond their Power to carry thereto, & that they were not engaged to carry at that Rate &c &c. But Meillet & Gladu who came with us finished the Dispute, by declaring it to be a Thing impossible for Men even lightly loaded to get down the Mountain without breaking their Limbs & that they could not think of such an Undertaking.

Although the *voyageurs* had refused to have anything to do with Hughes's first two plans, they were willing to listen to the third, probably because it involved no horseriding or bushwacking or backpacking, but took them back to what they knew best—paddling.

> The only hope that now remained was to return to the Saskatchewan near the Entrance into the Mountains, & there build a Canoe & try what could be done by that Means ... We therefore reloaded our Horses & resumed the Road we had come, & put up about 2 Miles N10W of where we started from this Morning.

The trip to the head of the North Ram River had taken seven days; the return to the North Saskatchewan took only three. On the evening of June 16, at a point about fifty miles upstream of Rocky Mountain House, they reached the North Saskatchewan River and crossed to where the Cree Indians had made a war tent several years before. This was a landmark that Thompson later called "The Little Plain of the War Tent" and mentioned often in his journals. Their camp was only a few miles downstream of Saunders Access—site of a canoe launch today and more than likely then.

Although they'd brought along enough birchbark to build a canoe, they had to spend days hunting for the right wood to make the frame. Thompson fretted about the time that was passing. A week went by, and the canoe still wasn't ready, though Thompson described it as "pretty well forward." Hughes, who was responsible for the affairs of the settlements along the river, decided he had to get back to the business of trading furs. Accompanied by one man and "our worthless Guide," all the horses (and no doubt the old Kootenay woman and The Rook's wife), Hughes departed for Rocky Mountain House on June 23. Thompson was left with eight men, an unfinished canoe, and the prospect of an upstream battle with the North Saskatchewan River.

The next day, construction of the canoe was complete, and the *voyageurs* started sealing the seams with gum. Three days of rain caused still more delay, but by June 26, Thompson and his men were equipped to continue the journey to the Rocky Mountains.

> During all this Time the Water had kept rising, & the River was now flush from Bank to Bank, bringing down great Quantities of Wood. We however set off, hoping that by the Line or the Pole we should be able to stem the Current ...

For three days, the *voyageurs* fought the North Saskatchewan. They soon abandoned paddling as useless, and attempted to line the canoe up the river. But towing the canoe from shore proved impossible—the banks were steep and stacked with debris. Getting into the water to tow it was unthinkable—the river was so deep and moving so fast, it would have swept the men away. They tried poling the canoe through the rushing water, but gained only a few miserable yards. They tried hauling themselves along by the trees on the riverbank, but the torrent flooding down defeated them. Finally, the exhausted men couldn't move the canoe another inch, and Thompson ordered them to where they could get ashore, most likely downstream near the mouth of Shunda Creek. After three days of unremitting effort, they'd advanced barely six miles up the river.

> [I] took two men with me to examine the River above us. We proceeded to nearly passing the first great Chain of Mountains, being about 5 or 6 Miles above where we left the Canoe; but instead of finding this Part better, to my great Disappointment we found it much worse: the River was every where bounded by Craigs, whose height was never less than 300 feet & often rose to 500 feet perpendicular above the level of the River.

Thompson and his men were looking at The Gap, a deep, narrow canyon that forces the North Saskatchewan to greater depths and higher velocities as it constricts to squeeze through the Brazeau Range. Thompson measured the currents of The Gap—at its slowest, the river was moving at nine miles an hour; at its fastest, twelve to fifteen miles an hour. The *voyageurs* are often credited with a paddling speed of six miles an hour, a rate that might have meaning on a mill pond. On the North Saskatchewan that June, paddling at six miles an hour meant they would have been moving backward, and as it was, the river brought them to a standstill. But once Thompson abandoned all hope of reaching the mountains and ordered the men to turn around, the river gave them a bonus. From The Gap to Rocky Mountain House, they shot down the North Saskatchewan at over ten miles an hour, paddling "no more than was barely necessary." Travel Alberta's *Reach Reports* estimate the time for this run at two to three days;[7] the *voyageurs* made it in five hours and fifty minutes.

Thompson arrived at Rocky Mountain House on June 30, to find he was a father. His daughter Fanny had been born on June 10, the second anniversary of his marriage to Charlotte. Thompson doesn't mention Fanny's arrival in his account of this journey, which in the end is a most peculiar document. Started as a journal, it changed to a diatribe, then a lament, and ended as a report to William and Duncan McGillivray, "Agents of the NW[t] Company." Thompson concluded that the only thing salvaged from this disastrous journey was a blueprint for the future.

> However unsuccessful this Journey has been, it has not been
> wholly without it's use ... Whoever wishes to attempt to cross the
> Mountains for the Purposes of Commerce ought to employ a
> Canoe, & start early in the Spring, say the beginning of May, from
> the Rocky Mountain House, the Water for that Month being low &
> the Current not half so violent as in the Summer ... In this Season,
> they would cross a great Part of the Mountains without any extraor-
> dinary Difficulty, and meet the Flushes of high Water where they
> would have need of it, that is, near the Head of the River—from
> whence there is said to be a short Road to the waters which flow on
> the other Side of the Mountain.

Thompson was bitterly disappointed at the failure of the expedition, but the consequences were more serious than he knew. Despite his blueprint, over five years would pass before he was allowed to make a second attempt to cross the Rocky Mountains. Thompson and his family stayed on at Rocky Mountain House for the winter of 1801–1802, but as soon as spring came, the North West Company ordered him north. His new job was to deal with two threats to the company's trade—the Hudson's Bay Company, which was taking a giant step to the north, and a new competitor who had emerged from an unexpected quarter.

That competitor was Alexander Mackenzie, newly returned from England. Mackenzie was now head of a group of renegade fur traders calling themselves the "New North West Company," but more commonly known as the XY Company. Named for the brand appearing on its bales, the XY Company was operating in the Athabasca Division, one of the North West Company's richest fur-bearing territories, and one where it had enjoyed a monopoly for twenty-four years. In order to concentrate on the threat posed by the interlopers, the Nor'Westers abandoned their attempt to develop a Columbia Division, stopped all western exploration, closed Rocky Mountain House, and sent David Thompson back to trading furs.

Northern Exile–
1802–1806

*For the next four years, David Thompson was
assigned to the northernmost regions of present-day
Alberta, Saskatchewan, and Manitoba. He put aside his
ambition to "expand my knowledge of the country," and took
up instead the routine life of a fur trader. Each winter, he
worked at his post, exchanging goods for the pelts brought
in by the trappers; each spring, he sent his canoes east
with the winter harvest of furs. Three times he made
the journey east himself, each trip bringing another
change in territory—first the Athabasca Division,
then the Churchill Division, and, at long last,
the Columbia Division again.*

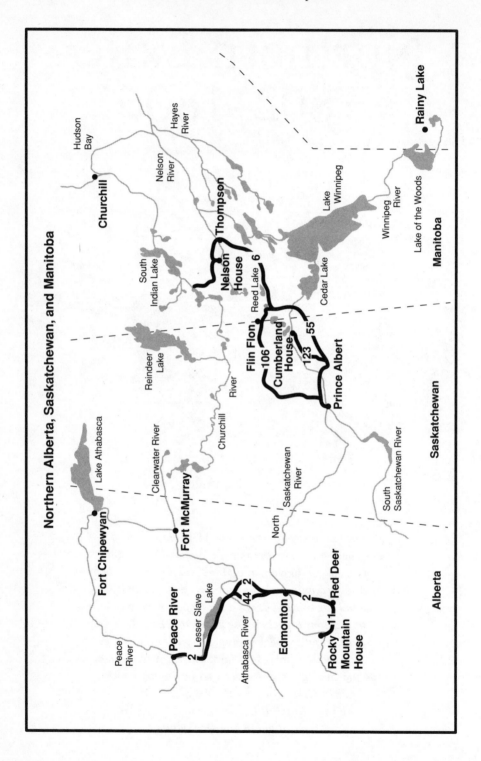

Northern Alberta, Saskatchewan, and Manitoba

THE NORTH WEST COMPANY DEALT IN A HOST OF FURS—FISHER AND FOX, otter and lynx, beaver and bear, wolf and wolverine, marten and mink and muskrat—but beaver dominated them all. In 1798 alone, the traders shipped 106,000 beaver pelts to Montreal, three times more than marten (which ranked second), and six times more than muskrat (a poor third).[1] So assured was the status of the beaver, its pelt served as a medium of exchange between the barter system of the Indians and the cash economy of Montreal. The price the company paid for a fox fur, for example, was based on its worth in "Made Beaver" (a prime pelt in good condition), and the price a Native paid for a gun or an axe was calculated the same way. In 1794 Duncan McGillivray listed some examples of the value the Nor'Westers assigned to their goods. Tabulated and edited for clarity, it read:[2]

Trade Item	Value in Made Beaver (MB)
Large Keg [liquor]	30 MB per keg
Long Guns	14 MB each
Fine Strouds [woollen cloth]	8 MB per fathom
Common Strouds	6 MB per fathom
Three-Point Blankets	6 MB each
Trenchers	3 MB pair
Medium Axe	2 MB each
Tobacco	3 MB per fathom
Balls [of shot]	1 MB for 20

Even the North West Company's coat of arms awarded top billing to the beaver. Surmounting the sailing ship, the moose's head, the canoeful of *voyageurs*, and the crusader's helmet, the company crest featured—not the typical lion rampant—but a humble Canadian beaver nibbling on a stick. Only a top hat could have ranked higher. Unbelievable as it seems, it was a fad in gentlemen's hats that drove the Canadian fur trade. A complex creation constructed of felted fur, the "beaver" made a fashion statement in the cities of Europe for more than two hundred years. This seemingly insatiable demand for hats built dozens of ships, hundreds of forts, and thousands of canoes. It spanned an ocean and opened a continent, created exports for Canada and business for Europe, and welded Indian, French, and Scot into a single massive enterprise called the North West Company. It also came within a whisker of wiping out Canada's national symbol altogether.

Long before it became the mainstay of the fur trade, beaver was an important source of food for the Indians, but since demand didn't exceed supply, even the common practice of destroying beaver lodges didn't seem to pose a threat to the species. With the coming of the fur trade, however, the picture changed. Demand for beaver soared, and as steel trenchers and axes arrived on the scene, the destruction of beaverworks took on a new efficiency. Duncan McGillivray described the ease with which he and his men eliminated an entire family.

> We found a Beaver lodge built on the side of a small dam—we
> resolved to work it, and began by cutting a passage in the dam in
> order to evacuate the water, and destroyed in a few hours the fabric
> which their ingenuity had been constructing for many years. We
> killed the whole of this family—4 old Beaver and as many young
> ones.[3]

Killing families of beaver was short-sighted, as the traders later realized when they moved to ban the practice. But as of 1794, when "traps of steel" started to replace the log deadfalls used by the Indians, the fur trade underwent another deadly increase in efficiency. Baited with castorum (scent from the beaver's own glands), steel traps led to overtrapping and its inevitable consequences: a shortage of beaver, poverty among the Indian people, and ever-lengthening supply lines for the company. As one region after another was trapped out, and one beaver population after another eliminated, the North West Company was forced to expand across the west and into the north—exploring more territory, building more forts, hiring more men—just to keep pace with the European demand for beaver.

That industrious little creature ultimately had its revenge. Today beaver colonies are well established wherever poplar groves and small streams occur together, which is to say almost everywhere on the Prairies. In agricultural areas, beaver are so numerous they're classified as a pest. They drop trees, dam streams, flood meadows, and take farmland out of production. In parks, too, they make their presence known, impairing the "natural" look of the trails with their incessant logging activities.

In the spring of 1802, Thompson and his family left Rocky Mountain House and travelled east to Fort William. At the annual meeting that year, Thompson was assigned to the Athabasca Division to "oppose" the competitors invading the territory—the Hudson's Bay Company and Mackenzie's newly formed XY Company. The Athabasca was a rich source of the finest beaver pelts in the country, and its defence was critical to the profitable operation of the North West Company.

In the fall, Thompson and his family travelled to northern Alberta, where they took up residence in an old post built by Alexander Mackenzie in 1792. Forks of the Peace River, now simply Peace River, was located about five miles downstream of the junction of the Smoky and the Peace. The post was extremely remote—practically at the western extremity of the North West Company's twenty-five-hundred-mile supply line—but the opposing forces were never very far away. Between them, the North West Company and its rivals had established a string of trading posts that reached from Peace River all the way to Fort Chipewyan on Lake Athabasca. In November Thompson mentioned passing a Hudson's Bay fort at Lesser Slave Lake, and in June the following year, he drily noted that the XY Company was building a new one only a hundred yards upstream of his own.

Wintering Nor'Westers and their rivals were generally on civil if not friendly terms—exchanging visits, celebrating holidays, and borrowing each other's books—but it was no holds barred when it came to trading furs. One indication of the intensity of the struggle that went on in the Athabasca Division was the flood of liquor that immediately started pouring north when the XY Company moved in. Although liquor was rarely a trade item, it was lavishly distributed among the Indians to lure them away from competitors. Author R.E. Pinkerton pointed out that when the battle for furs reached its peak, so did the volume of liquor imports.

> When the XY and North West Companies were at the height of their conflict [the Nor'Westers alone] sent 21,299 gallons into the Indian country ... After combining, the united companies sent only 10,800 gallons in 1806 and by 1808 had reduced that to 9,000.[4]

Caught up in the drive for furs, Thompson probably did whatever was necessary to boost the fortunes of the North West Company, including giving alcohol to the Natives. At the same time, it may have been these years of excess that finally turned him against using liquor as a bribe to trade, and led to his later resolve "... that no alcohol should pass the mountains in my company." Although Thompson often lamented the evils of drunkenness, it was Alexander Henry who detailed the havoc that liquor created. Noting that a "common dram shop" was a "paradise" in comparison, he went on:

Men and women have been drinking a match for three days and nights, during which it has been drink, fight—drink, fight—drink, and fight again—guns, axes and knives their weapons—very disagreeable ...

Grand Gueule stabbed Capot Rouge, Le Boeuf stabbed his young wife in the arm. Little Shell almost beat his mother's brains out with a club, and there was terrible fighting among them. I sowed garden seeds.[5]

Although liquor was the primary inducement to trade, it wasn't the only one. Guns and ammunition were a major attraction for the men, and the company's shipments also carried a complement of goods designed to appeal to women. Copper kettles and iron knives, awls and needles, cotton and woollen fabric (measured by the fathom), and blankets were all introduced early in the fur trade and soon became necessities. "Show them an awl or a strong needle," wrote Thompson, "and they will gladly give the finest Beaver or Wolf skin they have to purchase it." Lace, ribbons, earrings, brooches, and beads were welcome luxuries, and more than one *voyageur* put himself into hock with the North West Company buying trinkets and finery for his latest fancy.

During his stint at Peace River, Thompson still ranked as a clerk, and though he devoted his spare hours to recording his observations and working on his maps, his main responsibilities lay within the rhythm of the fur trade. When the snows came and ice closed the rivers, he spent his days trading with the Indian trappers, packing up furs for shipment east, and taking the occasional brief trip to relieve the monotony of a northern winter. When the rivers opened in the spring, he had his fur packs loaded into canoes, ready for the long haul to eastern Canada. But in 1803, Thompson didn't journey to Fort William. Instead, he devoted the summer to exploring the country around his post, and left the five-thousand-mile round trip to the wintering partners and the *voyageurs* who manned their canoes.

Each summer, fur brigades from all over the North West empire descended on Fort William, the company's western headquarters on Lake Superior. The *voyageurs* arrived from the Prairies with the winter harvest, exchanged their packs of furs for packs of British goods, then set out once more for the trading posts in the hinterland. Those who brought in furs from the Athabasca Division, however, rarely pushed farther east than the company's advance depot on Rainy Lake. Spring breakup and fall freeze-up set rigid limits on how far loaded canoes could travel in one season, and Fort William lay beyond the limits of the canoes from the Athabasca.

In the spring of 1804, Thompson and Charlotte left the Peace behind finally and forever. Now they travelled with two children—Fanny, who was almost three, and Samuel, who was born on March 5, 1804. Once again, Thompson had managed to absent himself. On the day young Samuel was born, his father was somewhere off to the west, visiting another "Rocky Mountain House" and surveying the upper reaches of the Peace River. Two days after he returned, he was hitching up a dog team to carry them to Lake Athabasca along the still-frozen river—presumably with Charlotte and her babies tucked up in the sled and himself mushing along behind.

During the two years Thompson traded in the Athabasca Division, the North West Company had shipped out more packs of beaver than the other two firms combined. Between his summer explorations and his route of departure through Lake Athabasca, he'd also managed to fit in a survey of almost the entire length of the Peace River.

From Lake Athabasca, Thompson and his family travelled on by canoe to Fort William, where Thompson planned to attend the North West Company's annual meeting. The meeting was notable for two reasons—a formal resolution banning Indian marriages, and Thompson's promotion to partner. For many years, the North West Company had condoned the practice of taking an Indian wife, both because it meant the traders had kinship ties to the tribes they dealt with and because the women made an economic contribution to the business of trading furs. At the annual meeting in 1804, however, the partners adopted a resolution prohibiting marriage to an Indian woman.

> No Partner, Clerk, or Engage, belonging to the Concern shall henceforth take or suffer to be taken under any pretense whatsoever, any woman or maid from any of the tribes of Indians now known or who may hereafter become known in this Country, to live with him within the Company's Houses or Forts and be maintained at the expense of the Concern.[6]

The fine for a violation was set at one hundred pounds. Several explanations have been advanced for this move on the part of the company: the increasing disenchantment of the Plains Indians with the fur trade; too many of the company's *voyageurs* leaving its service to settle in the west with their families; and a population explosion among North West dependants in the field. With respect to the latter, the partners had reason for concern. By 1810 the *Fort des Prairies* headquarters alone would boast a population of twenty-eight men, thirty-five women, and seventy-two children. The men, however, weren't expected to remain celibate or to survive in the wilderness without a woman's help, so the partners included an exception.

> It is however understood that taking the Daughter of a white man
> after the fashion of the Country shall be considered no violation of
> this resolve.[7]

The partners hoped the men would marry each other's half-blood daughters, thereby reducing the number of dependants living at the company posts. The original stricture was never applied to Thompson's Columbia Division, probably because in its early years there were no country daughters there for the men to marry.

At the same meeting, after seven years as a company clerk, David Thompson was officially elected a wintering partner and awarded two shares in the North West Company, each worth more than two thousand pounds sterling. On a more prosaic level, he was allotted an annual ration of four pounds of coffee, four pounds of chocolate, and six pounds of tea, double the ration he'd enjoyed as a clerk. But if Thompson had entertained hopes of being allowed to resume his search for the Columbia River, he would have been disappointed. Instead, the company sent him north again to take over the Churchill Division, a territory that Thompson disparagingly referred to as "Musk Rat Country." For some reason, the North West Company had been neglecting the Churchill, and most of the trade there had fallen into the hands of the Hudson's Bay Company. With the XY Company moving in as well, the partners had decided to take action.

After leaving Fort William, Thompson and his family travelled by canoe as far west as Cumberland House, a North West post on the Saskatchewan River that served as a supply depot. "It is at Cumberland House," Thompson wrote, "all the Pimmecan, and dried provisions of all kinds procured from the great Plains are brought down the Saskatchewan and deposited here." Peter Pond, an early Nor'Wester, is credited with the idea of using pemmican to supply the canoe brigades on their ever-lengthening journeys across the country. The recipe for pemmican was developed by the Indians, and its adoption by the Nor'Westers solved the trade's most pressing problem—an open water season so short that the *voyageurs* couldn't spare the time from their paddles to hunt for food.

Eventually, the inventory of pemmican along the Saskatchewan route was measured in tons, and the production of its ingredients by the Indians rivalled the trade in furs. The main ingredient was buffalo meat, stripped of its fat, then split, dried, and smoked over a small fire. The dried meat was pounded into a powder called "beat meat," a product so concentrated that all the lean meat on an adult buffalo went into the production of a single ninety-pound sack of pemmican. A second ingredient was fat—hard fat, stripped from the inside of the buffalo and melted to make "grease," and soft fat, separated in large flakes from either side of the backbone. Thompson recalled the qualities of melted soft fat in his *Narrative*, saying it "resembled butter in softness and sweetness," and went on to describe the process of combining the ingredients.

> The proportion of pemmican when made for best keeping is twenty pounds of soft and the same of hard fat, melted slowly together, and at low warmth poured on fifty pounds of Beat Meat; well mixed together, and slowly packed in a [rawhide] bag of about thirty inches in length, by near twenty inches in about four inches in thickness which makes them flat, the best shape for stowage and carriage.

The best pemmican had flavour and vitamins added in the form of dried berries, and an important summer task of the women was providing the berries. Today, berry picking usually means gathering a pailful for jam or pie, but the wives and daughters of the traders harvested their berries in bulk. They rode forth armed with buffalo robes, which they spread on the ground to catch the shower of berries—and leaves and twigs—that they beat from the bushes with a stick. The favoured berries were Saskatoons, also called serviceberries or Juneberries, which were abundant in the northwest and in many places still are. The *voyageurs* called the bush *bois de fleche* (arrow wood) because the Indians used its wood, which is both strong and straight, in making arrows. Although chokecherries were sometimes used to make pemmican, the Nor'Westers, who had to live on the stuff for months at a stretch, preferred their pemmican made with berries. Chokecherries are astringent rather than sweet, and though the women pounded the cherries, they didn't attempt to pit them, resulting in pemmican that was gritty with stones.

Thompson remembered pemmican as "wholesome" and "well tasted," but not every trader agreed with his assessment. He neglected to mention the dirt, sticks, and hair that completed the list of ingredients.

In the same passage, he illustrated (at the expense of the *voyageurs'* image) just how concentrated the fuel of the fur trade was.

> ... it is the staple food of all persons, and affords the most nourish-
> ment in the least space and weight, even the gluttonous french cana-
> dian that devours eight pounds of fresh meat every day is contented
> with one and half pound pʳ day.

Thompson set out from Cumberland House with a brigade of three canoes loaded with trade goods and provisions. He headed east to Manitoba's Cranberry Lake, where he left a crew to build a new post, then turned north toward the Bay's Nelson House, where he assigned a second crew to reopen an old one. From there, he dispatched a third crew even farther north to Southern Indian Lake, then moved downstream of Nelson House to start building his own quarters on the Nelson River. At an unidentified post called Musquawegan, Thompson and his family set-tled in for the winter.

Now that he was a partner in the North West Company, Thompson's duties changed and, in his view at least, probably not for the better. In addition to his own post, he found himself in charge of three or four outposts, and was often on the move, supervising the seasonal movement of goods and furs throughout the Churchill Division. This was country that Thompson knew like the back of his hand, territory he'd mapped years ago, and he must have spent at least some of his time dreaming about the unmapped regions that lay west of the Rocky Mountains.

While Thompson was working to get the Churchill Division run-ning again, the structure of the North West Company was changing. Liberated by the death of ruling partner Simon McTavish in July 1804, the Montreal partners made several unexpected moves. On November 5, they ended the cutthroat competition with the XY Company by forming a merger, which Thompson signed "by attorney," but didn't learn about until the following summer. Once the dispute with the XY Company was resolved, the partners turned their attention to a new threat south of the border.

In May 1804 Lewis and Clark had set out to explore President Jefferson's newly acquired Louisiana Territory. Purchased from France in a deal negotiated with Napoleon Bonaparte, the territory included most of the heartland of the future United States of America. Somewhere in this vast expanse, Lewis and Clark hoped to find a navigable route to the Pacific Ocean. It may have been nothing more than coincidence, but the attention of the Nor'Westers seems to have been arrested by this development. In 1805 they sent Simon Fraser to ascend the Peace River, cross the Rocky Mountains, and develop a territory that would later be named New Caledonia. Fraser was to build a series of company posts, open trade with the Indians, find the river thought to be the Columbia (which turned out to be the Fraser), and follow it to the Pacific.

If the Montreal partners intended to compete with the Americans, they'd made a mistake in burdening Fraser with the chores of the fur trade. In their defence, they could have had only the fuzziest notion of the geography west of the mountains—maps of the area were largely blank at the time—and they may not have grasped the scale of what they expected him to accomplish. Whatever the cause, the results were predictable. By the time Fraser set out on his expedition, Lewis and Clark were within striking distance of the Columbia River; as he built trading posts in New Caledonia, they were building Fort Clatsop on the shores of the Pacific Ocean; while he was working to establish the fur trade in British Columbia, the Americans were wintering on the Columbia. By 1808, the year Fraser finally reached the Pacific, Lewis and Clark had been gone for two years.

Despite their apparent concern about events on the Columbia, the North West partners gave no sign that they were ready to let Thompson have another try at crossing the Rockies. Instead, he was left to carry on in the Churchill Division for another winter. In his second trading season, Thompson changed his strategy. He closed Cranberry Lake and built a new post at Pukatawagan near Reindeer Lake, giving him three posts on the Churchill River, the Hudson's Bay Company's main route from Fort Churchill to the Athabasca. That fall, he moved south to build his own quarters on Reed Lake, next door to an abandoned post where he'd once wintered during his years with the Bay.

Even with all Thompson's efforts, the Churchill Division's fur take that winter was small. Still, before 1806 came to an end, he had other reasons to consider the year a good one. His third child, Emma, was born at Reed Lake House; the Hudson's Bay Company withdrew its forces from the Athabasca; and at the annual meeting at Fort William, John McDonald of Garth, now head of the *Forts des Prairies* Division, invited him to return to Rocky Mountain House and resume his search for the Columbia.

Howse Pass
–1807[1]

*David Thompson returned to Rocky Mountain
House in late October 1806, five and a half years after
his excursion up the North Ram River. He was now thirty-six
years old, Charlotte was twenty-one, and they had three young
children—Fanny, Samuel, and Emma—all under the age of six.
Thompson's historic journey across the Rockies lay more than
six months in the future, but preparations had been under
way since spring and would continue all winter. Past
experience, advance planning, new information, and
even Lady Luck herself all conspired to ensure
that this attempt would be a successful one.*

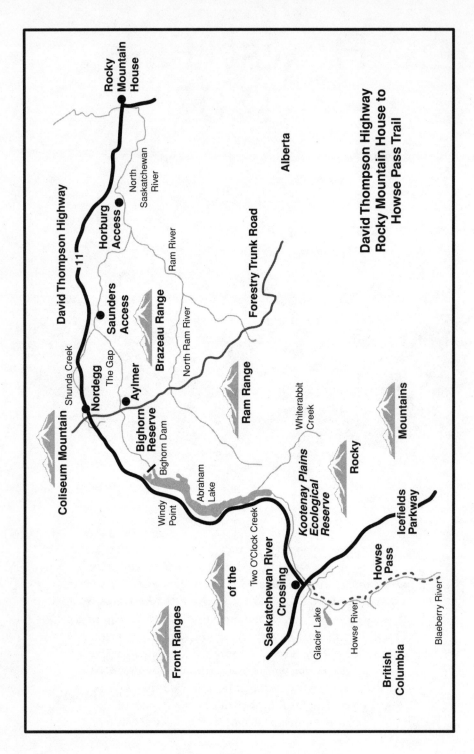

David Thompson Highway
Rocky Mountain House to
Howse Pass Trail

IF THERE'D BEEN A NORTHWEST NEWSPAPER IN 1806, THE JULY 27 edition might have carried the headline: "U.S. Army Foils Indian Attack." Although Captain Lewis and his men emerged from the skirmish unharmed, the Peigans never forgot that two of their braves had been killed. From that day on, they drew a distinction between the "Northern White Men" and the Americans to the south. Inspired by the massive swords carried by the U.S. Cavalry, the Peigans dubbed the Americans "Big Knives."

The knife that killed one of the Peigans was wielded by Reuben Fields, one of three men who accompanied Captain Lewis when he split off from the army's main Corps of Discovery to explore the Marias River. On a tributary of the river, Lewis and his men ran into eight Peigan war-riors scouting for a war party, and after a parley in sign language and an evening of smoking, the two groups camped together for the night.

Whether Lewis was extremely brave or merely reckless, he should have known that four white men wandering alone in Indian country were asking for trouble. In his defence, it could be argued that most of the Indians the expedition had encountered so far had been either peace-able or afraid. Unfortunately for Captain Lewis, the Peigans were nei-ther. They'd been part of the Canadian fur trade for decades and were more accustomed to inspiring fear than experiencing it. They were also somewhat spoiled by the Canadian traders' policy of winking at the larcenous habits of the young Peigan braves. Partly to keep the peace, but primarily to preserve the trade, the Nor'Westers tended to guard against thievery when they could and tolerate it when they couldn't. Captain Lewis, on the other hand, had no stake in the fur trade, no con-cern about customer relations, and, given his background, an under-standably conventional attitude toward theft.

The Peigans waited until dawn to make their move. At first light, one group seized the Americans' rifles, another rounded up the horses and took off with them. Fields, who hadn't been paying attention to his gun, jumped up, struggled with the Peigan who'd taken it, then stabbed the man to the heart with a hunting knife. Captain Lewis chased after the Peigans driving the horses, shouting at them to stop or he'd shoot. One man turned to face him, and Lewis shot him in the stomach. Six Peigans got away and rode to alert the war party. Lewis and his men fled toward the Missouri River, riding all that day and most of the night to escape the wrath that was bound to follow.[2]

This disastrous encounter translated into a stroke of luck for Thompson. When the Peigans near Rocky Mountain House got wind of the news that two of their braves had been killed, they swarmed south, hell-bent on revenge. As a result, the season's trade at Rocky Mountain House fell off. Only a few bands of Kootenays risked coming to the fort, and the usual steady trade with the Peigans declined to a trickle. According to historian Eugene Arima:

> In the 1806–07 trade season, the Pikani visited the post only a dozen times ... mostly in small groups of four to twelve men and with little to trade ... Thompson complains that their trade was "hardly enough to pay for the Rum."[3]

On New Year's Day, 1807, and again that March, Peigan Chief Kootanae Appee visited the fort, apparently to warn Thompson that the Peigans were prepared to cause trouble if he went ahead with his plans to cross the mountains. (A fanciful National Film Board of Canada re-enactment of the scene portrays a group of Peigans riding through a craggy Ontario landscape; a smiling Thompson greeting them in front of a picture of a fort; and a mounted Kootanae Appee grunting a warning to stay away from The Pass.) But even though Kootanae Appee was the Peigan war chief, he'd never shown much interest in declaring war on the North West Company; and if he'd come to Rocky Mountain House to deliver a warning, Thompson chose to ignore it.

After Kootanae Appee's second visit, the Peigans seemed to lose all interest in Rocky Mountain House, and by the time the expedition was launched in May, the threat of interference from that quarter had disappeared altogether. In his *Narrative*, Thompson acknowledged his debt to Captain Lewis.

> ... the murder of two Peagan Indians by Captain Lewis of the United States, drew the Peagan to the Missouri to revenge their deaths; and thus gave me an opportunity to cross the Mountains by the defiles of the Saskatchewan River ...

While Captain Lewis was sparring with the Peigans, John McDonald of Garth was making sure that this time the North West Company's bid to cross the mountains would be a successful one. In the spring of 1806, almost a year before the expedition set out, he decided to send a *Fort des Prairies* clerk to lead a work party across the Continental Divide to blaze a trail for Thompson. The man he chose for the job was Jacques Raphael Finlay.

Finlay (more commonly known as Jaco) was something of a free spirit, but he was also a man of many talents. During his years with the

North West Company, he worked as a clerk, interpreter, trapper, scout, horse trainer, and builder of canoes and forts. The country son of North West partner James Finlay and an Ojibwa girl, Jaco had grown up in the prairie posts, trained as a North West clerk by the time he was sixteen, and was associated with the company for more than thirty-five years. During five of those years, he often worked for Thompson, and even when he and Thompson were on the outs, Jaco worked around the fringes of the North West Company, making his living as a free trader and (some say) as a spy for the Hudson's Bay Company. Jaco was also an expert gunsmith. In later years, botanist David Douglas brought his gun to Spokane House for repairs and was surprised to learn that Jaco didn't speak English.

In the North West Company, clerks who spoke English were the exception rather than the rule. The company's partners were predominantly Scots (their meetings, according to historian Wilkins-Campbell, resembled a Gathering of the Clans[4]), but the language of the company's fur trade was French. The reason lay in the Nor'Westers' early history. In the mid-1760s, the company's forerunners had inherited the trade routes of the vanquished French and had taken on the French-speaking *voyageurs* to man its brigades of canoes. The fledgling firm also hired clerks who spoke French, and later expected its wintering partners to learn the language as well. Even Thompson spoke French and is said to have read the Bible to his men in that language, though his efforts are variously reported as extraordinary, eccentric, and (surely an exaggeration) execrable.

Jaco took up his assignment by travelling west to the Kootenay Plains, where he camped for the duration of the grazing season with his family, his horses, and two Ojibwa hunters. From this base, Jaco, a man named MacMaster, and two of Thompson's men headed up the North Saskatchewan. They followed the Howse River into the mountains, ascended Conway Creek, and crossed the Continental Divide through Howse Pass. From there, the men slashed a rough trail down the Blaeberry River and built two canoes for Thompson to use when he reached the western side of the mountains. In November Jaco turned up at Rocky Mountain House to report to Thompson and draw a map of where he'd been.

Thompson now had a clearer picture of an unknown road than he'd ever had before or, for that matter, would ever have again. He had his own knowledge of the North Saskatchewan River from Rocky Mountain House to The Gap in the Brazeau Range; he could draw on the information he'd gained in his conversations with the Kootenay Indians; and he had Jaco's map—a sketch of the land route to the mountains, the portage across the pass, and the trail down the other side. As if all that weren't enough, Boulard and Bercier, the two men who had crossed the Divide with Jaco's work party, would cross it again with the expedition.

This time events were running in Thompson's favour. It was his own experience, however, that produced the strategy for the journey, a strategy based on the blueprint he'd drawn up after the North Ram expedition fell apart. To guard against a repeat of that disaster, Thompson planned a two-pronged assault on the Rockies—one by river, the other by land. And, except for his resolution to take fewer men (in the end, he took just as many men, as well as three women and six children), he would follow his blueprint to the letter.

Trade may have been quiet that winter, but Rocky Mountain House was alive with preparations for the trip. Before spring arrived, a canoe had to be built, snowshoes constructed, hides stitched into mitts, caps, and moccasins, trade goods sorted and packed, and hundreds of pounds of pemmican manufactured to provision the journey west. The women would have been as heavily involved in the drive to get ready as the men, but Thompson's habit of writing sentences without subjects renders who did what a mystery. Nor'Wester Alexander Henry was Thompson's opposite. He recorded every detail of the routine at his post—men out haying, women off berrying, children chasing hailstones, himself shooting a dog for biting his little girl. Even the arrival of a newly hatched chick was duly recorded in his journal. But writing reports on the domestic routine simply didn't interest Thompson—his passion was the unknown.

During the winter, John McDonald of Garth paid periodic visits to Rocky Mountain House, possibly to make sure that two controversial liquor casks would be included in the inventory. Thompson had resolved that they would not, but in a heated argument with two of his North West partners, he'd been overruled.

> I was obliged to take two kegs of alcohol ... for I had made it a law to
> myself, that no alcohol should pass the Mountains in my company,
> and thus be clear of the sad sight of drunkenness, and its many evils ...
> but these gentlemen insisted upon alcohol being the most profitable
> article that could be taken for the Indian trade. In this I knew they
> had miscalculated; accordingly when we came to the defiles of the
> Mountains, I placed the two Kegs of Alcohol on a vicious horse; and
> by noon the kegs were empty, and in pieces, the Horse rubbing his

load against the rocks to get rid of it; I wrote to my partners what
I had done; and that I would do the same to every Keg of Alcohol,
and for the next six years I had charge of the fur trade on the west
side of the Mountains, no further attempt was made to introduce
spirituous Liquors.

This passage is just one example of Thompson adding "colour" to
his *Narrative* to increase its popular appeal. In this instance, he seems to
have inserted the story in the wrong chapter. According to the
Narrative, the argument with the partners took place in the summer of
1808, but the story itself says that the Columbia Division was free of
alcohol for the "next six years." Since Thompson worked west of the
mountains for only six years in total, it's more likely that he tangled
with his partners as early as 1806, when he was making up his load of
trade goods for his first venture across the mountains. It was during his
first trading season on the Columbia that a group of twenty-three
Peigans arrived at his new fort looking for alcohol. On that occasion, he
recorded that "as usual they asked for Rum & could not be persuaded
that we had none." Whether the tale of the broken casks is fact or fable
(it doesn't appear in his journals for either of the years in question), it
seems likely that Thompson's refusal to engage in the liquor trade dated
from his first year on the Columbia.

Thompson wasn't a drinking man, and he's sometimes portrayed as
the type who denies others a drink because he doesn't want one himself.
Thompson, however, wasn't quite that petty. He had, after all, a long
history of using liquor in the fur trade, and he also took a certain amount
of alcohol west of the mountains. His men expected their rum ration,
and Thompson expressed concern whenever the keg ran low, readily
admitting that "a dram" had often done them much good.

The journey to the mountains was slated to follow on the heels of
spring breakup, while flows in the North Saskatchewan were still low
enough for the *voyageurs* to make headway against the river's current.
The canoe that Thompson's men were working on was designed for
northern rivers, and one of its most useful characteristics was its ability
to keep going in low water. The "Canadian canoe" was developed by the
Algonquin Indians, and, according to aficionado Russ Gardner, refined to
such a state of perfection by the Woodland Cree, Montagnais, and
Ojibwa that it would "float on a wet handkerchief."[5] Nevertheless,
the canoe posed a problem. Though a light canoe would float in shallow water, a canoe carrying six men and close to a ton of trade goods
wouldn't.

By late winter, Thompson was anticipating the difficulty and, determined to preserve his early start at any cost, set his men to work building sleds to transport part of the load up the frozen North Saskatchewan. That year, the plan was feasible; in other years, it might not have been. As a rule, prairie rivers freeze to a flat, smooth surface (ideal for running dogsleds then and snowmobiles now), but the North Saskatchewan River is different. Its heavy rapids carve channels in the ice, break up the river below, and bury its downstream reaches in a jumble of frozen chunks. In 1810 Alexander Henry described a thaw that created blocks of ice stacked fifteen feet high, an effect that's sometimes seen to this day. But in 1806, the river must have been the same as any other prairie river—an icy highway covered in a blanket of snow.

Well before spring arrived, Thompson's men hitched up their teams of dogs, ran half a ton of trade goods about sixty miles upstream, and set up a cache on the riverbank. J.B. Tyrrell claims that all this was done very quietly, so the Hudson's Bay men at nearby Acton House wouldn't know what the Nor'Westers were up to.[6] Maybe so. But it's hard to believe that a cavalcade of excitable French Canadian *voyageurs* and their teams of unruly dogs could have headed up the North Saskatchewan River without the whole neighbourhood hearing about it. In any case, secrecy would hardly have been an issue. As early as the previous December, Hudson's Bay Factor James Bird had written a report that showed a considerable knowledge of the North West Company's plans.

> Mr David Thompson is making preparations for another attempt
> to cross the Mountains, pass through the Country and follow the
> Columbia River to the Sea ... the object of his enterprise is said to be
> to ascertain positively whether a Trade can be formed with that
> Country valuable enough to be worth pursuing thro' the difficulties
> with which it must be attended, and if it should, the uniting of the
> Commerce of the two Seas.[7]

Less than a week after spring breakup, the expedition to the mountains was already under way. For two days, one party after another set out from Rocky Mountain House, and by early afternoon on May 10, the fort lay abandoned. Thompson's journal entry for that date recorded the details of their departure.

At 9½ Am sent off Mr Finan McDonald & 5 Men in a Canoe with
Goods & Necessaries to the expedition ... Yesterday I sent off 2 Men
with 6 lean Horses, for want of better, with Provisions &c for the
above purpose. At 10 Am I set off with Bercier on Horseback ... but
could not get the Horses 'till 2½ Pm, when with very hard riding
thro' thick woods very much fallen down we arrived at the Round
Plain.

Crowded into this brief paragraph is a large cast of characters moving west in two separate groups—one grappling with the rapids of the
North Saskatchewan River, the other winding through the woods on
horseback. We see red-haired Finan McDonald, Thompson's clerk, taking charge of the canoe; Boisverd, Buché, Beaulieu, Lussier, and Le
Camble thrusting their paddles into the current; Boulard and Clément
riding on ahead with the "6 lean Horses" loaded with provisions. And
we can imagine the women and children who rode with them—
Charlotte Thompson and her three children (baby Emma on her back);
Lussier's wife and her three children; an Indian woman who (once again)
wanted to return to her people—and the pack of dogs trotting alongside.
Finally, we see Thompson and Bercier spending four and a half hours trying to find their horses, then putting in a hard ride to reach the expedition's encampment before nightfall.

Despite the complicated logistics, things seemed to be going well for
Thompson. Although he rarely bothered to record his moods (aside from
an occasional announcement that he was "vexed"), his journals for the
first leg of the trip indicate a man well pleased with the world. Forgotten
were the troubled days on the North Ram River when "all Nature
seemed to frown." On this journey, all Nature seemed to smile. The
morning the expedition set out, Thompson's weather report read, "A
very fine day," and the next morning it read the same. Although the day
after that was merely "a fine day," and the next brought a "morn of very
cold thick Snow," Thompson quickly started another string of very
fine days, his spirits apparently undampened by cloud, wind, or even
showers. Before two weeks had gone by, he'd come up with the upbeat
phrase "a day of flying cloud," and liked it so much he used it four times
over the next five days. By the last week in May, he was in such a good
mood, he happily declared the 27th, "A fine but stormy Day."

The women may have been less pleased with the trail along the
river. Thompson described it as "a very bad road," but from the point of
view of the women, who were accustomed to the open spaces of the
prairie, it must have seemed no road at all. The country had been

ravaged by fire and was clogged with the remains of burnt trees. Each day, the horses, with their long-suffering riders, clambered, lurched, jolted, splashed, and scrambled their way west; each evening, the women pitched the tents, cooked a meal, tended to the children, then retired to their tents until it was time to reload and set out again. The pace was agonizingly slow—often less than one or two miles an hour. They rode for three weeks through the wreckage of the forest before they reached open country at Kootenay Plains.

One of the few major landmarks named after Thompson is a modern road called the David Thompson Highway. The highway begins at the north end of the town of Rocky Mountain House, sweeps west for a hundred miles, and ends at Saskatchewan River Crossing in Banff National Park. From time to time, a highway sign will name a point of interest that happens to be near an area that Thompson also had a name for.

Thompson's Name	Today's Name for Where He Was
Lower War Tent	Horburg Canoe Access
The Round Plain	South of Chambers Creek Hills
The Long Plain	Southeast of Jackfish Creek
Plain of the War Tent	Near Saunders Access
Jaco's Brook	Shunda Creek
Upper War Tent	Beaverdam Campground, Nordegg
Kootanae Plains	Abraham Lake and Kootenay Plains Ecological Reserve
The Forks	Junction of the North Saskatchewan and Howse Rivers

Despite the promise of its name, the David Thompson Highway doesn't always follow in the tracks of its namesake. Between the fort and Horburg, Thompson's trail lay along the cliffs above the North Saskatchewan River; the highway runs parallel, but four miles farther north. In 1911 the tracks of the Canadian North Western Railway picked up Thompson's trail and followed it all the way to Nordegg; today grid roads and a fragment of Old Highway 11A still follow a similar route for about fifteen miles west of Rocky Mountain House Historic Park. The David Thompson Highway takes a different route, wandering at times even farther away from Thompson's trail than it does at its outset. Near Chambers Creek, for example, the highway arches north around a series of hills; Thompson's trail skirted the southern edge of these hills, more than six miles away.

As well as sheer distance, another barrier between the highway and Thompson's trail is the Rocky-Clearwater Forest. Over much of its length, the David Thompson Highway can best be described as "hemmed in." Relieved only occasionally by a tamarack swamp or a beaverworks, dense stands of pine and spruce confine the road, and the trail that Thompson travelled, the North Saskatchewan River beyond, and the broad valley where the river flows are all hidden from view.

As Thompson and his party rode the benchlands above the river, the *voyageurs* were fighting their way upstream against the force of its current. In the fifty miles above Rocky Mountain House, six sets of major rapids (with numerous lesser rapids scattered between) have earned this stretch of river a place in guidebooks such as Stuart Smith's *Canadian Rockies Whitewater*. But the *voyageurs* (quite apart from the fact that they were heading upstream) faced an even tougher job than the modern paddler. According to Travel Alberta's *Reach Reports*:

> Prior to the construction of the Bighorn Dam, the North Saskatchewan in this reach was known for its powerful rapids and was a challenge for the expert white water paddler. Flow regulation has resulted in a considerable alteration in the character of the river, generally taming its force ...[8]

Six years before, Thompson's crew had been overwhelmed by high water. On this trip, the river was low—fast-flowing and riddled with rapids, but shallow enough for the men to work in. The men could be forgiven, however, if they failed to consider this a benefit. Although they must have been in the canoe sometimes, they seem to have spent most of their time in the river. Again and again, they plunged into the frigid water to tow the canoe—hauling it along against the force of the current, battling one explosion of rapids after another, and ending each battle half-frozen and soaked. In a report to his partners, Thompson described what his men endured in getting the canoe up the river.

> The greatest Hardship of the People lay in being continually wet up to the Waist, exposed to cold high winds, & the water, coming direct from the Snows on the Mountains, was always so excessively cold as to deprive them of all feeling in their Limbs.

For five days, the *voyageurs* lived with the river, stopping each night to unload the canoe, build a fire, feed themselves, and crawl under the shelter of their upturned craft to get some sleep. On the morning of

May 16, they emerged from their latest round with the river near the mouth of Shunda Creek. Here they were joined by the hunters— Thompson's own and a visiting Cree named The Wolverene—who arrived the same morning with several loads of fresh meat. Thompson, his usual dashing style curbed by the assembly of women, children, pack horses, and dogs he had in tow, was the last to arrive.

> At 11 Am came to Jaco's Brook, where the Canoe & Men were wait-
> ing; [the hunters had] brought 2 Horse Loads of Meat—they had
> also killed a good Bull & a Red Deer. Got a quantity of the Meat
> split & dried for the use of the Canoe Men. The River is now very
> shoal & full of Rapids, but the Navigation is not worse than about
> the Fort below & for about 7 Miles above it. We now turn to the
> right to go up along the Brook ... the Mountains may be about 6 or
> 8M distant.

Thompson's mention of "Jaco's Brook" indicates he was starting to make use of the information on Jaco's map. Today, Jaco's Brook is called Shunda Creek, though it's had more than its share of names over the years. In addition to Thompson's sometimes calling it North Brook, Shunda Creek has been variously called Sinda Waptan (Stoney for "Mire Creek"), Mire Creek, Miry Creek, Big Fish Creek, and Fishing Creek.[9] Jaco's map also showed a "First or Last Ridge of Mountains," an outly-ing range of the Rockies now known as the Brazeaus. To get past the Brazeaus, the *voyageurs* had to take the canoe through the canyon known as The Gap, while the riders followed Shunda Creek. So far, Thompson had travelled a familiar trail, but once he turned aside from the North Saskatchewan River, he was entering new territory.

> Being now to go over Ground I have not yet passed, I will take the
> Courses, the best the nature of the thick woody Country will per-
> mit me. At 8¼ Am set off, Co S72W 6 or 7M—we followed the
> north Brook, very often crossing the Stream ... Put up at ¾ Pm as
> our Horses are very weak & poor—the first Grass is just showing
> itself in a few advantageous Spots.

The course of Shunda Creek marks Thompson's trail through the Brazeaus; the David Thompson Highway now follows a similar route along the Brazeau Bypass. The riders followed Shunda Creek for five days, and on their third night out, camped just east of present-day

Nordegg. An isolated community formerly known as the site of the Brazeau Collieries, Nordegg is better known today as the only stop on the David Thompson Highway that's open for business in the winter. Thompson's description indicates they were camped near today's Beaverdam Campground, between the "detached Mass" of the Brazeaus and the "tolerable even surface" of Coliseum Mountain.

> Camped at the upper War Tent, where the Nahathaways [Cree] formerly entrenched themselves ... the Woods are all green, but small; the foot of the Mountains [on the left] a^{bt} 1M or so from us—those on the [right] a^{bt} 3M, & the Land between is very swampy.

Game was plentiful in the Brazeaus, and Thompson and his hunters kept the people well fed with a steady supply of buffalo meat and an occasional porcupine. The horses were less fortunate. The "first Grass" was barely enough to keep them going, and they "fell down frequently with weakness & bad Roads." By the fourth day the riders had made it through the Brazeaus, and Thompson turned south to follow Shunda Creek past its headwaters. Two days later they were back on the banks of the North Saskatchewan. They set up camp, and Thompson started watching the river for the canoe.

After three days of waiting, the canoe still hadn't appeared. Impatient to move on, but with no way of knowing if the *voyageurs* had made it safely through The Gap, Thompson sent two men downriver to check out the cache of goods that had been brought up the river by dogsled the previous winter.

> As I was doubtful whether the Canoe & People had passed us or not, I sent down Clement & Bercier to go below along the Banks of the River to where the Goods of the Winter were put in Hoard. They went & found the canoe had passed ...

It's not clear exactly where the "Hoard" was, but a wilderness staging area that now goes by the name of Aylmer is a likely spot. Wherever the cache may have been, it wasn't very far downstream. Clément and Bercier were back the same evening to report that the *voyageurs* had already picked up their first load of goods and were well on their way to Kootenay Plains.

Aylmer

~ The staging area at Aylmer is situated southwest of Nordegg, where the Forestry Trunk Road crosses the North Saskatchewan River. The clearing there is large enough to unload a horse trailer, and the riverbanks are low enough to launch a canoe.

~ For Thompson's men, the main advantage of Aylmer would have been its location west of the Brazeaus. If the goods had been stored east of the Brazeaus, the *voyageurs* would have had to run The Gap twice, both times with the canoe fully loaded, and up a stretch of river that Thompson described as "much worse" than the river below.

The next day Thompson marched his party west to the junction of the North Saskatchewan and Bighorn Rivers and camped on land that's now part of the Stoney Indians' Bighorn Reserve. Here, on a small plain where there was grass for the horses, he stayed for a week to organize the final move of goods and people to the foot of the Rocky Mountains. On his first day in camp, he scouted the road ahead and discovered that Jaco's route followed a precipitous trail along a row of cliffs that towered above the North Saskatchewan River. Unwilling to trust his weak and weary horses on such a trail, Thompson started looking for an alternative.

> Bercier with myself went to find a Road to pass by that may avoid the high Banks of the usual Route—we found one, but finding a still better, we followed it 'till late without knowing where it ends ... [The next day] followed up the Road of yesterday—found it to be tolerable good & entirely keeps clear of the high Banks so dangerous to the Horses & Property.

The "high Banks" that Thompson was so anxious to avoid are now the site of TransAlta's Bighorn Dam. Constructed during the early 1970s, the dam backed up twenty-four miles of braided river, flooded part of the Kootenay Plains, and created a new body of water known as Abraham Lake. The damsite itself is first cousin to a gravel pit, but an extensive wall display in the Bighorn Information Centre commemorates Thompson's travels in North America. On the site's western edge, a landscaped viewpoint overlooks Abraham Lake. Painted a startling turquoise by its load of glacial silt, the lake is noted for being coldly beautiful, dangerously windy, and highly unpredictable. The David Thompson Highway runs along the slopes above its shoreline, and about five miles up the lake, Windy Point marks the boundary between the Alberta foothills and the front ranges of the Rocky Mountains.

On June 1, the expedition left the camp on the Bighorn Reserve, the *voyageurs* setting off to haul their last load up the river to Kootenay Plains, Thompson's riders mounting their horses to follow along shore. This was country the horses could handle, and the expedition started to put on a little speed. On the first day, the riders passed Windy Point; on the second, they rested the horses; on the third, they crossed the Cline River and were nearing an area now known as the Kootenay Plains Ecological Reserve. Thompson, who had never seen the valley of the upper North Saskatchewan before, was frankly enjoying the scenery.

> Co S22E 4M thro' the Kootanae Plains, where we put up near the Canoe & People at 1 Pm—we came fast on, often at a sound Trot. The Valleys, notwithstanding the rugged snowy appearance of the Chain of Mountains about us, are pleasant, & one might pass an agreeable summer in such places as we have come thro' the last 4 Miles ...

That evening the travellers reached Jaco's camp on Kootenay Plains, where they settled in to wait until the snow in Howse Pass had melted. Thompson didn't describe this camp, but judging from the distance the riders travelled, it was probably at the southern end of Abraham Lake near a ceremonial ground that the Indians had established alongside a stream now known as Two O'Clock Creek.

Two O'Clock Creek Campground borders the Kootenay Plains Ecological Reserve, a broad swath of prairie grassland cast up into the Rocky Mountains. Just south of the campground, the Siffleur Falls Trail leads into a landscape that looks much the same now as it did in Thompson's time. Generally dry, windswept, and covered in sand, the reserve manages to support an expanse of native grass, clusters of ground-hugging juniper and cranberry, and groves of spruce, pine, and poplar. As was true in Thompson's day, the grass cover is sparse and vulnerable to overgrazing—threatened then by the elk, deer, and buffalo (and Jaco's horses) that grazed the Kootenay Plains, and now by the large herd of elk that still makes its living there.

Although The Wolverene had headed north to guide the Indian woman to her people, between Thompson's crew, Jaco's family, and the two Ojibwa hunters and their families, the camp on Kootenay Plains housed thirteen men, five women, and a troop of a dozen children— quite aside from the herd of mares and stallions and the inevitable pack of dogs. Maybe Thompson was thinking the uproar at the camp was more than he could handle; maybe he was musing about that pass in the mountains, now only a two-day ride to the west; or maybe he figured the one would provide a handy refuge from the other. Whatever his thoughts, he hardly had time to record them. His stay on Kootenay Plains lasted precisely one day.

Travelling light and taking only Bercier and Buché with him, Thompson set off to follow the North Saskatchewan River toward the mountains. Somewhere near Thompson Creek, the three men stopped to camp, waking the next morning to find that the horses had wandered during the night and, except for one that had disappeared altogether, were quietly cropping grass on the far side of the river. Resigned to a change in agenda, Thompson decided they'd carry the baggage across the river and continue their journey on the south side. They gave up on the missing horse; "... as he is a stallion, we suppose he is returned to the Herds of Mares at the Kootanae Plains." On the other side of the river, the men reloaded the horses and rode west, crossing the Mistaya River in the early afternoon and arriving a short ride later at "The Forks," the junction of the North Saskatchewan and Howse Rivers.

> The Country is very mountainous & all nearly perpendicular, the
> Hills at the base of the Mountains are very wide & high, clothed
> with mostly small Firs & in places fine Grass for the Animals—
> there seems to be plenty of Buffaloe, Moose & Red Deer in the
> Summer, which however has not yet begun here. The Mountains
> are loaded with Snow, the continual rushing down of which makes
> a Noise like Thunder.

At The Forks, Thompson turned up the Howse River and, about two miles upstream, stopped to pitch his tent "on a most remarkable knoll." The *voyageurs* soon turned up with a loaded canoe, and Thompson wasted no time in getting rid of them. He kept Bercier and Buché with him and had Boulard stay behind, but as soon as the last of the goods had been delivered, he sent the canoe and the rest of the men back to Kootenay Plains, "there to live for the time the Portage is blocked up with Snow." He took up a quiet existence, and except for a few para-graphs about a three-mile ride up to Glacier Lake, his journal entries shrank to a series of terse notes about his daily routine.

Thompson's whole life seemed dominated by an urge to keep moving, yet he also had an inordinate capacity for waiting. When he'd left Peace River for Fort Chipewyan, for example, he'd started down the frozen river by dogsled. He then spent six weeks in the middle of nowhere, waiting for enough open water to launch a canoe. Later, he would repeat the performance on the Athabasca—insisting on crossing the Rockies in the dead of winter, only to sit in a hut for three months waiting for the Columbia River to open. His stay on the Howse River was shorter, but the pattern was the same: hurry up and wait. He occupied his time building boxes with Boulard, hunting occasionally (without any luck), and repacking some of the trade goods, all of it busywork and none of it critical. He made no move to visit the camp on Kootenay Plains. If he wanted something, he sent Bercier or Buché down with a message. A week went by, then a second week, then most of a third. Thompson stuck to his post—watching the weather, killing time, waiting for the snow to melt.

Today, a few miles short of where Thompson camped on the Howse River, the David Thompson Highway comes to an end at Saskatchewan River Crossing. Here motorists have the option of turning north up the Icefields Parkway toward Jasper or south toward Lake Louise. Straight ahead lies the trail that Thompson followed two hundred years ago, but to this day it has to be tackled either on foot or on horseback. Some Central Albertans would like to see the David Thompson Highway pushed another fifty miles west along this trail, up over Howse Pass and down into British Columbia, a route that would cut the present driving time between Saskatchewan Crossing and Golden in half. But because the proposed highway would require yet another fifteen-mile strip of pavement through Banff National Park, conservationists are adamantly opposed to the idea, a stand firmly backed by current Parks Canada policy.

Officially, the Howse Pass Trail now begins about three miles south of Saskatchewan Crossing at the Mistaya Canyon Trailhead—probably because the river's canyon was a better prospect for a modern bridge than the erratic flood plain at its mouth. Thompson, however, would have been down on the banks of the North Saskatchewan River, pursuing a course now followed by a bridle path called the Warden Creek Trail. Originating out on the Kootenay Plains, the trail crosses the Icefields Parkway near the warden station, fords the Mistaya River near its mouth, then winds along the flats on the south side of the North Saskatchewan.

In 1996 reporter Peter Verberg rode the Howse Pass Trail. A self-confessed greenhorn, Verberg put himself in the hands of the owner of the David Thompson Resort. The outfitter provided him with a sturdy mountain pony named either Tim or Willy (Verberg doesn't seem entirely sure which) and suggested that he try wearing pantyhose to cut down on the possibility of saddle sores (Verberg admits nothing). In an article he wrote for *Alberta Report*, Verberg described the fifteen-mile climb from Saskatchewan Crossing to Howse Pass.

> The trail wove in and out of ancient timber. A deer and her two
> fawns were grazing in the lush forage along the Howse River. Across
> the wide valley, a cabin built by the legendary outfitter Jimmy
> Simpson nestled in the trees. Over the next five hours, our sturdy
> horses forded numerous streams, trudged reluctantly through
> patches of muck, clambered up steep banks and toiled through thick
> bushes to get around fallen trees blocking the trail. Swarming mos-
> quitoes cut short our lunch at 4 p.m., and we reached the summit of
> the pass an hour later.[10]

On June 22, 1807, Thompson rode the same trail. The weather had been bad for days, and he had little hope that the pass would be open. "The Heights of the Mountains still present that cold clear shining white Snow which is never seen but in the depths of a rigorous Winter in a very severe Clime." It's quite likely, however, that the "snow" Thompson was monitoring was actually the Sir James Glacier on Mount Outram. If he'd waited for that to melt, he'd be waiting there still.

Probably more out of boredom than anything else, Thompson finally decided it was time to investigate. Early in the morning, he and Bercier saddled up their horses and started following Jaco's landmarks—"2 Bodies of Rocks" at the turnoff up Conway Creek, "Tent Poles & a marked Path" across Kootenay Pound, and the "Banks of blackish Gravel" that marked the entry to the pass. Within four hours, they'd ridden the last mile to the "Height of Land," found the pass wide open, and reached the headwaters of the Blaeberry River on the western side of the Rockies.

> At 9½ Am set off down the Rill Co SE 4M soon becomes a Brook
> ... Many Falls—the descent is every where very great ... we found no
> Snow whatever but the Grass somewhat long, the Leaves in the
> Willows somewhat large & all the appearance of Spring ... in all
> probability there is no snow to stop us in the rest of our Road.

This was what Thompson had been waiting for. First thing the next morning, he sent word to Finan McDonald to bring up the "People, Horses & rest of the Baggage, Provisions &c as soon as possible." Since the next leg of the journey was the portage over the mountains, the canoe was laid up at Kootenay Plains, and the horses that Jaco had been looking after took its place. In all, McDonald had to move something like two dozen horses up to Thompson's camp on the Howse, fully half of them riderless. The chore took him the better part of two days.

By the time the last of McDonald's entourage reached the Howse, it was seven o'clock in the evening. Thompson immediately started assigning "each two men three horses" and distributing tack and equipment. At 3:30 the next morning, he rousted the men out of bed and sent them out in the dark to round up and load the horses, and by six o'clock, a long cavalcade was winding its way up the trail along the Howse River. Only Finan McDonald stayed behind, charged with looking after the rest of the trade goods until the horses could be brought back for another load.

Close to thirty horses set out that morning, some loaded with freight and some carrying riders—Thompson, eight *voyageurs*, the two Ojibwa hunters and their wives, Charlotte and Mrs. Lussier, and, tucked among the baggage on the pack horses, eight or nine youngsters. Despite the shortage of men to manage the horses, the expedition reached the entrance to Howse Pass by early afternoon, and that night, Thompson and his people camped on the spine of the Continental Divide.

The trail from Thompson's camp to Howse Pass was just over twelve miles long, increased in elevation only about two hundred feet, and (including a two-hour delay when Thompson went off to chase after some mountain goats) took only seven hours to ascend. The trail down the Blaeberry River was another matter. Over thirty-five miles long, it dropped in elevation almost three thousand feet, and took Thompson's riders five full days to get down it. This was the trail that Jaco and his work party had cleared the summer before. It was about to be tried and found wanting.

The trail zigzagged down the Blaeberry Valley, sometimes following the river, sometimes crossing it, sometimes ducking away into the forest. Most dangerous for the men were the crossings. The Blaeberry was swollen by the suddenly melting snows, "always a Torrent which seemingly nothing can resist, always boiling with its velocity against the inequalities of the Bottom." Thompson rode ahead, sounding the river, searching for the safest places to cross. The men worked on foot, edging into the current at one crossing after another, clinging to the sides of the horses to keep from being swept away.

Less dangerous, but equally difficult, was the trail through the woods. There wasn't one day when Thompson and his men weren't hacking their way through the forest lining the Blaeberry, each day more laborious than the last. For the first two days, it was a toss-up which caused the most trouble—the perilous river crossings or the state of Jaco's trail. By the third day, it became apparent that the main obstacle to progress was the trail. On June 28 Thompson and his men spent over thirty-six man-hours clearing the road that Jaco was supposed to have cleared the summer before.

> ... went over a flat Point on the left tolerable open, then thro' quite pathless Woods & so thick set, that one may say the [sun] never saw their Stems, with hilly rocky Ground. Left our Horses, & Axe in hand four of us cut a Road thro' it, which took us a long time—at length by Noon we got to a low small flat Point, fine open Ground. Our Horses havg been loaded these 6 Hours, we stopped to refresh them & ourselves, from very heavy fatigue & Labour. After taking a mouthful of Pemmican 5 Men went off to cut a Road & it was 4¹/₂ Pm before they returned.

Thompson's men had mutinied for less, and that day, he lost all patience with Jaco's handiwork. In a report to the partners, obviously written in a fit of temper, Thompson blamed Jaco for all the difficulties they'd encountered on the trip down the Blaeberry Valley.

> From what has been said of the Road on the Portage, it is clearly seen that Jaco Finlay with Men engaged last Summer to clear the Portage Road, has done a mere nothing—the Road was nowhere cleared any more than just to permit Jaco & his Family, to squeeze thro' it with their light Baggage and it is the opinion of every man with me, as well as mine that Jaco ought to lose at least half his wages for having so much neglected the Duty for which he was so expressly engaged at £150 pʳ year, besides a Piece of Tobacco & Sugar, & a Clerk's equipment.[11]

Presumably Thompson meant "every man with me" except Boulard and Bercier, who must have been a trifle embarrassed by Thompson's indignation over the trail's shortcomings. In fairness to Jaco, it's quite possible that John McDonald of Garth didn't do a very thorough job of briefing him. The trail was evidently passable for riders. It was only when it came to getting a pack train over it that it proved inadequate—too close along the sheer cliffs, too narrow through the thick forest, and too often forcing "the horses... to jump with their loads over much wind-fallen Wood." Moreover, Thompson found the canoes that Jaco had left for him "unfit for carriage, but handy for light voyaging," yet another indication that the ton of freight that had to be transported had somehow been left out of the reckoning.

Author John Jackson maintained that, humiliated by Thompson's tongue lashing and the reduction in salary, Jaco quit the service of the North West Company.[12] Confirming the tongue lashing is problematic. Thompson did lash out on paper, but Jaco wasn't with him on the journey over Howse Pass and didn't appear on the Columbia until the following year, so it's unclear when a confrontation between the two men could have taken place. The reduction in salary is a different matter. If the partners had acted on Thompson's recommendation, the penalty may have been a matter of record, though Jackson doesn't substantiate this. Nevertheless, it's apparent that Jaco did have some kind of grievance. That year, he left the company to work as a free trader and may have been sufficiently aggrieved to lend a hand to the Nor'Westers' competitors. In later years, the map Jaco drew for Thompson turned up among the papers of the Hudson's Bay Company's Peter Fidler. According to Jackson,

> Seeking a way to support his young family, Jacco turned to the rival
> Hudson's Bay Company. The Edmonton House master, James Bird,
> was delighted to include him in a sly industrial espionage system
> that penetrated the Nor'wester system. Jacco's crudely sketched con-
> tribution to the early understanding of western geography was pre-
> served in the Edmonton journals and in the writings of Peter Fidler
> ... who had a map that was "drawn by Jean Findley in 1806."[13]

It was June 30 before Thompson's people finally ended their struggle with the trail down the Blaeberry. As they emerged from the wooded hills, they paused near a grassy marsh to rest the horses, then rode the last mile to the banks of the Columbia River.

Agnes C. Laut, writing in the early 1900s, once rode the trail up the Blaeberry and took advantage of the experience to describe Thompson's descent of the river. Laut's knowledge of geography was shaky (Rocky Mountain House was "somewhere" near Howse Pass), as was her knowledge of history (Joseph Howse "found" Howse Pass, but the Hudson's Bay Company kept it a secret). Whatever Laut may have lacked in knowledge, however, she more than made up for in imagination. Assuring the reader that "[i]t ought not to be necessary to say here that I know both regions traversed by Thompson well, very well, from personal travel,"[14] she launched into her version of Thompson's trip down the Blaeberry Valley.

> Hither came Thompson by a branch of the Saskatchewan and
> Howse's River and Howse's Pass to Blaeberry Creek ... On the
> Upper Blaeberry, Thompson constructs a rough log raft—safer
> than canoe, for it will neither sink nor upset—whipsawing two long
> logs over a dozen spruce rollers. A sapling tree for a pole, packs in a
> heap in the center on brush boughs to keep them free of damp, and
> down the Blaeberry whirls the explorer with his Indian guides ...
> Spring has set the torrents roaring. The river is a swollen flood that
> sweeps the voyageurs through the forests, past the glaciers [and no
> doubt over the fifty-foot drop at Blaeberry Falls], down to a great
> river, which Thompson does not recognize but which is the
> Columbia just where it takes a great bend northward [it doesn't] at
> the modern railway stations of Moberly and Golden.[15]

Mercifully, the author stopped short of claiming that Thompson had flagged down a passing train. Today there's a road up the Blaeberry River that does double duty as a logging road and recreational access for campers, hikers, kayakers, canoeists, and travellers on the track of Thompson. The Blaeberry Road isn't easy to find—the Moberly Branch Road on the TransCanada Highway is the turnoff—but a map available from the Forestry Service in Golden provides accurate distances and directions.

For three miles, the Blaeberry Road winds along the flats of the river, then starts to climb into the mountains. At one point, it creeps along a narrow ledge that might not be everyone's cup of tea. Higher up, warning signs by the roadside read "narrow winding gravel," and still higher, "steep narrow gravel—large RVs and Trailers Proceed at Own Risk." If the road were in fact gravel, it would be fine, but traces of gravel are rare. Most of the road is sand, a treacherous slime when it's wet.

Nineteen miles up the road, a short trail leads to a set of falls named after David Thompson. Here the forest has been stripped from the hills by "modern" forestry practices, but the Blaeberry is as untamed as it ever was. At Thompson Falls, the river tumbles over a series of ledges, churns through channels carved out of solid rock, then rushes away to plunge over the Blaeberry Falls below. One look at the Blaeberry River in full flood is enough to convince anyone that Agnes Laut was dreaming.

In one respect, though, Laut had it right. Thompson had no idea that the river he'd reached was the Columbia River itself. This was one occasion when he may have known too much. He'd calculated his own position, and knew he was north of the fiftieth parallel; but from his study of Captain Vancouver's account, he also knew that the mouth of the Columbia was near the forty-sixth parallel, almost a thousand miles farther south. Since this river was flowing northwest, he concluded that it wasn't the river he'd crossed the mountains to find.

What Thompson didn't know, couldn't have known, was that the Columbia flows northward from its headwaters for two hundred miles, makes a hairpin bend around the Selkirk Range, then flows southward over the rest of its journey to the Pacific. Convinced he was on a different river, Thompson called the Columbia the "Kootanae," unaware that he'd chanced on the Northwest Passage that Peter Pond had envisaged and that Alexander Mackenzie and Simon Fraser had laboured to find— the Great River of the West.

The Columbia River Headwaters –1807[1]

*When David Thompson crossed the Rocky Mountains
in the spring of 1807, the North West Company's Columbia
Division was an unexplored wilderness that happened to have
a name. It had no trading posts, no trade routes, no supporting
network of Indian hunters, trappers, and guides. Yet within
two months, Thompson and a handful of men had paddled
eighty-five miles up the Columbia River, opened trade
with the Kootenays, and erected Kootanae House—the
first trading post in the Columbia River Drainage.*

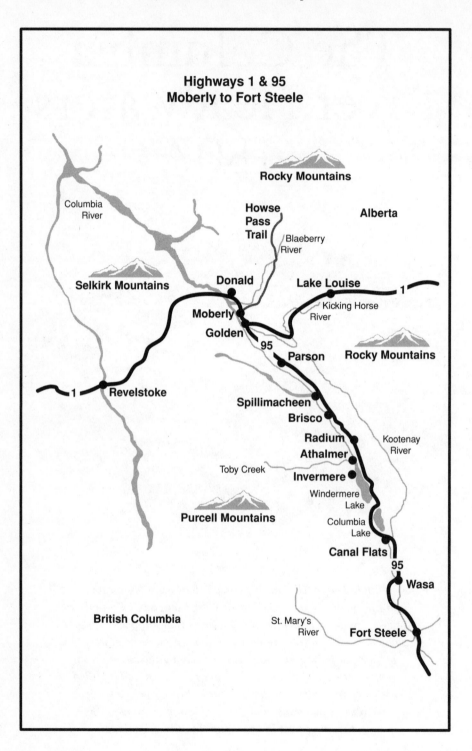

Highways 1 & 95
Moberly to Fort Steele

Columbia River

Rocky Mountains

Howse Pass Trail

Blaeberry River

Alberta

Selkirk Mountains

Donald

Lake Louise

Kicking Horse River

1

Moberly

Golden

95

Parson

Rocky Mountains

1 Revelstoke

Spillimacheen

Brisco

Radium

Kootenay River

Athalmer

Toby Creek

Invermere

Windermere Lake

Purcell Mountains

Columbia Lake

Canal Flats

95 Wasa

British Columbia

St. Mary's River

Fort Steele

LIKE OTHER GREAT RIVERS OF THE WORLD, THE COLUMBIA HAS HUMBLE ORIGINS. It begins life in the seeps of a marsh near Canal Flats, B.C., wanders through Columbia and Windermere Lakes, then flows northward along the floor of the Rocky Mountain Trench. The Rockies to the east and the Purcell Range to the west overlook the river's flood plain—a kaleidoscope of islands, lakes, ponds, marshes, and meadows in the summer; a study in black and white in the winter. This flood plain is known as the Columbia River Wetlands, one of the few remaining places where Woody Guthrie's Columbia is still free to roll on.[2]

Lying as they do under a major flyway, the wetlands are best known for their role as a stopover for migratory birds. Each spring, Canada geese, ospreys, eagles, and great blue herons nest along its shores; each spring and fall, trumpeter swans, hawks and ducks, coots and loons, grebes and gulls settle onto its waters by the thousands. During the winter, deer, moose, and elk move down into the valley, and at one time, late summer saw innumerable Chinook salmon migrating through the wetlands on their way to their spawning grounds upstream.

The Columbia Valley offered none of its bounty to Thompson. The spring migration of waterfowl was over, and the fall migration was months away. The animals that wintered in the valley had disappeared into the hills for the summer, and the Chinook salmon had yet to arrive. There were no herds of buffalo on the west side of the mountains, and no one there hunted for pleasure. Hunting was a grim business conducted for only one reason: survival. For two months, Thompson meticulously rationed what food there was and worried his people would starve.

Thompson's camp on the Blaeberry was less than ten miles north of Golden, B.C., not far off the route of today's TransCanada Highway. Thompson would one day map this north-flowing reach of the Columbia, but in 1807, he chose to turn south. Had he known that the river he called the "Kootanae" was actually the Columbia, he might have followed it downstream to its mouth instead of upstream to its headwaters, and reached the Pacific four years sooner than he did.

It's tempting to speculate that, if he had turned downstream, the first trading post on the Pacific might have been Britain's Fort George instead of America's Astoria, and Montana, Idaho, and Washington might have belonged to Canada instead of the United States. On the other hand, it's unlikely that Thompson could have altered the course of history simply by descending the river sooner. Eight months before he first set foot in the Columbia Valley, Lewis and Clark's Corps of Discovery had already reached the Pacific Ocean.

If anyone arrived at the mouth of the Columbia River too late, it was

Captain George Vancouver. In 1792 the captain sailed his ship *Discovery* up the west coast, carrying a directive from the British Admiralty to keep a sharp lookout for the mouth of a major river. As it happened, Vancouver did come within sight of the Columbia, but dismissed its outflow as a collection of small creeks. He then sailed north, only to dismiss the Fraser River delta as a series of unnavigable mud flats. (The captain was not, as Bernard DeVoto put it, "a lucky man with rivers."[3]) By the time Vancouver sailed south again, he was five months too late. American sea captain Robert Gray had spotted the Columbia, sailed the *Columbia Redidiva* across the bar, and named the river after his ship.

Thompson stayed at the camp on the Blaeberry for twelve days, organizing the shift from horseback to canoes. He sent four men and twelve horses back over Howse Pass to fetch Finan McDonald and the rest of the trade goods, then dispatched Bercier and Clément south to search for the Kootenays. Meanwhile, he and his two remaining men started work on a large canoe to transport the goods up the Columbia. Five days later, Bercier and Clément returned with three young Kootenays in tow, and five days after that, McDonald arrived from the pass. The next day was July 12. Everyone was back in camp, the canoe was finished, and Thompson was ready to load.

> Agreed with Boulard & the three Kootanae Lads to take the Horses
> up to the Kootanae Lake, while the whole of us took up the Goods
> & Baggage in 2 small & one large Canoe. I set off in one of them
> with a Man & the other small Canoe, also 2 Men, the large canoe 4
> Men & Mr F. McDonald—at 3½ Pm set off.

Thompson's journal carried few details about his first journey up the Columbia. Most entries show a man distracted by the daily quest for enough birds and fish to make a meal for seventeen people. Since Thompson was "obliged to paddle," he deferred his usual surveys to a "more convenient time," and his mileage record tends to have gaps in it. Although his course took him past three major streams—the Kicking Horse River at Golden, the Spillimacheen River across from Spillimacheen, and Toby Creek near Invermere—the only one he named was the Kicking Horse, which he called the "Rapid River." He made a detour into the Spillimacheen, but made no attempt to name it, and he didn't even mention passing Toby Creek. The other thing he didn't mention was the women, so we have to imagine the ghostly presence of Charlotte, Mrs. Lussier, and six children seated somewhere in the canoes.

Thompson's journal says little about the landscape bordering the river, but a report he later wrote for his partners described the changing countryside as the canoes followed the Columbia south.

Here it may not be amiss to state the nature of the Country. This of the Kootanaes is a Valley of from 6 to 12 Miles wide, if we compute from Mountain to Mountain, but if only the level space, it will seldom exceed 2 Miles, being the Ground occupied by the River, it's Islands, small Lakes & Marshes ... As one approaches the Lakes, the Woods of this almost impenetrable Forest, become gradually less close ... & soon ... open clear Ground for Horses ... a fine Meadow of Hill & valley & Gullies with Hemlock planted upon it as it were for Shelter against the heat & bad weather.[4]

Before Thompson's arrival in the Columbia Valley, Native trails traversed the hillsides, and not long after he'd left, the canoes of the early missionaries followed his course up the Columbia River. In the mid-1880s, the Canadian Pacific Railway reached Golden, the first steamboats appeared on the Columbia, and, anticipating an influx of settlers, the B.C. government started construction of the "Colonization Road" between Golden and the old mining town of Galbraith's Ferry. In 1890 the mining town was renamed Fort Steele by the North West Mounted Police, and by 1913 the Kootenay Central Railway had linked Fort Steele to the main line at Golden. Today, however, travel by river and rail has given way to travel by road, and the towns and villages in the valley are connected by a ribbon of blacktop called Highway 95.

Highway 95 runs south out of Golden through a countryside that supports a blend of ranching, recreation, and forestry. Settlement of the Columbia Valley has been light, and little has happened to alter the pleasant scenery Thompson described to his partners. Fine weather still brings those days he characterized as "warm dry hazy & smoky." In Thompson's time, the smokiness was caused by fires set by the Kootenays; today it's caused by the burners associated with sawmills.

There are, of course, other changes. At Nicholson, Parson, and Brisco, low bridges now span the multiple channels of the wetlands, and a crossing at the village of Radium Hot Springs leads to a high viewpoint overlooking the flood plain below. Outfitters in the valley offer for our amusement what Thompson did for a living—trail riding, mountain climbing, running whitewater in a canoe—as well as the more sedate pastime of an evening float through the Columbia River Wetlands.

Thompson's destination was Windermere Lake, about seventy-five miles south of Golden. Today a town called Invermere stands on the northwestern shore of the lake, and in the background looms "Nelson's Mountain," which Thompson named when he first learned (two years after the fact) that Admiral Nelson had been killed at the Battle of Trafalgar. "Invermere on the Lake" appeals to tourists and retirees alike, and one of its attractions is the quiet preservation of its David Thompson heritage. For many years, Invermere was home to the David Thompson Memorial Fort, and though the fort is gone now, a collection of materials dealing with Thompson's first days on the Columbia is housed in the Windermere Valley Museum. Just north of town, on the Toby Creek Road, a stone cairn marks the small clearing where Thompson built Kootanae House.

By July 17, Thompson was camped only a few miles downstream of the mouth of "Kootanae Lake." The next morning, he had everyone up at daybreak, and before five o'clock, the men had loaded the canoes and were paddling the last leg of their week-long journey up the river. The canoes swept past the mouth of Toby Creek, then plunged into the fast-moving current of the channel downstream of Windermere Lake.

> At noon, arrived at the Kootanae Lake ... it has a fine appearance:
> the Banks are high say 200 ft, all Meadow, with straggling Trees & d°
> in Clumps; the Water is very clear & the Country on the whole has
> a very romantic appearance.

Brave words on Thompson's part, but the last thing he needed was a romantic appearance. What he did need was a reliable food supply, horses to help with the logging, and a piece of flat ground to build on. For weeks, he had none of them. Food had grown so scarce that his people had made themselves sick eating the putrefied carcass of a wild horse. Later, Boulard would arrive from the Blaeberry camp with only four of the twenty-odd animals he'd been charged with ("hav⁸ left all the others behind from the badness of the Roads & his being a complete Rogue"). And so far as Thompson could tell, the lake's towering cliffs offered no suitable site for a trading post.

> Early set off to look for a Spot to build a House ... Found no fit place
> for several miles, returned & crossed over to the SW⁴ but also no fit
> Place—& I was obliged to pitch upon a Spot ab⁴ 200 [feet] above
> the level of the Lake, where a few straggling Pines may be got to
> build with.

Judging by Thompson's description, his initial building site was high above Lake Windermere (two hundred feet is comparable to the height of a twenty-storey building). It was probably on the east side of the lake, not very far from its outlet. He must have identified the spawning grounds in the Columbia just downstream, since he was convinced that there'd be good fishing nearby. If he'd stayed where he was for a month, he might have been proved right. Today, the community bordering the lake's outlet is called Athalmer, but in the early days of settlement, it was known as "The Salmon Beds."

That afternoon, the men hauled all the goods to the top of the cliffs and the women set up the tents. They were scarcely settled in before the first band of Kootenays arrived.

> Talked a long time with the Kootanaes, but find by their informa-
> tion that little can be done in the present circumstances. The
> Country is extremely poor in Provisions beyond us, & even about
> us, & nothing larger than a Chevreuil, whose weight when poor may
> be about 50 lbs & when fat ab^t 70 lbs—& we are in all 17 mouths to
> feed.

Despite their own hardship, the Kootenays did their best to supply Thompson with provisions—dried meat, berries, the occasional *chevreuil*—but it was never enough. The men set nets in the lake, but the nets came up empty, and even Finan McDonald ("who is the most clever") rarely speared more than a few small fish. As a result, the warehouse went up with the men on short rations, often too weak to work hard and, some days, too weak to work at all. In the report to his partners, Thompson indicated he had seriously debated allowing some of the men to return to the prairie posts.

> The men were now so weak, that however willing, they actually had
> not the strength to work, & some of them told me that two or three
> days more of Famine would bring them to the Ground. I deeply felt
> for their Situation & my own, but was determined still to wait a few
> Days before I could consent that any should return.[5]

Nevertheless, within two days of their arrival, Thompson and his men were felling timber, skidding logs, and raising the walls of a warehouse, "but the wood is very heavy & large ... got it half up." By July 23, the walls were raised, the gable ends finished, and the poles cut for the roof. But with each day that went by, Thompson grew increasingly dis-enchanted with his hastily chosen site.

> Being now better acquainted with the Country ab[t], which is full of
> Ravines & Gullies capable of concealing Armies from our View &
> rendering us liable to an Attack every minute—which, should it
> happen, we must perish with Thirst only—I resolved to see if any
> place more eligible could be found ere we advanced too far in the
> Building intended, as the prime Objects for which we built here
> have deceived us—viz the Fisheries—for we get nothing, besides
> having no Wood worth while to build with.

Thompson's disappointment in the fishery meant the Chinook run was much later than he'd anticipated. His worries about an attack stemmed from his belief that, sooner or later, the Peigans would arrive on the scene, and his comment about perishing from thirst reflected his concern about the site's extreme distance above the water.

Today Thompson could have built near the lakeside, but in 1807, he may not have had that option. He reached Windermere Lake at a time of year when the water was high, during a fluvial period known as the "Little Ice Age." Although the climate in this part of the Columbia Valley is now classed as semi-arid, in Thompson's day it would have been much wetter, and there's a good chance that the low land around Athalmer, which is still prone to flooding, was lying under water.

Thompson could see for himself several disadvantages to his posi-tion, but the Kootenays who were arriving to trade emphasized just how dangerous it was.

> After some Conversation, they told me plainly that the Situation of
> the Building was bad, as it was far from water & open to the insult of
> the Peagan ... I had long thought this myself ...

The Kootenays may have pointed out that the Peigan War Road, which followed the east side of the valley, was too close to the ware-house for comfort, but whatever argument they used, they finally convinced Thompson he'd be better off elsewhere. By that time the warehouse was almost finished—the door cut, the shelves up, and the goods moved inside—but the bark the men had collected to finish the roof was never laid. During the last week of July, Thompson halted work on the warehouse. He dispatched Bercier, Clément, and Le Camble north to search for the horses that Boulard had left behind, and started looking around for a building site where his settlement would be less vulnerable.

On July 28, Thompson went scouting for a new location. Taking two men with him, he headed north by canoe, following the Columbia downstream. For the first time since he'd arrived in the valley, luck was on his side. Only a mile or so downstream of the lake, he found what he was looking for: "an eligible Spot on the Kootanae River, in a commanding Situation, the water quite near." Thompson's "situation" was a patch of even ground (smaller, but not unlike the setting of Rocky Mountain House), about twenty feet above the confluence of Nelson's Rivulet (now Toby Creek) and the Columbia River. Satisfied that he'd found a safer place to build, Thompson headed back to camp.

> On my return I found everybody under the alarm of a Band of
> strange Indians hav^g pursued the Women who were out gathering
> Berries &c. I directly ordered the Men to fill the Kettles with Water
> & get all ready for defence—but it fortunately turned out to be only
> 3 Kootanae young Men, who in a frolic gave a fright to the Women.

The panic created by the young Kootenays indicated a camp in a state of nerves, and Thompson decided the sooner they moved the better. By seven the next morning, the men had lugged the goods down the hillside and were loading the canoes, and by noon they'd ferried two loads of merchandise, lumber, and baggage down the river. Late afternoon found them felling trees and hauling logs up to the new site.

Thompson's first priority was to build another warehouse. He was still short of horses, and with three men away on a search for the animals, he was down to five men—Beaulieu, Boisverd, Lussier, Boulard, and Finan McDonald. Nevertheless, by the first of August, the warehouse was up, shelved, and stocked. The entire job, including cutting and hauling the logs, took them less than three days. Since food was still in short supply ("only 4 lbs of poor Scraps for this day"), Thompson gave his men a few days off to go fishing.

On August 5, things started to look up. That day, Boulard killed a black bear and her cub, and the men sent north arrived with the missing horses. The following morning, work started on the "Dwelling House." Actually two buildings in one, the "House" was partitioned into Thompson's room and a hall used for trading. By that evening, the walls had been raised to the "intended height" of six and a half feet. The next day saw the gable ends raised to accommodate the pitch of the roof, the roofbeam installed, and the poles cut for the rafters.

By August 11 the men had roofed the building in bark, chinked the log walls inside and out with mud, and were laying the last stones of the fireplace in Thompson's room. The following morning, some of the men paddled up the river to split out wood for the floor "& sent it down the River piece by piece which we caught as it passed." Over the next few days, they laid the split logs, round side down and notched to fit over "sleepers" (timbers laid on the ground to form a foundation), then levelled the flooring with an adze, built the doors, and covered the windows in parchment. On August 15 Thompson recorded a landmark in the development of the Columbia Division: "Took up my Residence in my room."

Over the next three weeks, Thompson and his men erected three more buildings. First they built the hall and the men's house—both equipped with stone fireplaces and wooden floors. Then they constructed what Thompson called a "Hangard." At that time, the British used the word to mean "carriage house," but Thompson probably meant *hangar*, the French word for "shed." The traders usually built sheds to store meat, but given the limited number of buildings at Kootanae House, this one may have served a number of functions. One possibility is a smithy, another is a tack room, where saddles could be hung out of reach of the busy teeth of a wolverine.

More than a hundred years later, B. G. Hamilton, one of Invermere's early residents with an interest in history and archaeology, wrote to the Reverend E. Smythe at the Rectory in Trail, B.C. Hamilton wanted to know whether some remains discovered on Canterbury (Invermere) Point might be those of an old fur trade fort. In January 1911 Reverend Smythe replied. The remains were those of his own residence, he wrote, then went on to describe another site on Canterbury Point.

> On the top of the hill east, which looks south up the lake, is the old HBCo's fort. When I first came to Canterbury, there were the remains of two old chimneys, and the burnt square of the stockade ... also in rummaging round I found a few brass HBCo buttons ...[6]

For some reason, Hamilton didn't go looking for the old Hudson's Bay fort. He seemed more interested in the Reverend's postscript.

> PS I speak of the fort as the HBCo, but of course it might be the NWTCo, still it was known as HB by Baptiste Margeau, and other old Indians. I may say there are the remains of another fort north of Toby Creek ...[7]

Reverend Smythe's recollection was the first indication that Kootanae House had once stood above Toby Creek. Hamilton started looking around for clues to the site, and by 1912 he'd found several. He sent a report of his findings to W. Denison Lyman, a history professor at Whitman College in Walla Walla, Washington, and enclosed a sketch of the site that outlined the boundaries of the stockade and marked the locations of four "ovens."

> I have been making a critical examination of the ground myself. These have resulted in my being satisfied that the works and remains are those made by a white person. We have discovered pieces of charred wood showing evidence of auger holes and work having been done with an axe ... Charred pieces of timber and piles of scattered bones may be found in several places within the radius of what are shown as ovens on the small tracing which I am enclosing herewith. All evidences on the ground would go to show that whatever wooden erection there had been had been early destroyed by fire which may account for no mention being made by travellers through that part.[8]

Hamilton's ovens were the bases of the Kootanae House chimneys. Their locations seem to correspond to Thompson's comments on the layout—two fireplaces fairly close together (his own and the one in the trading hall), a third on the other side of the compound (the men's house), and a clay firepit (not mentioned by Thompson) that may have been located outdoors. Hamilton's report and his accompanying sketch are now part of the David Thompson display in the Windermere Valley Museum.

Hamilton sent a carbon copy of his report to a geographer named J. B. Tyrrell, who was living at the time in Toronto. During the late 1800s, Tyrrell had worked for the Canadian Geographical Survey, and the maps he'd used to explore the northwest had been drawn by David Thompson. Curious about the man behind the maps, Tyrrell tracked down Thompson's papers and managed to rescue them from obscurity, a piece of detective work that gave him access to Thompson's journals and enabled him to buy the handwritten copy of the *Narrative*. In the years that followed, Tyrrell became not only Thompson's first editor and biographer, but his greatest admirer as well.

Ten years after Hamilton discovered the remains of Kootanae House, the Canadian Pacific Railway and the Hudson's Bay Company cooperated in the construction of a replica of the fur trade fort. The intent was to create a tourist attraction. The "fort" went up on Canterbury Point, the same point, you'll recall, where Reverend Smythe picked up the Hudson's Bay buttons. Although the Bay had apparently had a fort there at one time and was a sponsor of the project, for some reason the name of a Nor'Wester was bestowed on the replica. It was called the David Thompson Memorial Fort. Although the replica attracted few tourists, it served for twenty-five years as Invermere's community centre and dancehall. By the mid-1940s, however, Invermere had built another community facility, and the Memorial Fort fell into disuse. It was still standing in 1957, when Mabel Jordon (who was researching an article on David Thompson monuments) visited Invermere, but years of neglect finally rendered the aging structure too dangerous to ignore. Local support for its restoration was lacking, and the replica was burnt down.

As well as being keenly interested in the archaeological remains of Kootanae House, J. B. Tyrrell also tried to determine the position of the warehouse that Thompson had abandoned. Using an average of the two observations Thompson recorded at the site, Tyrrell concluded that the original warehouse had stood on Canterbury Point. That conclusion would result in some curious developments.

Over the years, the long-standing presence of the replica led to Canterbury Point being nicknamed Fort Point, and memories of the Memorial Fort merged with Tyrrell's assertion that Thompson's first warehouse had once stood there. As a result, Invermere's "fort history" became scrambled. Some Invermere residents believe Thompson camped on Fort Point, others believe he put up his warehouse there, and still others believe he built Kootanae House there. Not surprisingly, Fort Point came to be so strongly associated with the name of David Thompson that the *Columbia Valley Guide* captioned a 1922 photo of the Memorial Fort: "Hudson Bay Fort, Invermere, B.C. Built by David Thompson, the fort was located on Fort Point in Invermere."[9]

Thompson's journal, however, indicates he was never anywhere near Fort Point, and Tyrrell's assertion that the warehouse stood there was little more than a guess. Two of Thompson's observations of latitude were no guarantee of accuracy (as Tyrrell himself well knew), and Thompson's calculations of longitude were even more approximate. In this instance, he recorded the degrees and minutes of his longitude, but no seconds, making it unlikely that Tyrrell had enough information to distinguish east from west on a lake as narrow as Windermere. In any case, Thompson stated that he "found no fit Place" on the western side of the lake, and that he'd built his first warehouse at the top of a two-hundred-foot cliff, probably somewhere on the level ground between the Invermere airport and the brow of Athalmer Hill.

In 1916 Tyrrell finished editing Thompson's *Narrative*, and the Champlain Society became the first to publish the manuscript. Distribution was strictly limited to the society's archives and its members, but for Christmas that year, Tyrrell sent a single copy to B. G. Hamilton in Invermere. This first edition of the *Narrative*, now approaching one hundred years of age and correspondingly fragile, is displayed under glass in the Windermere Valley Museum.

Near the end of August 1807, the long-awaited Chinook salmon run arrived. On the 27th, Thompson reported "several salmon seen." Two days later, Finan McDonald went night fishing and speared five salmon, "one of them weigh[ing] 26½ lbs." Over the next few weeks, the catch continued to increase in quantity, but progressively declined in quality.

> Mr F. McDonald & 4 Men from spearing of Salmon—they
> brought 7 d° but they are very poor, quite exhausted with spawning
> & the vast dist^{ce} against a very Rapid Current from the Sea hereto.
> One of them, poor as it is, weighed 34½ lbs.

By mid-September, the men were spearing more fish than the people needed. Thompson had nine salmon split, but judged them so "Meagre and flabby" that he doubted they would dry. Game had started to move down into the valley again, and once there was fresh meat in camp, the people lost interest in fish. As the run went on, Thompson pronounced the salmon "too meagre to be eaten but by People who are starving which, thank Heaven, is not our case at present." For some time, he'd been feeding the surplus to the dogs, and on September 18, three of the dogs died.

> The Kootanaes had often warned us of the fatal Effects to Dogs if
> permitted to eat raw Salmon which, they said, constantly 9 times
> out of 10 were sure to bring on the Death of the Dog—we had paid
> no attention to this Point, as thinking it the Effect of Superstition.
> But for about 6 days past our Dogs have been dying, & this day
> made their exit ... they became dull & lethargic, always lying down
> in some lonesome place & sleeping, refusing all food, & scarcely
> after the 3rd day lifting their Head even at the voice of their Master,
> never of their own Will getting up—except when, urged by extreme

Thirst, they ran down to the Brook & drank heartily ... When near dying, they almost always retired to some dark & there quickly expired.

Salmon Poisoning Disease

~ Far from being the effect of superstition, the Kootenays' caveat is still in effect today. The *Merck Veterinary Manual* carries a warning about Salmon Poisoning Disease (SPD), which it defines as an "acute, infectious disease of canids in which the infective agent is transmitted through the various stages of a fluke in a snail-fish-dog lifecycle."[10] The entry gives the same ratio of deaths the Kootenays gave, and differs from Thompson's description only in terms of vocabulary.

~ "Signs appear suddenly, 5–9 days after eating infected fish and usually persist for 7–10 days before culminating in death in up to 90% of untreated animals ... It is accompanied by depression and complete anorexia in virtually all cases ... Dehydration and extreme weight loss occur ... Currently [1986], the only means of prophylaxis is to prevent the ingestion of uncooked salmon, trout, steelhead, and similar fresh water fish."[11]

The same day the first salmon arrived, so did the first band of Peigans. Kootanae House was still defenceless. The men's house wasn't finished, and the stockade had yet to be built. In anticipation of the visit, Thompson had moved all his best horses well to the north of the fort, but he wasn't looking forward to renewing his acquaintance with the Peigans.

> About 2 Pm, 12 Peagan young Men & 2 Women arrived ... I had expected them long ago, & it must be their Policy to be highly dis-pleased with us for being here, as we thus render all the Indians independent of them over whom from time almost immemorial they have held in dependence or as enemies & destroyed them. They have it in their Power to be very troublesome to us, & even to cut us off ...

The young Peigans didn't stay long. Four days later, they were away, picking off three of the Kootenays' horses as they went. Two Kootenays rushed off in pursuit, loudly protesting the theft. The Peigans ignored the protests, hung onto the horses, and fired a few shots at the Kootenays. "The Kootanaes in return fired on the Peagans ... then flew back to the Ho[use] & put all their Goods &c under our Protection." That night the Kootenays camped close to the fort, armed and ready for trouble.

No sooner had the fourteen Peigans left than word came that thirty more were on their way. Thompson was annoyed. "They have nothing to trade, & only come to see what they can get & how we are situated; it is fortunate I am not off on Discovery." Nevertheless, the size of the approaching band was grounds for caution. Thompson immediately started erecting a stockade around the buildings of Kootanae House.

In his *Narrative*, Thompson wrote dramatic accounts of the Peigan presence. One described the people at Kootanae House enduring a three-week seige; another evoked a picture of a massed force of three hundred Peigan warriors advancing through what is now Crowsnest Pass. On that occasion, Thompson claimed he sent the Peigan chiefs an offering of tobacco, which Kootanae Appee, the war chief, arranged "thoughtfully" on the ground, then said: "If we proceed, nothing of what is before us can be accepted." Another of the three chiefs, "wistfully" eyeing the tobacco, made a long speech, then "cut the end of the Tobacco, filled the red pipe, fitted the stem, and handed it to Kootanae Appee." The three chiefs smoked, the three hundred warriors rode back over the pass, and Kootanae House was saved.

It was J. B. Tyrrell who pointed out that Kootanae House never was under seige, and who tactfully commented that, in this respect, Thompson's memory had "failed him somewhat."[12] Tyrrell had noticed that the account in the *Narrative* bore little relationship to Thompson's daily record. For the same reason, the tale of the three hundred Peigan warriors is probably suspect as well. According to his journal, Thompson viewed the comings and goings of the Peigans as less a menace than an unmitigated nuisance.

The visitors not only had a habit of commandeering provisions that the Kootenays brought to the fort, but they gambled all day and the Kootenays gave up hunting to sit in. They pilfered the Kootenays' "little property" until the Kootenays lost patience and "pitched away" and, to add insult to injury, the Peigan presence was driving off trade. When a band of Flatheads headed for Kootanae House heard their enemies were on the road, they turned around and went back to Montana.

Thompson spent his days urging the Peigans to leave, "as we wish them off from here very much," and on September 13, his wish was granted. "Hunger," commented Thompson, "makes them decamp."

> After the major part were gone I learnt that some of them had
> threatened that we should not be a long time here, & had told the
> young Men not to steal Horses now, as they should have them all in
> a short time. I spoke to those few who loitered behind: they denied
> any Intention of the Chiefs of bringing on a Quarrel but owned the
> young Men would be glad of it, that they might have a Pretence to
> plunder all Parties ...

News of the North West trading post was gradually filtering through
Columbia country, and on September 16, a group of Flatbows from
Kootenay Lake arrived at Kootanae House. The Flatbows were famed for
their great skill in bow making, and though Thompson sometimes called
the Kootenay River the Flatbow, he usually referred to the Lower
Kootenays themselves as the "Lake Indians."

The Lake Indians told Thompson they'd travelled overland, crossing
the Purcell Range that stood between the Columbia Valley and
Kootenay Lake to the west. For some reason, Thompson gathered that
they'd followed the Columbia River through the mountains, but their
return path "by the foot of Nelson's Mountain" indicates they'd probably come through Earl Grey Pass at the headwaters of Toby Creek. The
Lake Indians seem also to have told him that the Kootenay and the
Columbia Rivers eventually meet (which they do). Thompson was
instantly mustard-keen to go and see for himself.

> I wished them to conduct me directly as far as the junction of
> McGillivray's River [the Kootenay] with the Kootanae dº [the
> Columbia], but they said they had left their Families far on this Side
> that Place, that the Season was too far advanced, & that not one of
> them were Men of consequence—that Ugly Head, their Chief, was
> the most fit Person to apply to, as he was best known to the neigh-
> bouring Indians & most respected.

Thompson was forced to possess his soul in patience. Nine days
went by before Chief Ugly Head (so-named for his curly hair) appeared
at Kootanae House. After a long conversation, Thompson appealed to
the chief to lead him down "McGillivray's River" to its junction with
the "Kootanae." In translation, this meant Thompson wanted to travel
the southward loop of the Kootenay/Kootenai River to its junction with
the Columbia River, a return journey of approximately seven hundred
miles. Although Thompson had gleaned some knowledge of the two

rivers from the Lake Indians, it's doubtful he grasped the sheer scale of the journey he was proposing. It's also doubtful that Chief Ugly Head understood exactly what Thompson had in mind.

After much discussion, the two men agreed to make the trip, but they disagreed about when they should leave. Thompson wanted to wait a month, time enough for him to ensure that Kootanae House was well provisioned and safely enclosed by a stockade. Chief Ugly Head insisted they leave at once, before the weather was too cold and the snow too deep in the mountains. Thompson didn't seem to realize the implications of that remark. Maybe he was preoccupied with the timing, which from his point of view could hardly have been worse. Finan McDonald and four men had left Kootanae House just days before to make a supply run over Howse Pass. This meant the women and children would be protected by only three men, one of them the feckless Boulard, "useful as an interpreter in these troublesome times, but good for nothing else." To add to Thompson's concerns, Kootanae House was still vulnerable to attack—the buildings were all up, but the stockade wasn't—and he was acutely aware that the Peigans could come back any moment.

> I again hesitated to go now, as while the weather is moderate the
> Meadow Indians [Peigans] may attack and destroy the Settlement
> here—but the Old Chief assuring me with the other old Men that
> they did not think an Attack at this Season was to be apprehended,
> I agreed to go off with the Lake Indian Chief in a few days.

Thompson was anxious to explore the Kootenay River to find out whether it was navigable. Some of his sources said it was; others said only in part. The prospect of "penetrating farther" finally overcame his misgivings, and on October 2, he left the three *voyageurs* in charge of Kootanae House and rode south with Chief Ugly Head.

Their route lay along the east side of the valley, and by five o'clock the same afternoon, they'd passed Windermere and Columbia Lakes and were making their way along the eastern edge of Canal Flats. That evening they reached the Kootenay River—"we quickly forded it over a bottom of fine large Gravel"—and rode along the east side of the river. Early the next morning, they crossed the Kootenay again, "very good bottom & only deep to the belly of the Horse," and continued their ride along its west side.

Thompson was obviously in his element. His journal entries for the trip are lengthy, varied, and rich in detail, and descriptions, directions, and distances appear once again in his record. By early afternoon on the second day, the two men had ridden about seventy miles and had reached the "Torrent Rivulet." This was the St. Mary's River near Fort Steele, and here Chief Ugly Head unaccountably left the banks of the Kootenay and turned to ride west. Disturbed by the increasing distance between themselves and the river, Thompson mentioned his problem to his guide.

> As me & my Guide converse together partly by signs and partly by words, I supposed that when we left McGillivray's River it was only to cut across some long winding Point of the River & presently fall upon it again ... but my Guide now gives me to understand that the Road he is on leads direct thro' the Mountains before us, & always at a great dist^ce from the River ...

This plan didn't suit Thompson at all. His intent had been to explore the Kootenay River, and Ugly Head's shortcut through the Purcell Mountains wouldn't bring them back to its banks for almost a week. For the first time, Thompson realized that the march to the lake country and back was going to take him seventeen or eighteen days.

> As seeing the River & how far it is navigable is one of my present Objects, & not crossing barren Mountains, this Route renders useless the best half of my journey; besides, the length of Time, which in these perilous times I cannot spare from my new settlement, is a very material Point—I shall therefore proceed no farther on this Route ...

The next day (Thompson grumbling to his journal about wasted time, useless roads, and his guide's slow horses), the two men set off to retrace the route they'd followed south. On October 6 they reached Kootanae House, where Thompson found everyone safe but rattled. All summer, the Peigans had been in a fighting mood. They'd plundered Fort Augustus to equip themselves for war and provoked a battle with the Flatheads that cost them fourteen men. Now rumours were swirling around Kootanae House that the Peigans had declared war on the Kootenays for arming the Flatheads, and on David Thompson for supplying the guns.

Thompson's reaction was to concentrate on fortifying Kootanae House. In his absence, the men had cut two hundred logs and hauled forty of them up to the building site. Over the following weeks, they completed the stockade and erected bastions on two of its corners. On October 27, 1807, Thompson wrote *finis* to the project: "Sawed Boards for the Gate & made it &c—thank Heaven we have now fully enclosed ourselves."

The Kootenay/ Kootenai River –1808[1]

By the spring of 1808, David Thompson had dedicated more than a year to gaining a foothold on the Columbia. His job as a fur trader had claimed all his time—transporting goods, building a post, coaxing the Kootenays to bring furs. Despite all his efforts, however, returns that winter were small, and when spring arrived, he decided to open trade with the Flatheads in Montana. Just weeks before he was due to leave for Rainy Lake, he descended the Kootenay River for a second time, but between a rendezvous gone awry, a guide who lost his nerve, and a countryside inundated by flood waters, little of the expedition went according to plan.

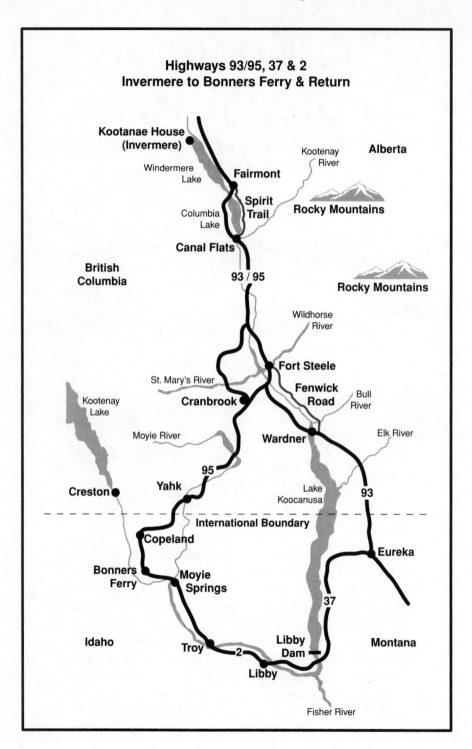

Highways 93/95, 37 & 2
Invermere to Bonners Ferry & Return

Kootanae House
(Invermere)

Kootenay
River

Alberta

Windermere
Lake

Fairmont

**Spirit
Trail**

Rocky Mountains

Columbia
Lake

Canal Flats

**British
Columbia**

93 / 95

Wildhorse
River

Rocky Mountains

St. Mary's River

Fort Steele

**Fenwick
Road**

Bull
River

Kootenay
Lake

Cranbrook

Moyie River

Wardner

Elk
River

95

Lake
Koocanusa

93

Creston

Yahk

International Boundary

Copeland

Eureka

**Bonners
Ferry**

**Moyie
Springs**

37

Idaho

Troy

2

**Libby
Dam**

Montana

Libby

Fisher River

UNLIKE THE IMPULSIVE JAUNT WITH CHIEF UGLY HEAD, THOMPSON'S SECOND journey down the Kootenay River was well planned. The month before he set out himself, he sent Boulard and Boisverd south to search out the Flatheads and urge them to work beaver. He chose four *voyageurs* (Beaulieu, Lussier, Le Camble, and a new recruit named Mousseau) to man his canoe, and set up a rendezvous with the Kootenays, who were making the same trip on horseback. He also made sure he wouldn't have to worry about the families at Kootanae House. Charlotte and Mrs. Lussier (both with three children and expecting their fourth) were left in the care of Clément, Bercier, and Finan McDonald, his most trusted men.

Critical to the venture was the rendezvous with the Kootenays. For the first part of the journey, Thompson and his men would travel by canoe, but for the last part, they'd have to travel on horseback. The Kootenays had told Thompson about their own route into Flathead Country (a trail he later called the "Kootanae Road") and agreed to supply the horses he would need and a guide to show him the way.

As usual, Thompson wrote an account of his journey down the river and, as usual, strings of his "courses" render it virtually unreadable. When Barbara Belyea edited the *Columbia Journals*, she omitted strings that were longer than ten and replaced them with the total in brackets, but even this simplified version of Thompson's notation barely penetrates his thicket of numbers. Even though none of the courses downstream of Montana's Fisher River exceeded Belyea's limit of ten, the passage is no more readable for that. A sample, dated May 5, 1808, reads:

> Obs^d Doub Merid Alt^{des} of [sun's] LL Lat^{de} 48°:22':24" N Varn by the [sun's] Transit 17½° East—this Obs^n is at end of Co S50W 1/6 M close above Rock [Fisher] River. At 2¾ Pm set off, Co West ½ M strong Rapid run on the right—good S69W ¼ SR—mid good SW ¾ M + ¼ R S75W ½ M the River only 150 Y^{ds} wide, but bold & deep. West 1/3M N86W ¾ M R + ¼ M N65W 1/3M N30W 1M NW ½ M S70W 1/5M S40W 1/3M sight tolerable high snowy Mountains on the left, say 3000 ft perpend S48W ½ M S34W 1/3M S8W ¾ M S70W ½ M R N72W ¼ M S87W ¼ M R N80W 1M S60W ¼ M NW 1M N82W ½ M mid of Co put up at 5½ Pm to shave & wash ourselves &c.

These strings are enough to tax anyone's patience, but those Belyea excluded are much worse. They number in the teens, twenties, and thirties, occasionally soar over one hundred, and constitute the main reason Thompson's writings attract few readers. When Elliott Coues undertook to edit the journals, Thompson's adventures ended up as footnotes to those of Alexander Henry.[2] Even J. B. Tyrrell, a geographer himself, balked at translating the journals. He summarized them in a preamble titled "David Thompson's Itinerary,"[3] and went on to present the more reader-friendly *Narrative*. But as intimidating as even short strings might be, Belyea was right to include them. In some ways, the picture of Thompson frantically scratching down data is more intriguing than the journey itself.

On April 20, 1808, six men left Kootanae House and paddled a loaded canoe into the winds gusting down Windermere Lake. Along the cliffs fronting the lakeshore, Thompson rode through the rain, mounted on one horse and leading six others. The trip down the Kootenay involved two portages simply to reach the river—one to bypass the stretch of the Columbia between Windermere and Columbia Lakes, the other to cross the flats separating the Columbia and Kootenay drainages. Both required horses.

A three-hour ride brought Thompson to the "Head of the Lakes River," where he rejoined the men handling the canoe. Thompson knew this short reach of the Columbia well, so well that he changed his name for it with every fluctuation in the river. Sometimes it was "the River of the Lakes," sometimes it was "the Rivulet between the Lakes," and sometimes it was "the Brook between the 2 lakes." That morning he wavered between "Rivulet" and "Brook." Either way, the water was too low for a loaded canoe. The goods would have to be carried.

The horses took on the packs, and Bercier and Clément started off on the eight-mile trek to Columbia Lake. Thompson continued up the river in the canoe. Over the next few hours, he jotted down 125 courses and still had time for a description.

> The first part of this Rivulet had water enough for us, & plenty of
> Beaver; the mid part, full of embarras [logjams] which took us
> much time to make a passage thro' them; the latter part, shoal
> rapids. Pines along this Brook but in patches & generally small, &
> each side extensive Swamps, Ponds & Marshes. Beaver less plenty as
> we advance, but their marks are every where.

Today this reach of the Columbia flows through the Riverside Golf Course at Fairmont, B.C. According to the Riverside brochure, the developers' first priority was "to ensure we always will enjoy what mother nature has given us." But a golf course is what it is, typically mother nature with a facelift. The bridge over the Columbia at Fairmont illustrates the contrast between Thompson's river and the one that now serves as a water hazard. On one side of the bridge, the Columbia wanders among a welter of rushes, grasses, and willows, floods into new channels whenever it needs more room, and wears the appearance of wetland habitat. On the other, it winds among manicured fairways and under ornamental bridges, flows meekly between the berms and riprap that confine it, and bears an uncanny resemblance to an artificial spawning channel. Which, whether by good luck or good management, it is. Each fall, during the last week of September, hundreds of thousands of Kokanee salmon spawn and die in this well-trained reach of the Columbia.

That evening Thompson and his men camped near the south end of the golf course, and the next morning, the goods went back into the canoe for the trip up Columbia Lake. Once again, Thompson stayed with the canoe while the men in charge of the horses followed a precarious track along the east side of the lake. Thompson had ridden this road with Chief Ugly Head the previous fall and knew what his men were in for.

> [The Road] is tolerable good 'till the end of it, when it crosses rocky Hills & follows the shelves of a steep Rock Hill, at the end of which the Path, always narrow, becomes still more so among black broken fragments of Rocks. This Lake is always pretty close to the foot of the Mountains, which leaves but a small space for the choice of Road & often none at all.

Between Invermere and Fairmont, Highway 93/95 now follows the east side of Windermere Lake, but at Columbia Lake, the highway's designers (in apparent accord with Thompson's assessment) decided to route the road along the west side. This stretch of highway overlooks Thompson's course up Columbia Lake—"a fine Sheet of Water: deep, clear, without Reeds, Rushes &c"—as well as the woody hills on the far shore where the horsemen had their trail. Today these hills are protected habitat (no camping, no hunting, no motorized vehicles), but what is known as the Spirit Trail still winds there, and modern-day hikers still tackle the ten-mile trek between Fairmont and Canal Flats.

Canal Flats is the name of a small community, but it's also the name of the two-mile expanse of flat land that separates the Columbia and Kootenay drainages. It was once the site of a canal, the brainchild of one William Adolph Baillie-Grohman who'd noted, as Thompson had before him, that the elevation of the Kootenay River is about six feet higher than that of Columbia Lake. By the mid-1880s, Baillie-Grohman had come up with a scheme to dig a canal across the flats and divert the Kootenay River into Columbia Lake. His intent was to get rid of the water that flooded the Kootenay bottomlands each year; his motive was the sale of the reclaimed land to the settlers three hundred miles downstream. All went well until the interests on the receiving end of the water kicked up a fuss. When the federal government got wind of the scheme, it vetoed the proposed diversion, and Baillie-Grohman's master plan was retooled into a less profitable, but infinitely more costly project—a system of locks to provide passage for steamboats and keep the water nobody wanted where it was.

In 1808, however, there was no canal. The only way to navigate the flats was to hoist the canoe and carry it.

> At 10 Am put the Goods ashore & began to carry, the Horses taking the Goods & most of the Canoe Men for the Canoe. The first part of the Portage being bad & wet, lost much Time & the first Trip took us 2½ H, the next 2 Hours, when we got all over by 3½ Pm ... Gummed the Canoe & dried several Things wetted by the Horses sinking in the Swamp close to the Lake ... This Portage I name McGillivray's Portage; its course S28E 2M full.

In the course of his travels, Thompson scattered the McGillivray name throughout the northwest, and though it survives here and there, in the case of the portage, it hasn't. On Highway 93/95, near Thunder Hill, a historical marker overlooks Canal Flats, in memory of the explorer who put the flats on the map and the entrepreneur who did his best to exploit them. Nearby, the remains of the Baillie-Grohman Canal lie alongside Thunderhill Road. Slow-moving water still slides down the ditch, under the highway, and into Columbia Lake.

Once Thompson's crew reached the south end of the portage, Bercier and Clément headed back to Kootanae House with the horses. Thompson and his four *voyageurs* reloaded the canoe and pushed off into "McGillivray's River." For the moment, the mountains were hanging onto their snowload—the river was only sixty yards across and barely deep enough for the canoe. The next day the river grew steadily broader and deeper, but it was still in a mild mood, "every Point a rapid but not strong, with pieces of easy Current." For the rest of the day, the current favoured every stroke of the paddle, and the canoe swept swiftly southward, with Thompson absorbed in recording every nuance of the size, direction, and character of today's Kootenay River.

From Canal Flats, Highway 93 follows Thompson's route south. The highway often doubles with other roads, but "93" is the number to keep an eye on when you're following the Kootenay River. Between Canal Flats and Wardner, the highway crosses the river at Canal Flats and Skookumchuk; just north of Wasa; and at Fort Steele and Wardner. All five crossings lie along Thompson's route.

By the evening of the second day out, the canoe was more than thirty miles downriver. The men camped for the night just north of Fort Steele, where they stayed for a day to wait out a heavy rain.

> ... where we are camped the Points are of fine Meadow, & the first Ground I have seen that I think has sufficient moisture to form a Garden for Herbs. The Woods of the Country are fine Red Fir, Fir Pine, very fine Mountain Larch, & along the River Pines, but of the swampy kind; the low Points have small Aspins & Willows.

This is where Thompson was when he'd turned back with Chief Ugly Head, so he was already familiar with two tributaries that run into the Kootenay at Fort Steele. He named the one flowing from the east "Skirmish Brook," and the one flowing from the west, "Torrent Rivulet"—now the Wildhorse and St. Mary's Rivers. It's not surprising that neither of Thompson's names lasted. In the East Kootenays, the fur trade had a brief presence, and within fifty years or so, the Wildhorse gold rush burst onto the scene. The new era brought new names, and the old ones, if anyone ever knew them, were forgotten. Thompson's "Lussier's Rivulet" still lives on as the Lussier River, but farther south, two more of his choices have faded away. The "Bad Rivulet" and the "Stag River" are now the Bull and the Elk.

The twentieth century brought even more change. For ninety miles south of Wardner, the river that Thompson travelled is no longer a river, but an international reservoir known as Lake Koocanusa. Backed up by the Libby Dam in Montana, nearly half the lake lies on the Canadian side of the border, the remainder on the American side. Although the name might be taken for an Indian word, it's actually a species of acronym. Alice Beers of Rexford, Montana, won a contest to name the lake by adding together the first syllables of Kootenai and Canada and the intials USA. In Canada, only back roads approach Lake Koocanusa, but just north of Eureka, Montana, Highway 37 heads west to Rexford, then follows the lakeside south to the Libby Dam.

On April 25, Thompson passed the mouth of the Elk River to reach the Tobacco Plains. His men paddled across the forty-ninth parallel (a prosecutable offence for watercraft today) and crossed into the state of Montana.

> ... Beautiful Meadows on both Hands, even to the very Mountains
> on the left ... a very fine Country ... This is the Place where the
> Indians speak so much of growing their Tobacco, & we named them
> on that account the Tobacco Meadows.

For some reason, Thompson thought he was approaching the point where he was supposed to meet the Kootenays. The *voyageurs* put ashore and fanned out to check both sides of the river. Thompson, who had sprained his knee, hobbled a mile and a half south to the "Fine Meadows Rivulet," where he came across "the Marks of six Lodges" and a trail that led away to the south. But the people themselves were gone. Later that day he and his men camped briefly near the mouth of the Tobacco River to "dry and arrange" the canoe, then paddled south for a few more miles, hoping to catch up to the Kootenays.

As the river entered the gorge between the Salish and Purcell Mountains, Thompson decided against going on. He was to meet the Kootenays at a "Narrows," and since the river downstream afforded "no considerable Narrows" for as far as the eye could see, he assumed he would meet them "hereabouts," a misunderstanding that was to alter the entire scope of his journey. On April 29, he wrote " ... we suppose part of the Kootanaes still behind, but what Route they will take to the Flat Head Country is unknown to us." Uncertain about where the Kootenays were, Thompson decided to hedge his bets. He sent Beaulieu and Le Camble south (on foot) after the Kootenays, who were ahead, and kept Lussier and Mousseau with him to wait for those he assumed were behind.

They waited for five days, most of them hungry ones. They had no horses, and though they hunted on foot, angled for fish, and set traps every night, they came up with nothing but a skunk and two beavers. By the fifth day, Thompson was sounding disheartened: "am so lame of the Knee as to be obliged to walk with a Stick ... & our subsistence this day was a Dram of Rum & half a Partridge p^r man." But early the next morning, a lone Kootenay called to them from the far side of the river. Thompson knew him as Le Monde, one of the men from Kootanae House. Le Monde was leading two company horses he'd found straying, and Thompson promptly sent him out hunting. Over the next three days, Le Monde shot a small *chevreuil*, a buck *chevreuil*, and a "Kind of

Tiger." Despite his concerns about the elusive Kootenays, Thompson was intrigued. He'd never seen a mountain lion before.

> ... he was 3 feet high, long in proportion his Tail 2 ft 10 In—of a
> Fawn colour, Belly white, very strong-legged & sharp Claws ...
> Found the Tiger very good food, & yields as much Meat as a
> Chevreuil.

The next day Thompson decided he had to move on. Le Monde had probably told him that there were no Kootenays on the road behind him, and his only hope of finding them was to catch up to those ahead. Thompson tried to talk their hunter into coming with them, but Le Monde refused, "on acc^t of his Family & rugged Country," though he promised to look after the company's horses. At noon Thompson and his two remaining *voyageurs* pushed off down the Kootenai on their own, travelling slowly "to look after my 2 Men who are on the scout after Indians." As the canoe rounded the Kootenai River's big bend, Thompson lost sight of the Indian trail Beaulieu and Le Camble were following. He later noted that it continued along the north side of the river, but on that day he didn't spot the changeover and was worried he'd missed his men. He backtracked a couple of miles and put ashore just upstream of the Fisher River, where Highway 37 now crosses the David Thompson Bridge.

> Find^g a fire but newly extinguished, we supposed our 2 Men to have
> slept here—we fired several Shots but without answer. I sent a man
> on each Quarter, & ab^t 2 Hours after one of them returned with the
> 2 Men sent on the Scout, quite fatigued & half starved, hav^g found
> no Indians, & only a chance Partridge for food. We staid an Hour to
> refresh them.

Thompson never did find the Kootenays, primarily because "Narrows" is a relative term. If he'd continued south from the Tobacco River for another forty miles or so, he'd have come across a narrowing in the Kootenai so dramatic he couldn't have mistaken it. In later years, it was dubbed Souse Gulch, site of today's Libby Dam. Souse Gulch was less than three miles from the head of the Kootenays' trail to Flathead Country, and whether Thompson was aware of it or not, his two scouts had camped only a stone's throw away from the Kootanae road. From the big bend of the Kootenai River, the road followed the Fisher River south into the Cabinet Mountains, then tracked the Thompson River all the way to the Clark Fork. In years to come, the road played a role in the development of Montana's fur trade, and Thompson would eventually ride parts of it as he travelled between the Kootenai River and his post on the Clark Fork.

In the spring of 1808, however, the Kootanae Road was an unknown quantity, and even if Thompson had known it was there, he wouldn't have risked the vagaries of an Indian trail when he had the certainty of a river. Once he realized the Kootenays had gone, he gave up his plan to visit the Flatheads. He ordered his men to launch the canoe, opened his journal, and devoted the next three hours to filling another page with notes on the course of the Kootenai River.

From the David Thompson Bridge, Highway 37 follows close along the banks of a smooth, broad Kootenai River, polished to a preternatural clarity by the presence of the Libby Dam. Seventeen miles later, the road crosses the river again and comes to an end at Libby, Montana, where a display in the town's heritage museum recalls Thompson's travels in Montana. A large-scale reproduction of his map of the area forms a backdrop for a fur trade display, and a small-scale map in the museum's collection shows Thompson's version of the route of the Kootanae Road.

Between Libby and Troy, the Purcells to the north and the Cabinet Mountains to the south close in to create a narrow pass that forces the Kootenai River, Highway 2, and the Burlington Northern Railway into tight quarters as they squeeze through the limited opening. This was one of the unnavigable reaches that Thompson's sources had warned him about. In a river now riddled with rocks, the *voyageurs* dodged through the rapids, went "down with the line" on the left, shot an "Isle of Rock & Embarras" on the right, and came to a halt on the brink of Kootenai Falls. Ahead, the river roared through a canyon—foaming against boulders, plunging over ledges, boiling between islands of stone.

For the better part of a day, Thompson and his crew searched for a way past the barrier. Dismissing the south side of the canyon as "impracticable," they crossed the river to examine the north side: "we found it very bad indeed but practicable with much care & precaution ... " He sent the men back to the canoe to ready it for the portage, warning them not to start carrying without him, and stayed to explore the cliffs ahead. He finally concluded that the precipitous route offered "nothing extraordinary" except the difficulty of getting back down again.

We began carrying at 3¼ Pm with light Loads & went abᵗ 1 Mile
over a terrible Road, along Side of a steep Hill nearly perpend, walk-

ing wholly among small fragments of black broken Rock that had
rolled from the Summit. Our Height at times was ab^t 300 feet above
the River ... the least slip would have been inevitable destruction, as
the steepness of the Rock allowed no return ... Each Trip took
1½ H, & by 6¾ Pm we had got most of the Cargo to the Brook,
where we put up.

Today only the trails of sure-footed animals follow Thompson's
route along the cliffs, but the Kootenai River still pours through the
canyon, the only major falls in the American northwest to escape being
harnessed for electricity. A popular "point of interest," the falls are a fif-
teen-minute walk from the parking lot on Highway 2—over a well-
beaten path, across a mesh-covered bridge, down three flights of
expanded-metal stairs, and along a tree-lined trail to the edge of the
river. To paraphrase Thompson, the route offers "nothing extraordinary"
except the difficulty of getting back up again.

From Kootenai Falls, Highway 2 follows Thompson across the state
line between Montana and the Idaho Panhandle. Just short of Moyie
Springs, the road crosses the riotous Moyie River, a name Tyrrell suggested was an anglicized version of *mouillé*, the French word for "wet."
Before the month was out, Thompson would be floundering among the
upstream reaches of "this terrible River," but he said nothing of passing
its confluence with the Kootenai.

Nevertheless, he couldn't have been very far from it. He noted steep
cliffs, poplar-covered flats, and a broader and smoother Kootenai, a
description that reflects the setting of the mouth of the Moyie River.
Curious about why Thompson ignored its lower reaches, we stopped for
an hour to investigate. At its confluence with the Kootenai, the Moyie
resembles a small lake, but up on Highway 2, a lookout peers into a
canyon that would make a sky jumper giddy. Idaho's second highest
bridge spans this chasm, and a dam that's higher than Niagara Falls
drops the Moyie over its spillway. By no stretch of the imagination could
the lower Moyie have ever served as a trade route, one possible reason
for Thompson's indifference to its presence.

On the morning of May 8, 1808, Thompson ended his journey in the
vicinity of present-day Bonners Ferry, where he found ten lodges of
Kootenay and Lake Indians camped by the Kootenai River. On the hill-
top above the town, a historical marker now welcomes Thompson and
recalls the day of his arrival.

DAVID THOMPSON

COMING FROM CANADA, THE FAMOUS MAP MAKER AND TRADER FOR THE NORTH WEST COMPANY EXPLORED THIS AREA AND RIVER IN 1808.

On May 8 somewhere near here, Thompson's famished party, all
sick from eating "much tainted" antelope, met ten lodges of Indians
who could give them only "a few dried Carp (of last year's catch!)
and some moss bread ... but acceptable to the hungry."

The account was taken from Thompson's *Narrative,* but his journal
is more explicit. For reasons of his own, Thompson did call the tainted
meat "antelope," though his journal says it was *chevreuil.* Somewhere
near Troy, Montana:

Found part of a Chevreuil, which the Eagles had more than half
devoured—it was almost putrified, but as we were without Food,
we were necessitated to take what remained, altho' we could hardly
bear the smell—at 6½ Pm put up as the Men had tasted nothing all
day & were much fatigued. Boiled our rotten Meat—we eat of it
but all of us became quite sick, & fatigued as we were ... could not
sleep.

They passed this sleepless night six and a half miles upstream of
Bonners Ferry, at their camp near the mouth of the Moyie River.
Although the circumstances make the honour a dubious one, David
Thompson seems to have been one of the first guests to pitch a tent at
the Twin Rivers Canyon Resort.

Among the Lake Indians at Bonners Ferry were some of Chief Ugly
Head's people, and Thompson had no sooner reached their camp than he
was dispatching messengers in all directions to carry the news of his
arrival.

As soon as I landed, smoked with the Indians for a few Minutes,
when I got one of them to set off with Tobacco to the Flat heads &
the Old Chief, to be here as soon as possible—a Horseman also set
off below to a Camp of Lake Indians who are to be here the
Morrow or so.

Bonners Ferry isn't usually counted as an official North West post, but it's flagged on Thompson's map with an italicized "NWCo," his symbol for posts that were. Although he later had cause to revise his opinion, initially he seemed quite taken with Bonners Ferry. The day he arrived, he sketched a pretty picture of the trees edging the river banks: "Poplar, Aspin, Thorn, Choak Cherry, small Plane—the Woods in half Leaf & the Blossoms already falling off the Arrow Wood." That night, he "Obs^d for Longitude by Capella, Arcturus and Regulus," and added the future location of an American town to his map of "The Province of Canada."

For over a week, Thompson had been keeping a wary eye on the level of the Kootenai River. At Tobacco Plains, he'd recorded an overnight rise of six inches; at Bonners Ferry, he measured an increase of four and a half feet in two days. Despite the rapidly rising water, two days later he had his men back on the river again, paddling north toward Kootenay Lake to "see if any eligible Place can be found for a Settlement." By that time, only ten yards of river bank remained, "& the rest to the foot of the Mountains & southward one extensive Lake."

Early the next morning, the canoe crossed the border into Canada, and Thompson came in sight of the south end of Kootenay Lake near Creston, B.C. For four hours, they paddled among the back lakes (Leach Lake, Duck Lake, and the Six-Mile Slough), looking for the Lake Indians. At eleven o'clock in the morning, they found them. Thompson and his hosts soon got down to the business of trading. He expensed eighteen inches of tobacco, and traded goods and ammunition for a moose skin, thirty-five furs, three good horses, and four of the Lake Indians' famous bows. The horses were for the return journey to Kootanae House; the bows were a gift for Duncan McGillivray, who had left the field and retired to Montreal. Thompson had no way of knowing that his friend's "vile disorder" had finally defeated him, and that McGillivray had died on April 9, only five weeks before.

Duncan's Bows

~ Thompson's Lake Indians were well known amongst other tribes as skilful makers of bows. *Arrow Lakes Indians* presents a description of how these highly prized weapons were constructed.

~ "The double-curved bow was ... made of red cedar or yew wood. It was about 4 feet long and recurved on either side of the hand grip as well as the tips ...

~ "The wood was cut when the sap was running and then was

> soaked for several days. When the wood was soft, it was
> shaped and bound tightly to another piece of straight wood.
> ～ "Wedges were then driven in to form the curves and the bow
> was left to season. After seasoning ... the two arcs of the bow
> were wrapped tightly with wet sinew. This tightened as it
> dried and added toughness to the wood.
> ～ "The bow was then polished and might also be decorated."[4]

The Lake Indians told Thompson there was a second camp of their people "ab^t the mid of the Lake," and that this midpoint was where the Kootenay River left the lake to flow west to another great river. Thompson would have known or guessed that this great river was the Columbia, yet he turned back without making any attempt to reach it. Over the years, more than one author has muttered about this apparent lack of enterprise, but Thompson had his reasons for not bothering.

The first was the nature of the river itself. On its final rush to the Columbia, the Kootenay River drops 360 feet in less than 50 miles, and, in Thompson's day, stepped down to the Columbia over a series of impassable falls. The Lake Indians had warned him that the descent to the Columbia required five difficult portages, one of them twenty miles long. Today five dams—Corra-Linn, Upper Bonnington, Lower Bonnington, South Slocan, and Brilliant—capture the Kootenay's power and control its drop to the Columbia. The dams have created a broader, smoother, and often deeper river that's well adapted to an afternoon's paddling, but no more a navigable route to the Columbia now than it was then.

The second reason was the rigid schedule of the fur trade. Although Thompson believed the route down the Kootenay was unnavigable, it did cross his mind to make sure. But his men had grown weak on their diet of dried fish and moss bread, and the season was rapidly advancing. Even if his men could have summoned the strength, the 180-mile side trip would have taken well over a week. Thompson didn't have a week to spare. He had a 5,000-mile trade run to make before freeze-up, back to Kootanae House to pick up Charlotte and the children, across Howse Pass to the Prairies, east to Rainy Lake House to deliver his furs, then west to the Columbia again with a new load of goods, and he was already a month late.

Thompson talked two of the Lake Indians into delivering the horses to Bonners Ferry, then set off on the return trip upstream. The Kootenai River had now risen six feet, and every effort to move the canoe was overwhelmed by the force of the current. The *voyageurs* gave up on the river and paddled and portaged their way south among a series of back lakes, lakes that just a few days before had been meadows. By the time they reached Bonners Ferry, the whole country lay under water, including Thompson's camp and all the Indian trails his customers needed to reach it.

> These Lakes brought us to our old Campment, which is now under water—we camped at 11 Am at a detached high Knowl & here received the disagreeable News of the Flat Heads & Kootanaes being unable to come here, on account of the flooding of the Country—thus all my fine Hopes are ruined ... [the next day] Conversing much ab' the Country, & tried to make an arrangement to go to the Flat Head Country, but all to no purpose.

Floods of this magnitude were a common occurrence on the Kootenai for centuries. The Lake Indians tolerated the moods of the river, paddling their canoes through a world that could turn to water without warning. To the white settlers, however, the floods were a menace. To safeguard their settlements, the lands around Bonners Ferry and Creston were extensively diked (for over fifty miles at Creston alone), but in the years the river went on a rampage, summer was a season of sandbagging. These were the floods that inspired Baillie-Grohman in 1886, the floods that made history in 1894, the floods that inundated the entire countryside in 1948. In 1951 the U.S. Congress authorized the construction of the Libby Dam, but ten years would pass before Canada and the United States signed the necessary treaty. Still another decade went by before the Libby Dam went in and the Kootenai's reign as a wild river was over.

The flood seemed to bring home to Thompson the enormity of the task he faced in developing the Columbia Division. His small company of men was dwarfed by the size of his territory, and though he covered more miles and incurred higher costs than any other North West trader, his partners made no allowance for either. Unless headquarters granted him more leeway, Thompson could envision the Columbia Division going under, and with it all hope of completing his map of the west. On May 17, he drafted a letter.

> The Flat Heads &c &c were only 12 day's March from us last Winter and the Lake Indians only 6 days & yet both as completely shut up by Mountains as if they were on the other Side ... the Waters

rising in the summer have nearly the same effect ... We are too few to
separate ourselves—last Winter I had only 7 Men & it is not likely I
shall have more this Winter ... I labour under many disadvantages
which only Time and a generous assistance can overcome.

It's not clear whether Thompson ever sent this letter, but he wasn't
the only Nor'Wester to reproach the senior partners for their penny-
pinching. Simon Fraser had also argued for more "generous assistance"
in opening the country west of the Rockies, and from his post in the
northern interior of B.C., he too had written a letter.

To form establishments this summer certainly depends upon us—
but to render them productive, will depend on the attention you
Gentlemen pay them ... tho few of you can imagine what it costs to
feed the people in this quarter, there are none of you but know that
exploring new countries and seeing strange Indians is expensive was
it only to procure a welcome reception.[5]

On May 19, just eleven days after his arrival, Thompson was gearing
up to leave Bonners Ferry. He planned to avoid the Kootenai River by
crossing the Purcell Mountains, riding the same trail he'd refused to follow with Chief Ugly Head the previous fall. For this trip, Thompson and
his men had a guide, albeit an unwilling one. While the men were loading the horses, their young Kootenay was off pleading with his people to
send someone with him. Nobody volunteered. The old men "made
Speeches to encourage the young Men," but they might as well have
saved their breath. "None," Thompson commented drily, "were found
hardy enough."

Despite Thompson's insistence that "we are too few to separate ourselves," he and his men were already scattered across two of today's
American states as well as a Canadian province. Beaulieu would stay in
Idaho for the winter, leaving Thompson with only three men (and one
recalcitrant guide) for the journey to Kootanae House. By mid-afternoon,
the horses were loaded and ready to go. Rightly anticipating a rough trip,
Thompson left his survey instruments with Beaulieu.

... we set off with our Kootanae at 2¼ Pm. But the Hills were so
steep & so high that the Loads slipped continually off the Horses, &
it was 4¼ Pm before we got to the top of the first Banks. Hav^g gone
abt 2M our Guide found himself very uneasy, seated as he was on a

loaded Horse, & requested to go back to procure a light Horse of
his own.

The request was a reasonable one, but Thompson was immediately
suspicious. He let the young man go, but anticipating an attempt to
"give us the slip," he sent Mousseau along with him to make sure he
found his way back.

Today Highway 95 has replaced the trail to the top of the "first
Banks," but anyone familiar with the road that climbs out of Bonners
Ferry—a six percent grade, two runaway lanes, and warnings to trucks
to "gear down"—will recognize the hill that signalled the beginning of
Thompson's journey. From the top of the hill, the highway follows his
route north toward Copeland, an early settlement now largely aban-
doned except for its grain elevator, then turns east to enter the Purcell
Mountains.

Highway 95 shares Thompson's trail through the Purcells with the
Crowsnest Highway, the Canadian Pacific Railway, a pipeline, and a
power transmission line, a neighbourliness among linear facilities that
indicates there's still only one way through. Most of the route lies
within the Moyie Valley, even today a natural tapestry of streams,
meadows, and trees, bounded by forested mountains.

At nine in the evening, Mousseau returned with his charge, but he
might as well have left him behind. Although their young Kootenay was
a keen hunter, he showed little interest in a career in guiding. For three
days, his clients barely saw him. The first day he was off fetching his
horse; the second day he faded away at the first stream crossing, "leaving us to go on the best we could"; the third day he produced a *chevreuil*
for a late breakfast, only to announce he was going hunting again. At
that point, Thompson put his foot down. He told his guide he had to
stick with them, then looked on in amazement as the youngster "threw
himself on the Ground quite sulky and threatened to leave us." As is
often the case, the tantrum had the desired effect. Thompson gave in and
their guide left them, setting off "as if to hunt."

We also went off, but finding a Morass before us, we were obliged to
return back to where we breakfasted to try & round it to the east[d].
Here we found our Guide, who also returned & was eating the
singed Skin of the Chevreuil. It immediately struck me that he was
about to desert: he rose up and begged us to stay here while he
would go & visit the Country for the best way to pass ...

That was the last they saw of their guide. Thompson waited until 10:30 the next morning, hoping the "Scoundrel" would turn up, but he finally had to admit what he already knew—it wasn't going to happen. He dispatched Mousseau and Lussier back to Bonners Ferry to try and recruit another guide.

At the time, Thompson was northeast of Copeland. He'd crossed "Beaulieu's Brook," now known as Mission Creek and had set up his camp a few miles farther on. Stuck there for three wearisome days, he brooded on their "forlorn situation" and passed the time wandering around, "examining the Country" and engaging in "sad reflections." This air of helplessness was utterly unlike Thompson, but his knee had gone again and he could hardly walk, which may have affected his outlook. Nor would the time he was wasting have helped to lighten his mood. Under the tutelage of their wayward guide, the expedition had advanced less than twenty miles in three days (six days, counting the waiting). But on the evening of May 24, Thompson's gloom lifted.

> While I was wandering about ... my 2 Men returned with Ugly
> Head for a Guide, thank God—they came at 6 Pm. He has received
> payment for this Service: 1 Capot [cape] of 4 Ells, 1½ Y^{ds} of com
> Red Strouds [woollen cloth], 1 large Knife, 1 small Axe, 10 Balls &
> Powder.

In view of the arduous journey ahead, the services of Chief Ugly Head would have been a bargain at any price. The next morning, he marched Thompson and his men east for a mile, across Mission Creek again, and along the route of Highway 95 for about eight miles. Here the highway ducks south around a height of land and heads for the Moyie River, but Chief Ugly Head chose to turn north. Late in the afternoon, the riders came to the Little Moyie, which Thompson described as "the most northern Scource of the McDonald's River." Fording the Little Moyie held them up for an hour and a half, but after a seven-mile trek "thro' pathless Woods," they reached "McDonald's River," now the mainstem of the Moyie itself. They camped for the night a few miles short of present-day Yahk, B.C. With a guide who knew where he was going, they'd covered seventeen miles in a single day.

Once the riders started following the Moyie, however, even their guide was at a loss. The river had crested its banks, flooded across the floor of the valley, and drowned long stretches of the Indian trail. By May 26, there wasn't a piece of dry land left on the south side of the river. Chief Ugly Head eyed the higher ground of the mountainside, but decided it was "too bad to be passed by Horses." Thompson agreed. The legs of the horses were already so badly cut up "we may trace them by the Blood only, poor Animals." The chief sent Thompson's crew to search out enough wood for a canoe, but by morning he'd changed his mind. Horses or no horses, they'd have to head up the mountainside. Thompson complied, even though he knew the chief's assessment of the route would prove accurate. "We went on in a terrible Road—our poor Horses suffered most cruelly from the Rocks and the Woods."

The party rode northeast for two days, upslope and down, but "always along McDonald's River." On the afternoon of the second day, Ugly Head found a remnant of the trail that led across the river. They forded the Moyie and rode for a few miles over "tolerable Ground," but were soon forced back up onto the mountain again: "as usual made very little progress from climbing & descending, at other times to the middle in water." For the whole of the third day, they struggled through the forest and splashed through the streams along the west side of Moyie Lake. That evening they reached the Moyie River again, "& here by one Means or another we must cross it."

Early began to throw down large Trees for a Bridge, but the Current always broke them or swept them away. One of them was a very fine Larch of ab^r 2 fms round & its Butt lay abt 8 Y^{ds} in the Ground, but the Current turned it round & swept it off without the delay of even a minute. At 11½ Am, seeing all hopes were vain, we desisted ...

For the next six and a half hours, the men tried to cross the river by fording it. They managed to get across four channels on horseback, but were stymied by the volume of water that poured through the fifth. They unloaded the goods in midstream, "standing Knee deep in exceeding cold water & the whole Embarras shaking with the violence of the current." Ugly Head and Lussier swam their horses across and laboured until six o'clock dropping trees onto the logjam, only to watch as the Moyie snatched them away like straws. In desperation, Thompson tied the packs up in blankets, secured them with a line, and threw them into the river.

We then crossed everything we had, except a Parcel cont^g ab^t ½ Pack of Beav^r, 2 very fine Bear Skins & all the little Property of Lussier & Le Camble, which was totally lost by the breaking of the Line. We then crossed on Horseback by 8 Pm, all safe thank God.

We camped on the waters Edge hav^g had a Day of extreme Danger
& hard work—I hope we have now done with this terrible River.

Early the next morning, the men spread everything out to dry, then
rode "thro' close burnt Woods & over high Points of Rock" to emerge
into open country that was "more level & much better ... everything
about us is green." They trotted northeast for nine miles and stopped to
rest by a stream somewhere southeast of today's city of Cranbrook. By
evening, they'd reached the Kootenay River, where they camped and
built a canoe. At noon the next day, they crossed to the east side of the
river, landing on today's Wardner-Steele Road (probably closer to
Wardner than to Fort Steele). For the next three hours, they rode the trail
Thompson called the "Peigan War Road."

The Peigan War Road

~ The Peigan War Road emerged from the Crowsnest Pass
and descended the Elk River Valley to follow the Kootenay
River north. Part of it traversed the same countryside as
today's Fenwick Road.

~ Fenwick Road is an offshoot of the Wardner-Steele Road,
so you can drive it from either end. From the Wardner end,
take the Fenwick Road turnoff when you reach the Kootenay
Trout Hatchery; from the Fort Steele end, turn right shortly
after you cross the Wildhorse River Bridge.

~ Fenwick Road follows close along the Kootenay River,
through a mixture of forest and ranchland that looks much
the same now as it did when Thompson rode by nearly two
hundred years ago.

~ Although the Peigan War Road crossed the Kootenay several
times, most of it seems to have lain on the east side of the
river. It's quite likely that the Spirit Trail between Fairmont
and Canal Flats was once part of the same route.

Today a gravel offshoot of the Wardner-Steele Road follows the trail
through the landscape Thompson described: open-grown stands of ponderosa pine and Douglas fir, fields of dry native grasses, clusters of trem-
bling aspen and cottonwood down by the river. Fenwick Road is the only
road that follows this reach of the Kootenay, just as it was the only road
then. Needless to say, Thompson was uneasy sharing a trail with the
unpredictable Peigans, and Chief Ugly Head was worried enough to go
the rounds whenever they stopped for the night. But only once was the

silence of the War Road disturbed. Thompson's men heard a shot and "Passed the night under arms." Otherwise, they travelled in peace.

The difficulties arose at the river crossings. Both the Wildhorse and the Lussier were roaring with runoff, and precious time ticked by as the men threw down more trees to make bridges. At Canal Flats, the Kootenay was too deep to ford and too broad to bridge, and more hours were lost in building another canoe. This time, Chief Ugly Head took charge of construction and crafted the canoe himself, a job that occupied all of the morning and much of the afternoon.

> Early our Guide began his Canoe but taking extraordinary pains did not finish it 'till 2½ Pm, when we began crossing the River. By 5 Pm were all landed on McGillivray's Portage thank Heaven. Here we bid adieu to our humane Guide, without whose manly exertions, Perseverance & Attention we had certainly never been able to have reached this Place. He descended McGillivray's River in his Canoe & we went on over the Portage ...

On June 8, 1808, Thompson reached Kootanae House to find it deserted. Finan McDonald, Clément, and Bercier had already set off for Howse Pass, taking the women and children with them. Thompson stopped to look around for his wood canoe, but "the wind & Current had carried it off." The riders went on, leaving the "old House now desolate" behind. They spent the night in a field, then rode into the wetlands, following a sometime trail. Like every other river in the country, the Columbia was sprawling over its banks, and the trail soon disappeared into the "Lakes of Grass & Water." The packs on the horses (already wetted, by Thompson's estimate, some fifteen or twenty times) were in danger of another soaking. He had the horses unloaded and ordered Le Camble and Lussier to ride on ahead. He and Mousseau stopped for a day to build yet another canoe.

Two days later Thompson finally caught up to his family. He "found all safe," but encountered a tale of more days with nothing to eat. "They have had but poorly at times in Food," he wrote, "& have eat most of the Dogs &c." Although Charlotte seems to have had plenty to worry about while Thompson was gone, any relief she may have felt when her husband returned was short-lived.

Thompson's children rarely appear in his journals, but on the climb to Howse Pass, he wrote about them twice in a matter of days. When the horse carrying Fanny (now aged seven) and Samuel (aged four) tried to buck its load, Thompson's journal entry was brief and to the point: "One

of my horses nearly crushing my children to death from having his
load badly put on, which I mistook for being vicious; I shot him on the
spot and rescued my little ones." (We're left to speculate about
Charlotte's reaction to this strategy, which could easily have brought the
horse crashing down on the children.) Then, as they neared the pass, a
second crisis:

> At 3 P.M. we reloaded but missing my little Daughter [probably
> Emma, now two] & nowhere finding her, we concluded she was
> drowned & all of us set about finding her—we searched all the
> Embarras in the River but to no purpose. At length Mr McDonald
> found her track going upwards. We searched all about & at length
> thank God at 8½ P.M. found her about 1 Mile off, against a bank of
> Snow.[6]

Over the next two days, the travellers crossed Howse Pass and
descended the trail to Kootenay Plains, where Thompson ran into
another delay—the canoe laid up for the winter was useless, crushed
beyond repair by the heavy snows. Luckily enough, a band of Iroquois
trappers proved willing to trade, and Thompson soon had the canoe he
needed. Women and children, baggage and packs were bundled aboard,
the *voyageurs* dug in their paddles, and the canoe fled into the rapids of
the North Saskatchewan River.

Thompson was pushing the pace. He still had a four-thousand-mile
trip ahead of him and July was almost upon him. By that evening, the
canoe was at Rocky Mountain House, and by the next, it was another
sixty miles downriver. Thompson stopped just long enough to leave his
family at Boggy Hall, then he was back in the canoe, headed for Rainy
Lake House.

Boggy Hall

- ~ The exact site of Boggy Hall hasn't been found, but its
  general location is known. It stood on the west side of the
  North Saskatchewan River, a few miles southeast of present-
  day Lodgepole, Alberta.
- ~ In 1811 Alexander Henry described the remains of the fort:
  "At this place we had an Establishment a few years ago ... but
  Beaver getting scarce we abandoned the place in the Fall of
  the year 1808, the remains of the building stand ... about half

---

> a Mile from the River, through a thick Woods which must
> have made it very tedious getting water at this post in the
> Winter season.
> ～ "The situation of the House is very pleasant, having a
> beautiful Meadow on one side, sufficiently large for a horse
> race, the whole is bound in by tall Poplars, Aspen and pine."[7]

While Thompson was away, Charlotte gave birth to their fourth child, a son named John, who was born at Boggy Hall on August 25, 1808. It's likely, however, that only three of the Thompson children were with Charlotte. About this time, Thompson had arranged to send Fanny to school in Montreal. Now that Charlotte was back on the North Saskatchewan, she was among her relatives. Her brother Patrick was stationed at Boggy Hall, and though Sir George Simpson maintained that Patrick Small was "kept sober by the dread of being turned out of the service only,"[8] Charlotte had her sister-in-law to rely on.

Thompson's journey to Rainy Lake took him three and a half months. On October 3, 1808, he arrived to greet his newborn son, but once again his visit was short. By the next day, he'd dispatched his canoes up the North Saskatchewan River and was saddling up for the ride to Howse Pass. Charlotte was now twenty-three, and she'd travelled with her husband since she was barely fourteen. That fall, however, she was left behind for the first time. A few months later, Boggy Hall was closed, and Charlotte and the children moved to a more permanent establishment. At the time, it was known as Fort Augustus; today it's the city of Edmonton.

Considering the sum of events on the Columbia, the separation of the couple isn't surprising. It's easy to imagine a trader hampered by his domestic responsibilities, and a wife who'd had her fill of living on the edge. Maybe they came to an agreement—he'd travel alone as he worked to establish the Columbia Division, and Charlotte and the children would stay on the Prairies until he got the job done. Although the reason is a matter of speculation, the result is a matter of record. Charlotte Thompson never ventured into the field with her husband again.

Lake Pend Oreille–1809[1]

David Thompson's first year west of the Rocky Mountains came close to being his last. His meagre harvest of furs had cast doubt on the commercial value of the Columbia Division, and his Montreal partners had contemplated shutting it down. Thompson forestalled this disaster by asking for two years to prove his territory, a time limit that trapped him in an early version of catch-22. Unless he increased his returns, he'd lose his chance to map the Columbia, but the effort to increase his returns would cost him the time he needed to explore it.

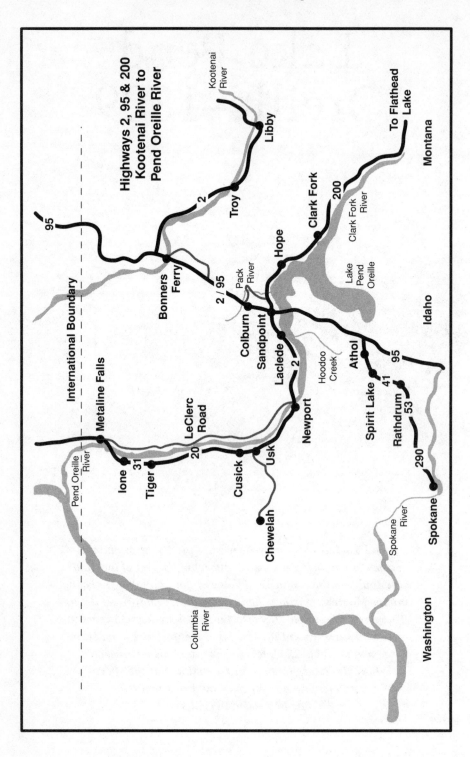

Highways 2, 95 & 200
Kootenai River to
Pend Oreille River

DURING ITS FIRST YEAR OF OPERATION, THE COLUMBIA DIVISION HAD SUFFERED a critical shortage of manpower, but by the fall of 1808, Thompson had mustered enough personnel to man two winter posts. He kept James McMillan and a crew of four (Lussier, Parizeau, Brière, and Buché) with him at Kootanae House, and dispatched a second crew (La Gassé, Méthode, Mousseau, and Crépeau) to Lake Indian Country with a loaded canoe. In charge of the expedition was Thompson's right-hand man, Finan McDonald.

Officially, McDonald was a company clerk, but his duties that winter were far from clerical. He set off for Bonners Ferry on November 7, only to have his canoe "taken in the ice" of the Kootenay River. He hiked back to Kootanae House, started off again with a string of horses, and managed to make it as far as Montana. Too late. Winter blew in and buried the trail in snow, and when his horses bogged down, McDonald was forced to give up. Somewhere along the Kootenai River, he and his men pitched their tents, built themselves a storage shed, and holed up for the winter.

As for the location of McDonald's camp, there are as many opinions as authors. Some place it at the head of Kootenai Falls, others wave vaguely at "somewhere upstream," and still others put it as far up the river as Libby, Montana. This last location, which Thompson noted on a later journey up the Kootenai, is most likely, and it was a good spot for a trading post. It stood only seventeen miles west of the confluence of the Kootenai and Fisher Rivers, a crossroads of Indian trails leading south into Flathead Country, north into Kootenay Country, and west into Lake Indian Country. Judging by McDonald's fur take that winter (he managed to out-trade Thompson), it's likely he was in a similarly strategic position.

In addition to the men stationed at the trading posts, two others (Beaulieu and Boulard) were still in the field. Thompson now had almost double the number of men he'd had the year before, as well as an unexpected bonus in the person of Jaco Finlay, who turned up on the Columbia that fall. Any hard feelings between Thompson and Jaco seem to have evaporated, but Jaco, as usual, was keeping his distance. He camped for the winter with his family and his horses half a day's ride north of Kootanae House.

For six months, Thompson barely stirred from Kootanae House. He put in a quiet winter trading with the Kootenays and filled his spare time going for walks, riding his horse, and writing up his "thoughts on the country." On December 11, he "transcribed Captn Lewis's acc^t of his journey to the Pacific Ocean." On the whole, it must have been a dull winter, but with spring came the payoff. Between McDonald's post and his own, Thompson's division had generated fifty-five packs of furs, a haul that was likely to pacify his eastern partners and was guaranteed to pique the interest of the Hudson's Bay Company.

The spring of 1809 also brought tragedy to the people of Kootanae House. Mrs. Lussier died near the end of April, only six months after her fourth child was born, and the men's last melancholy duty before leaving for Rainy Lake was her burial. When Thompson headed for Howse Pass with the fur harvest, he took Lussier's youngsters with him as far as Jaco's camp, where he left them in the capable hands of Mrs. Finlay. For the Finlays, the burden of an abruptly expanded family soon paled into insignificance. While Thompson was away, the Peigans swooped down on Jaco's camp, raided his herd of horses, and left his family with little more than the clothes they stood up in.

Until that spring, the Bay men had looked on "Mr. Thompson's" Columbian venture with amused tolerance, but a shipment of two and a half tons of furs was no laughing matter. True to his policy of following wherever the Nor'Westers led, James Bird promptly sent Joseph Howse on an exploratory trip to the mountains. Thompson, however, had his own policy—staying one jump ahead of the Hudson's Bay Company. Although he'd escorted the fur pack as far as Fort Augustus, once he heard what Howse was up to, he decided against travelling on to Rainy Lake. He sent James McMillan east with the canoes, spent three weeks visiting his family, and returned immediately to his post on the Columbia. Within a month of the Bay's tentative move toward the mountains, he'd abandoned Kootanae House and moved his operation, lock, stock, and barrel, into the American northwest.

Accompanied by Finan McDonald and followed by Jaco Finlay, who was hunting on horseback, Thompson descended the Kootenai River for a third time. On August 29, he landed at the head of a trail near Bonners Ferry, a trail that led from the river to Idaho's Lake Pend Oreille. Initially, Thompson called this overland route "The Great Road of the Flat Heads," but on his map he labelled it "Lake Indian Road." It's not clear where the road began. Thompson merely noted that it was a good twenty-five-minute walk from "our old campment of last year."

At 11½ Am we arrived at the Great Road of the Flat Heads & camped as it is here we must procure Horses to take us to the Flat Head River where we hope, please Heaven to pass a good quiet Winter.

Thompson's "good quiet Winter" was destined to last all of two months; meanwhile, he camped by the Kootenai River to await the arrival of the Flatheads who were bringing the horses. A week later, the Indians reached Thompson's camp, and on the afternoon of September 6, fourteen horses carrying riders and packs struggled for three and a half hours to crest the cliffs of the Kootenai River Valley.

> ... went to the foot of the High Banks S15E 3M. At 11½ Am we had much Trouble to get up it, the Horses often rolling down with their Loads. At length by 3 Pm we had got all up, taken a mouthful to eat & reloaded & set off.

The "Great Road of the Flat Heads" led into a thick forest of pine, fir, and spruce. Thompson found the trail "good yet narrow," and though he complained that cutting away small trees to widen it slowed their pace, they'd covered twenty-five miles by the evening of the second day. It was now September 7, and autumn was in the air. Ice was forming on the margins of the streams, and the leaves on the cottonwoods were starting to fade and fall.

The next morning the riders reached the "Portage River," so-named because Thompson considered the ride to Lake Pend Oreille a portage. Apparently, those who came after him agreed—the Portage River is now known as the Pack. Once the riders reached the river, they followed it for half a mile, forded it, then rode the remaining seven and a half miles through the forest and out onto the flats of Lake Pend Oreille. At the lakeside, another helpful band of Flatheads waited. Thompson had the horses unloaded and close to a ton of "Lumber and Goods" stowed in the Flatheads' canoes.

It's often said that Thompson pioneered the route of Highway 2/95 between Bonners Ferry and Sandpoint, but the highway tends to run southwest, and Thompson consistently gave his direction as southeast. This may be one occasion, however, when Thompson's directions should be taken with a grain of salt. Highway 2/95 lies within the Purcell Trench, and it's highly unlikely that he (or the Flatheads before him) would have forsaken this natural passageway for a rugged climb into the Cabinet Mountains. Since he was vague about where he started out, it's difficult to follow Thompson's trail for the first twenty miles of his ride, but he must have paralleled the highway over at least part of the distance. His description of the trees lining his trail matches that of the woods that lie east of the highway. Within these woods, the Paradise Valley Road winds today, offering a close-up of the forest that Thompson rode through. The road begins in downtown Bonners Ferry and, at several points, rejoins the main highway to Sandpoint.

Twenty miles south of Bonners Ferry, Highway 2/95 crosses the Pack River Bridge, and two miles farther on, the Colburn-Culver Road loops into the landscape Thompson travelled. Although the surface of the road isn't always as smooth as it could be, the detour makes a pleasant drive through a lightly settled landscape of meadow and forest. Three miles into its run, the Colburn-Culver Road crosses the Pack River, then turns south for another three miles to cross it again. In its uppermost reaches, the Pack is a swift mountain stream, but lower down it's a sandy, lazy river curling its way through a tangle of trees and brush. This is the reach that Thompson described as "15 Y^{ds} wide, deep & very easy Current," now a favourite among paddlers who prefer their rivers mild.

After the Colburn-Culver Road crosses the Pack River for the second time, it continues south for another three miles and comes to an end at its junction with Highway 200. A few miles to the east, Highway 200 catches up to the river, crosses it, then bends to oversee its final ramble across the Pack River Flats. As the highway skirts the northern shore of Lake Pend Oreille, it overlooks the railway lagoon where Thompson loaded his packs into the Flatheads' canoes.

Once all the goods were safely stowed, canoes and riders pushed on up the lake for four or five miles, but in mid-afternoon, Thompson called a halt: "put up at 2½ Pm, the Wind blowing too hard for the Canoes to hold on." The two parties camped by the lake for the night, and early the next morning, they tried again.

> The Wind moderating, the Canoes got off & we following, but the Wind rising, the Canoes were obliged to lighten & reload part of the Horses. We all at length arrived in safety, thank God, at the mouth of the River where we camped for the Night. They all smoked—say 54 Flat Heads, 23 Pointed Hearts & 4 Kootanaes—in all ab^t 80 Men.

This large encampment, which included not only the men, but their families as well, was located at the easternmost edge of Lake Pend Oreille, near the delta of the Clark Fork River. First thing in the morning, Thompson and two Flatheads left the camp to paddle the lakeshore, scouting for a likely site for a trading post. About eight miles down the lake, they came to a rocky peninsula jutting from the eastern shore, "a place somewhat eligible but labours under the want of good earth." Even though the stony ground promised difficulties, Thompson was satisfied he'd found his building site: "got all the Goods embarked by the Flat Heads & landed the whole by 3 Pm."

Largely because of J. B. Tyrrell's abiding faith in Thompson's numbers, it was once thought that Idaho's first trading post stood only a mile or so from the mouth of the Clark Fork River. Whatever Thompson's numbers said, the first clue to the post's location lay in his words: "Took a walk around the Peninsula on which we are, which took me 4 Hours." In 1923 an aged blind Indian who remembered seeing the house chimneys as a boy helped searchers find the stones that established the old fort's position. It stood on a rocky promontory now known as Hope Peninsula.

Today Hope Peninsula is shared by Samowen Park (camping and picnicking in the woods along the lakeshore), the David Thompson Game Preserve (overrun by small deer that the preserve's namesake would have rated as "poor"), and a scattering of privately owned acreages. Since the remains of the fort lie on private land, no attempt has been made to publicize their location, but at East Hope, a historical marker and a stone monument stand in memory of David Thompson. Erected in 1928, the monument is located on the Hope Frontage Road, a short detour off the north side of Highway 200.

Thompson would name both his new post and the lake it overlooked after the Kalispels, whose name he rendered as "Kullyspell." Since Kullyspell House was established in the heart of their country, the choice was an appropriate one. In Thompson's day, the Kalispels were a seminomadic people, travelling in small bands during the summer and settling in larger encampments for the winter. According to Robert Carriker's history of that people:

> The Kalispel ranged widely over lands below the forty-ninth
> parallel ... west as far as Mount Spokane in Washington, south to
> Lake Pend Oreille in Idaho and east to the Clark's Fork River of
> Montana ... It has been estimated the tribe roamed an area over
> four million acres in breadth.[2]

In later years, the French traders had their own name for Kullyspell Lake—they called it *Lac Pend d'Oreille*. The phrase has been taken to mean "earring" (*pendiller* is French for "to dangle" and *oreille* means "ear"), presumably in reference to decorations worn by the Kalispels. It's often denied that the Kalispels ever wore earrings (or that the Nez Percé ever pierced their noses or the Flatheads ever flattened their foreheads); nevertheless, Carriker's book includes a 1910 photograph of a Kalispel man wearing large "ear pendants" that look like they're made of shell.[3]

An alternative suggestion is that the traders named the lake for its unusual shape. Seen from the air, Lake Pend Oreille takes the form of a giant ear. Those who disagree maintain that the lake is so large (forty-five miles long and up to six miles across), the earthbound traders couldn't possibly have known what shape it was. Yet on Thompson's map, Lake Pend Oreille stands out, not merely because it's big, but because it's drawn in the shape of an ear.

Today Lake Pend Oreille attracts scores of vacationers keen on boating, sailing, and fishing its waters. Idaho's largest and deepest lake is cradled in forested mountains, and on its western shore stands the city of Sandpoint, the hub of the Pend Oreille tourist industry. Down on the lakeside, a cluster of modern hotels presides over City Beach, a broad spit of land that Thompson called Sandy Point.

By September 12, 1809, the construction of Kullyspell House was under way, and Thompson's assessment of the "want of good earth" was rapidly proved correct.

> Began our Warehouse. The Ground is so very full of small Stones
> that the Holes for the Posts &c &c is a long time making—got the
> Posts & Needles ready, & threw down a Red Fir of 2 fms round to
> make a Canoe for fishing &c.

Over the next two and a half weeks, the men laboured to get the warehouse up, but compared to the speed at which they'd built Kootanae House, the work proceeded at a snail's pace. It took two days just to dig in the posts and raise the walls two and a half feet: "the Wood is so very heavy that it requires the force of 4 or 5 Men to lift a single piece of 10 or 11 feet." The next day the walls went up to the "intended height" of seven feet, but it would be a week before "Mr McDonald hung the Door." Yet another three days would go by before the men finished mudding the roof and moved the goods into the warehouse.

Although construction was slow, Thompson had reason to be pleased. Word of his new trading post was spreading like wildfire, and entire days had to be set aside to deal with the customers who flocked to his camp with furs and fish, meat, and horses to trade. During the weeks the men were trying to get the warehouse up,

> 16 Canoes of Pointed Hearts passed us & camped with the other
> Flat Heads ...

Spent much of the Day in trading with the Indians who brought ab^t 120 or 130 Skins ...

Traded ab^t 20 Skins ...

3 Canoes arrived last Night & put up at the Island ...

Indians arrived with ... ab^t 1¾ Packs & much Berries ...

Traded a Horse for 15 skins value ...

Traded 3 Horses which now makes 7 for the company ...

15 strange Indians arrived from the west^d; they are quite poor in every thing ...

2 Green Wood Indians arrived; they made me a present of a Bear Skin, 1 Beaver d° & 5 Rats, with 2 parcels of dried Fish & 2 Mares—for which I shall pay them ...

The Pointed Hearts were the Coeur d'Alènes, the Green Woods were the Nez Percé (a people that Lewis and Clark knew well), and the fifteen strangers were the Kalispels. In Thompson's terms, "quite poor in every thing" meant the Kalispels lacked kettles, knives, axes, and guns, and were prime targets for trade. Before they went away, he showed them how to stretch a variety of skins "& they promised to be here by the time the Snow whitens the Ground."

At some point in the past, a Lake Indian Chief (probably Ugly Head) had told Thompson about a river that joined the Columbia downstream of its confluence with the Kootenay. This river was the Pend Oreille, and Thompson now found himself talking to the people who made their home on its banks. The Kalispels confirmed that their river flowed north and west and that, yes, it did join the Columbia. For Thompson, the news came as a revelation, and less than two days after his visitors left, he was saddling up to ride west. But what a time to choose. The construction of Kullyspell House was barely under way, customers were arriving in droves, and he was due to meet James McMillan on the Kootenai River within the next three weeks.

The river now called the Pend Oreille was only one segment of a much longer river that Thompson named "The Saleesh." His rendering of the Saleesh drainage encompassed Montana's Flathead Lake (which he called Saleesh Lake), the downstream reaches of the Flathead River, the section of the Clark Fork from the mouth of the Flathead River to Lake

Pend Oreille, the lake itself, and the entire length of the Pend Oreille River.

Naming watercourses is often an arbitrary business, and modern cartographers have adopted a different view. On today's maps, the Clark Fork and the Pend Oreille are two different rivers. The Clark Fork rises high in the Rocky Mountains near Anaconda, Montana, and flows westward for over three hundred miles to empty into Lake Pend Oreille. As it exits the west side of the lake, the river is reborn as the Pend Oreille, a 114-mile-long watercourse that sweeps through northern Idaho and Washington and falls into the Columbia just north of the Canadian border.

On the Prairies, roads tend to ignore rivers unless they're forced to cross one, a consequence of the inflexible grid system laid down in the days when the West was carved into homesteads. In the mountainous terrain west of the Rockies, however, virtually every major river valley has a road in it. As a result, most of Thompson's ride down the Pend Oreille is tracked by a collection of highways known as the Pend Oreille Scenic Byway.

In Idaho the byway arches around the northern bays of Lake Pend Oreille as Highway 200, follows the Pend Oreille River southwest as Highway 2, then swings northwest to cross the river into Washington. From Newport, the byway follows the river north, first as Highway 20 and then as Highway 31, through a memorable sportsman's paradise nicknamed Washington's "Forgotten Corner."

Thompson rode away from Kullyspell House on September 27, 1809, a "blowy cloudy Day" that foreshadowed a week of rain. Taking only Beaulieu and an Indian lad with him, and carrying no goods other than a small gift or two and a length of tobacco, he set the pace along the lakeshore at a brisk trot. Once again, he was in that expansive mood that always seemed to visit him whenever he slipped his leash. At Kullyspell House, Thompson's daily record had been a bare-bones trade journal, noting only who arrived, who left, who did what, and when they did it. But once he reached the Pend Oreille River, his writing underwent a sea change. Line after line, paragraph after paragraph, he flooded his text with details. The following passage is a only fraction of what he wrote as the river unrolled before him.

> The River is here ab^t 350 to 400 Y^{ds} wide, very easy Current
> & shoal near the Shore ... Killed 1 dwarf Goose & 3 Partridges—
> many Swans, Geese, Ducks & Cranes ab^t the head of the River
> & all along hereto ... The woods of Poplar, Aspin, Cedar, different

Firs & Fir Pine, with a few White & Red Pines—Plane & Alder & a variety Shrubs &c—many fine grassy Points & Bays all along the River & the Grass every where quite green, hav^g sprung up since the water has lowered.

The weather that morning was dreary—cool and damp, the mountains shrouded in cloud—but Thompson's spirits seemed undampened. The leaden sky was no use to a surveyor and his compass lay in pieces, a catastrophe that earned scarcely a mention. He tracked his course by glimpses of sun, checked his position if he could see the stars, and kept a careful record of his mileage.

About twelve miles west of Sandpoint, the riders passed Seneacquoteen Crossing, an Indian ford that Thompson would note on the ride back, and where a historical marker near Laclede now stands. In 1864 Seneacquoteen connected the pack trains of the Wildhorse gold rush to the wagon trains rumbling south. For Thompson, it was a temporal crossroads. To the north, the Wildhorse Trail followed the same route he'd ridden with Chief Ugly Head in the past; to the south, it followed a road he would ride in the future.

Thompson called this overland link between the Spokane and Pend Oreille Rivers the Skeetshoo Portage. The portage involved a seventy-five-mile ride—up the Spokane River for twenty-five miles, across Rathdrum Prairie, and down Hoodoo Creek to the Pend Oreille River. In 1811 he took two and a half days to make this ride; in 1813 a fur trader named Ross Cox polished it off in a mere eight hours. In fairness to Thompson, it should be noted that Cox's mount was *Le Bleu*, a famous racehorse of the time.

That night the three men camped about five miles downstream of Laclede. The next morning was foggy and cold, and no sooner had the fog lifted than the sun was lost in the clouds. The riders trotted on to the northwest, and by mid-morning, they'd crossed the Priest River and were riding through a blur of rain toward the first set of falls on the Pend Oreille River.

... went West 5M N80W 2M to the Falls which are in 2 Channels separated by an Isle of Rock on which is the Portage of ab^t 20 Y^{ds}, seemingly good—safe ... Held on N70W 1M ... Refreshed our Horses & took a Meal. Rain then coming on, we camped & the Rain soon became tolerable heavy—shaved, wrote off my Journal &c &c. Ther +64° Rained all the evening.

On Thompson's map, these falls are labelled "carry." The portage he envisaged wasn't along the shore, but over the "Isle of Rock" that divided the falls in two. Part of the rock is still there today, lodged midway in the structure of the Albeni Falls Dam.

The Albeni Falls Dam is a hydroelectric facility that backs up twenty-five miles of the Pend Oreille River and utilizes Lake Pend Oreille as a reservoir. Its presence has created a broader, deeper, more placid river than the one that Thompson surveyed, and in its protected marshlands, the waterfowl he once held in his gun sights now lead a less precarious existence. The staff at Albeni Falls are aware that David Thompson inspected their damsite, and a historical sign in the visitors' centre commemorates the day of his visit.

Just west of the dam, the Scenic Byway crosses the Pend Oreille River, then turns north toward the Washington communities of Usk, Cusick, Tiger, and Ione. Thompson, however, didn't cross the river. He cut through the woods and rode the route now followed by the LeClerc Road. Immediately before the Scenic Byway reaches the bridge leading to Newport, the LeClerc Road sets off to the right. It follows the river north, crosses the last remaining fragment of the Kalispels' traditional lands, and provides access to the recreational country on the east side of the Pend Oreille.

> The Ground is very dry & finely hilly, but very much of it level & the high Hills seemingly distant, but we cannot see to any dist^{ce} on acc^{t} of the bad weather ... having from 7 Am to Noon kept always on a jog Trot except in a few places & the Road has been in general good. At Noon we came to where the River seemingly falls into wide marshy Ground—here we saw the Tents of a few Indians.

The tents were pitched on a plain on the far side of the river, possibly on the same plain that now borders Calispell Creek near Cusick. In later years, a missionary known as Father DeSmet would refer to the people who lived there as the "Kalispel of the Bay." The "wide marshy Ground" that Thompson described was probably the bay as it looked in the fall when the river was low.

The Indian lad accompanying Thompson called to the people on the far side of the river, and they sent a canoe to ferry the youngster to their camp. An hour later, a group of men, women, and boys paddled across the Pend Oreille. The oldest man "according to custom" made a speech and presented the travellers with a gift of root bread, dried salmon, and boiled beaver. In return, Thompson dispensed a few feet of tobacco and gave the old man "a Steel & 2 Flints." As soon as the ritual was complete, Thompson got down to what he was really after—information.

> I inquired of the Road before me; they say there is only another Fall
> to go to the Columbia of which they drew the Chart. This was good
> news to me, who expected to have heard of ab' 1½ days' March of
> Falls & no navigation among them as the Lake Indians had
> informed me ...

As it turned out, the Lake Indians were better informed about the lower Pend Oreille than the Kalispels, but that isn't surprising. Thompson's Lake Indians were the Lower Kootenays, the same people who'd warned him about the difficulty of the five portages between Kootenay Lake and the Columbia River. Their familiarity with the route indicates they'd descended the Kootenay themselves, and once on the Columbia, they'd have been only thirty miles upstream of the mouth of the Pend Oreille. Since the Kootenays came at the Pend Oreille from below, so to speak, they were in a better position to know what the lower river was like than the Kalispels, few of whom had ever visited it.

Thompson didn't realize that until later. He assumed the Kalispels knew their own river and was more than willing to accept their word that only one fall interrupted the road to the Columbia. One problem remained.

> [The Kalispels] inform me that the Road thereto is very bad for
> Horses. I requested the loan of a Canoe & one to guide us, to which
> they readily consented & we are to go the Morrow ...

The canoe Thompson proposed to borrow was known as a sturgeon-nosed canoe, a unique design with blunt ends that rode flat on the water instead of curving upward. This canoe kept a low profile, as both stern and bow were submerged when it was loaded. It's said the design allowed the Kalispels to cope with the large windswept surface of Lake Pend Oreille, their unusual craft ducking under winds and riding over waves that would swamp a conventional canoe.

Thompson eyed the canoe the Kalispels brought him with misgiving, pronounced it "old & nearly useless," and asked for another. The Kalispels produced a second, almost as decrepit as the first, and Thompson, Beaulieu, and their guide pushed off down the Pend Oreille River. That morning they paddled for four sodden hours. Between a leaking canoe and pouring rain, everything on board was soaked. They spent the afternoon gumming the canoe and drying their gear, and after a damp night on the riverbank, they set off again. For three hours, they paddled down the river, swept along by a "steady, sometimes a swift Current," but there was still no sign of the falls. Thompson was running out of time. He'd been absent from his post for a week, and the Columbia seemed as remote as ever.

> I asked our Guide if we were near the Falls, but he informed us he had never passed in a Canoe. We found we had no Time to go any great distance & therefore began our Return, as we shall have barely time to get to McGillivray's River before the Canoes arrive [from Rainy Lake].

When he turned back, Thompson was only forty miles from the Columbia River. Eight miles ahead, the Pend Oreille churned through Box Canyon, but had he gone on, the canyon's rapids would have been the least of his problems. Beyond, lay an aquatic obstacle course: a drop over Metaline Falls, a wild zigzag through the tight-walled Z Canyon, another drop where the Boundary Dam now spans the river, another at the Seven-Mile Dam, and still another at the Waneta Dam—all crammed into the short stretch of river that stood between Thompson and his goal.

In the late 1800s, the steamer *Metaline* travelled the Lower Pend Oreille River, but never as far downstream as the Columbia. The *Metaline* could make it through Box Canyon (one traveller maintained "The trip down took 2 minutes, but it took 2 weeks to get back up"), but Metaline Falls marked the downstream limit of navigation. And if the falls hadn't, Z Canyon would have. About five miles downstream of the falls, the towering walls of the canyon closed in, forcing the river into a twisted slot a mere eighteen-and-a-half feet across.

Today the Lower Pend Oreille wears a milder countenance. Metaline Falls and Z Canyon are no longer barriers to navigation. All kinds of pleasure craft cruise the river, but it still isn't a navigable route to the Columbia. Although dams have calmed the rapids, tamed the canyons, and drowned the falls, they constitute barriers in themselves. The Box Canyon Dam interrupts the run down the river, and the Boundary Dam terminates it. Another ten miles downstream, Canada's Waneta Dam, fantastic in its utilitarian ugliness, is planted firmly across the mouth of the Pend Oreille River.

Thompson didn't seem unduly discouraged by the premature end to his trip. He spent the return upstream with his notebook on his knee, jotting down strings of notations, marvelling at the snow on the mountains, puzzling over the absence of game, and continuing his inventory of the woods and waterfowl along the shores of the river.

Two days later he was back on his horse and headed for Kullyspell House, still stubbornly convinced that he'd found a navigable route to the Columbia. The following spring he made another flying trip down the Pend Oreille, this time with a guide who'd been down the river before. They made it to within three miles of Metaline Falls, then paused for a consultation.

> My new Guide who had once been here pointed out the Country to us. Ab^t 3M below us was ... a high steep Fall ... he told us they left their Canoes a little dist^ce this side of the Fall & by Hands & Feet got along the steep rocks to the Fall, beyond which no Indians ever penetrate except a few to gather Red Ochre, which is very fine & in plenty among the Mountains ... he assured us that beyond the Great Fall ... is little else but terrible Cataracts bounded on each Side by high Crags ... [4]

His guide's words finally convinced Thompson that the Lake Indian chief had been right. On this second attempt, he'd come within twenty-nine miles of the Columbia, but he might as well have been on the moon. When it came time to draw his map, he wrote off the lower reaches of the Pend Oreille River with a single word—"unnavigable."

It must have crossed Thompson's mind that every tributary of the Columbia seemed to be guarded by impassible falls. In his conversations with the Kalispels, however, he learned of a smaller river that seemed more promising. That river was the Colville, which lay west of the mountains bordering the Kalispel homeland. The Kalispels were great travellers, and one of their excursions was an annual trek to take part in the salmon harvest at Kettle Falls. They told Thompson about a trail that led across the mountains, descended to the Colville, and followed the river to its confluence with the Columbia.

Between Usk and Chewelah, Washington, the Flowery Trail Road now takes much the same route through the Colville National Forest. The road is paved, but parts of it can be closed in winter, and though it often turns up on road-maps, it's rarely named or numbered. In the best of all possible worlds, Thompson would have followed that road through the mountains and reached the mouth of the Columbia two years sooner than he did. As usual, however, he was overdue elsewhere. In the hectic world of the fur trade, Thompson had no more time for roads than he had for rivers.

The Clark
Fork–1809[1]

*Well before Kullyspell House was completed, David
Thompson was building Saleesh House on the Clark Fork
River, and by the following spring, he was planning a third
post on the Spokane. His strategy would establish a North West
post in three of today's American states—one in Idaho, one in
Montana, and one in Washington. During the construction of
the Kullyspell and Saleesh posts, he was usually on the scene
or chasing around his territory, but the post on the Spokane
River went up in his absence. In April of 1810, suddenly and
inexplicably, Thompson packed up his books and
baggage and departed for Montreal.*

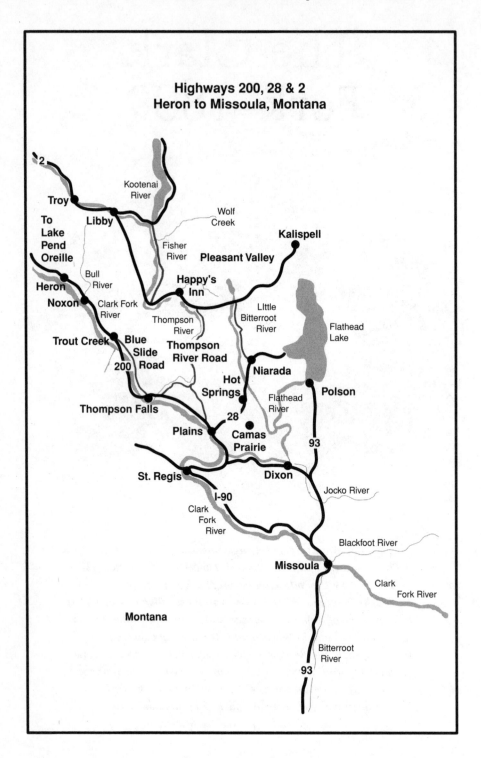

Highways 200, 28 & 2
Heron to Missoula, Montana

THE TERRITORY THAT THE NOR'WESTERS CALLED "THE COLUMBIA DIVISION," the Americans considered to be part of "Oregon Country," an enormous tract of land that lay between the Rockies and the Pacific and extended from the northern boundary of California to the tip of the Alaskan Panhandle. Britain and the United States had a long-standing agreement to "share" this territory, an uneasy alliance forged two years after Captain Gray claimed the Columbia for the United States and Captain Vancouver claimed it for Britain.

Five months after Captain Gray sailed into the Columbia, Captain Vancouver dispatched Lieutenant William Broughton, commander of the brig *Chatham*, to explore the lower reaches of the river. Broughton returned to report that he'd ascended the river for a hundred miles and had no reason to believe that Gray's ship had ever left the arm of the sea.

Many years later, Thompson pointed out that the outflow of the Columbia is fresh water, that an arm of the sea is salt, and that Broughton may have known a lot about oceans, but he didn't know much about rivers. Vancouver, however, accepted Broughton's report as gospel and precipitated the international squabble over the Columbia "which the Yankee sea captain Robert Gray claimed to have entered, which Captain Vancouver said Gray had not entered, which Lieutenant Broughton most certainly had entered."[2]

When Thompson made his move into Oregon Country, the stew over the Columbia had been simmering for fifteen years, and would simmer off and on for thirty-seven more. Thompson knew perfectly well he was trading in joint territory, and his drive to build forts had a political tinge (he later argued his "settlements" bolstered Britain's claim to the American northwest). It's unlikely, however, that he ever believed his timely arrival at the mouth of the Columbia would resolve a dispute between nations.

During his first year in Oregon Country, Thompson had more on his plate than a quest for an elusive river. Once again, he was starting from scratch in unfamiliar territory, and once again, his own ambitions would be pushed aside in favour of the demands of the fur trade. Unlike Vancouver, Thompson didn't have the British Admiralty behind him, nor was he backed by an American president as Lewis and Clark were. As a working partner in a company, he was answerable to the other shareholders, a group of men who persisted in the quaint notion that they were in business to make a profit.

A second year of striving to make a profit left Thompson little time for anything but his job. The journey east to Rainy Lake House—always too long to be practical and now even longer—consumed half his year. In an effort to free up some time, he appealed to the partners for a shorter run for his furs, and at their meeting in July 1809 (which Thompson didn't attend), they handed down their decision. Couched in language typical of annual meetings, it read:

> ... that the trade hereafter to be carried on, to the district beyond the Rocky Mountains, known by the name of Columbia, shall be precisely on the same footing as the Trade to Athabaska—that is— that the Canoes for that quarter with the Returns shall come annu- ally to Lac La Pluye [Rainy Lake], and there take the Outfit, as otherwise it would be attended with too great an Expence to the Compy ...[3]

In a nutshell, the answer was no. To add to Thompson's frustration, he was bitterly aware that the North West Company was no longer will- ing to support his explorations. "The Partners of the Co[y] allow of no fur- ther discoveries," he wrote that fall, "but only trading posts upon a small scale and I have means for nothing else." The result was an explorer who lacked a mandate to explore.

Thompson, being Thompson, explored anyway. One indication he was "off on discovery" that fall was the bizarre route he followed to meet the goods canoes that were returning from Rainy Lake. A ren- dezvous may have been necessary (McMillan and his crew had never been to Kullyspell House), but the route Thompson chose was less so. Instead of heading north along the Pack River portage to the Kootenai River (a ride of less than forty miles), he rode southeast up the Clark Fork, turned northward across the valley of the Little Bitterroot, and fol- lowed the Fisher River to its junction with the Kootenai. This ride, according to Thompson's own record, was over 160 miles long, every inch of it through unexplored territory.

On October 11, 1809, only four days after he got back from his excur- sion down the Pend Oreille River, Thompson left Kullyspell House to meet McMillan's canoes. He set out at 10:30 in the morning, the late start, as usual, dictated by a missing horse. Once again, he travelled light and took only three men with him—Beaulieu, an Indian lad to hunt, and the lad's father as guide.

By mid-afternoon the riders had rounded the eastern shore of Lake Pend Oreille and climbed to the top of the "river Hills." Looking back, Thompson could see the "House Point" six miles down the lake; ahead, only the forested ridges of the Cabinet Mountains. Thompson's party rode on through the woods for three hours, then camped for the night a few miles shy of the Idaho/Montana state line.

> Put up on the tops of the hills with Snow for Water ... the
> Mountains are about 2 to 3M distant & loaded with Snow—we see
> from the Camp with a Birds eye View the Road of tomorrow S80E
> 5M thro' seemingly thick Woods ... the River appears deep, with a
> strong Current.

The river was the Clark Fork, and the snow-laden mountains were the Bitterroots, a range that faces the Cabinets across the Clark Fork Valley. The "Road of tomorrow" was a trail later known as the "Old Kootenai Road." Thompson didn't think much of the early stages of this trail. For twenty-five miles, the riders wound through thick woods that "every where want clearing," and picked their way along a beach "composed of sharp ugly stones." Now climbing, now descending, "cutting off the ups & downs of the bad Road," they progressed at barely three miles an hour, and the vagaries of the route challenged even Thompson's ability to judge distances. "Hereto," he wrote after two hours of following the river, "I think we may have come 4½ M on a Line, but not more, but much more in turnings & windings."

Today Highway 200 pursues Thompson's trail from Idaho into Montana. The modern highway winds almost as much as the ancient trail, and settlement along it is scanty, most of it in small communities on the far side of the river. Where Thompson's riders mounted a rocky slope, the highway cuts through, and where the riders took to the beach, the highway is hidden in the Kootenai Forest, but a few reminders of Thompson's ride up the Clark Fork remain.

The first is about five miles upstream of Idaho's Cabinet Gorge Dam. Here Thompson paused in his ride to watch a band of Flatheads dipnetting "Herrings" from the rapids in "great quantities." The numbers and the season suggest the herring were mountain whitefish, migrating upstream to spawn in the tributaries of the Clark Fork. Thompson traded a foot of tobacco for twenty of the small fish, and named the spot "Herring Rapid." Today the Heron Rapids, as they came to be called, lie under the reservoir behind the Cabinet Gorge Dam, but the name still serves a secluded community called Heron.

Six miles upstream of Heron, Thompson stopped to rest the horses, then forded the Bull River. Here he came across Jaco and his family, but he didn't stop. "We have drove hard on," he wrote, "in hopes of finding Grass for the horses." He pushed on for another three hours and camped for the night "on a low point close above a strong Rapid." Three years later, the Pacific Fur Company's Ross Cox added more detail: "A great barrier of stone split the Clark's Fork River into two channels of churning rapids about seven miles upstream from the mouth of the Bull River ... [The stone] acquired the name Rock Island."[4]

For over seventy years, these rapids were known as the Rock Rapids, but when the Northern Pacific Railroad came through in the 1880s, the name changed. Just downstream, one of the rare flats on this reach of the Clark Fork became the site of a railway camp. The camp was called Noxon (apparently the name of the engineer in charge of construction), and Rock Rapids became known as Noxon Rapids.[5] The community of Noxon, its houses and businesses still strung along the now vanished tracks, survived the loss of the railway, but once the Noxon Rapids Dam went in on the Clark Fork, Thompson's "strong Rapid" disappeared.

Fourteen miles farther on, where Highway 200 crosses the Noxon Reservoir, Thompson noted "a Brook of 6 y[ds] from the south[d]." Today the "Brook" is much wider (a result of backflooding from the reservoir), and Trout Creek is better known as the name of a small town. Thompson and his riders didn't cross to Trout Creek; they stayed on the northeast side of the river and turned aside to follow a different road.

> At 7½ AM set off & held on mostly on a jog Trot 'till 11½ AM but we had so very many high Hills to ascend & so much of our Road full of small Stones & our Horses feet are so very tender from bad Roads that we have not come more than about S50E 10M ... At 1¼ PM set off & held on 'till 2¾ PM—Say S50E 4½ M—as we had a good road and jogged well on ... we stopped at the end of a fine Plain ab[t] 1½ M long, where we found about 40 Horses feeding but no Person in care of them—here we put up at 4¼ PM.

Today parts of Thompson's trail are overlain by the Blue Slide Road, twenty miles of scenic back road that climbs high above the river to wind along the edge of the mountain. The road is little used, and though patches of it are in bad repair, most of it is smooth gravel or pavement. Heavy forest alternates with open-grown trees, the Vermilion River and a host of small streams come tumbling from the hills, and the Blue Slide still lies where it fell when it slipped from the slopes years ago. At the road's highest point, an overlook offers a sweeping view of the Clark Fork Valley below.

The Blue Slide Road rejoins Highway 200 at the "fine Plain" where the forty horses grazed unattended, now the site of Thompson Falls, Montana. Within a month, Thompson would be building a post there, but on this trip, he stopped only long enough to camp. In the evening he scouted ahead, noted the Thompson River and the "close Mountains" beyond, and laid out his course for the next day.

On Thompson's map, the Kootanae Road (the same road he'd refused to tackle the year before without the help of the Kootenays) links the Clark Fork and Kootenai Rivers. The trail followed a natural corridor through the Cabinet Mountains for approximately eighty miles. Beginning well east of Thompson Falls, it joined the Thompson River above the rocky canyons of its lower reaches, then followed the river upstream to its headwaters in the Thompson Lakes. From there, the road crossed a divide into the Fisher River Valley and followed the Fisher downstream to its confluence with the Kootenai.

Thompson apparently missed the entrance to the Kootanae Road. Instead, he drifted off to the east and went on a long ramble through the Camas Prairie Basin, a landscape where the trails were so poorly defined his guide lost the way half a dozen times in less than sixty miles. For once, Thompson was restrained in his criticism—he used the word "ignorant" only once—but the guide ditched his demanding client as soon as he got him to the Kootenai River.

Thompson and his three riders set out from Thompson Falls on October 15. They forded the Thompson River and rode southeast, but after four hours on the road they'd covered just seven and a half miles. "We have had," Thompson commented, "a very high Point of Rocks to go up and down so that we have not made a dist^{ce} equal to the Time." That remark is a typical Thompson understatement. More than seventy years later, "Bad Rock," as it came to be known, was dynamited to make way for the Northern Pacific Railroad, but early travellers who encountered it never failed to comment on its difficulties. Lieutenant C. Grover, who surveyed the route in 1853, gave Thompson's "high Point of Rocks" full value.

About the middle of the day we came to a place called 'Bad Rock,' where a mountain cliff crowds itself into the river, and the trail winds up its jagged side in a serpentine course to the height of about five hundred feet, and down an equally precipitous face on the other side ... ropes were made fast around [the horses'] necks, and by dint of pulling from above and whipping from below, one by one we forced them up. All these extraordinary proceedings amused Paul [the guide] very much, and he frequently exclaimed 'Es-em-mowela,' (bad rock).[6]

With Bad Rock safely conquered, Thompson rode out onto a "very fine Plains ... & a great extent of Meadow Knowles." Tyrrell called these prairie hills the "Horse Plains";[7] today they're the site of a small town called Plains. As the names testify, Thompson and his riders had left the forested Cabinets behind and emerged into open country.

Highway 200 runs through the gap where Bad Rock once barred the way and follows Thompson's route past the settlements of Eddy and Weeksville to Plains, Montana. The sudden change from mountain to prairie is startling. Thompson's "Meadow Knowles" are high hills cloaked in natural grass, hills so smooth and treeless they might have been shaved by a giant hand. Until Thompson reached Plains, his course was consistently southeast, but now he turned northeast and crossed a divide into the rolling lands of the Flathead Indian Reservation.

> ... we came down the Hills to the Plains fine & extensive for the Country, to the SW^d they are bounded by the River & a Range of high snowy hills—to the North^d the Meadows & Hills of d^o appear extensive—Thro' the Plains to a Ridge of meadow Hills East 5M on a round Trot ... very fine Road but our real Road ought to have been more to the north^d ...

This ride brought Thompson to today's settlement at Camas Prairie. From there, he trotted northeast for another two miles, then turned northwest. Highway 28 now follows Thompson's trail onto the Flathead Reservation, and though the highway runs "more to the north^d," it parallels his route for about thirty-six miles. Near the towns of Hot Springs and Camas, Thompson was off to the east, riding a "Sterile White Plain," the sage-covered flats of the Little Bitterroot Valley. The valley, now marginal ranch land, is dry, sandy, open, and bounded by hills. The only crop is irrigated hay, and the soil, as Thompson noted, is white. The curious can explore this country by turning east along the Sloan Road. The junction is less than half a mile north of the turnoff to Hot Springs.

Six miles farther on, Highway 28 crosses the Little Bitterroot at Lonepine, not far from where Thompson crossed it himself, then continues to Niarada. Here the highway swings sharply east toward Flathead Lake, but Thompson stayed on his northwest course, crossing a divide of "fine Hilly Ground," and riding down into Pleasant Valley.

Today a gravel road follows much the same route from Niarada to Highway 2, a distance of about twenty miles.

According to forestry supervisor Ralph Space, writing in 1959, the riders crossed Pleasant Valley, skirted the east side of Wolf Mountain, then followed Wolf Creek to its confluence with the Fisher River.[8] This description matches Thompson's own—he crossed an open valley of brooks and meadows, encountered a stream coming from the northeast (Wolf Creek), and rode southwest "always along the Brook" to the Fisher River. He reached the Fisher just nine miles south of its confluence with the Kootenai. There, for the first time, he came across the Kootanae Road shown on his map.

As Thompson and his men rode north on the Kootanae Road, the weather grew progressively colder. Rain and sleet gave way to showers of snow, ice was forming on the ponds, and wherever the ground was damp, it was frozen. But the rills trickling from the mountains still flowed, and the river they fed grew steadily larger until it had doubled in size. The riders trotted along at a good pace "over hilly & sometimes stony Ground," and in the early afternoon of October 20, much to Thompson's relief, they came to the confluence of the Fisher and Kootenai Rivers.

> ... at 1½ PM set off & went on the same Course ab^t 1M when
> thank God we came to the River—across the River we saw 2
> Canoes & a Tent of Indians, upon calling they came & crossed all
> our Things &c—here we found also Forcier & Roberge who
> informed us Mr McMillan & Canoes were 3 Points below.
> I immediately set off with Roberge & in the evening arrived, where
> I found Mr McMillan. All the People well thank God ...

McMillan was camped near Libby, where Finan McDonald had set up his "hangard" the winter before. The next morning an expedition of horses and canoes loaded with packs set off down the Kootenai River. The following day, the men tackled the portage around Kootenai Falls, and the day after, reached Bonners Ferry and the northern end of the Great Road of the Flat Heads. On October 23 Thompson dispatched five riders with a message for Finan McDonald, who was still holding the fort at Kullyspell House. On October 27 the riders returned with twelve horses. The next morning, Thompson and his men loaded up for the Pack River Portage, and by October 30 they'd reached the post on Lake Pend Oreille. Two days later Thompson was gone again.

Leaving Finan McDonald in charge once more, Thompson saddled up for his second trip up the Clark Fork. This time there would be no aimless wandering. He was headed for the present-day site of Thompson Falls, where he planned to build a post to serve the Flatheads. With him went a six-man crew (Beaulieu, Boulard, Crépeau, Forcier, La Gassé, and Roberge) and James McMillan as clerk. The November weather had turned decidedly wintry, and by the second morning on the trail, the bad road of three weeks before was even worse than it had been the first time.

> A tolerable fine day. Much snow every where on the Ground—at 7½ AM set off & went on along the high Hills, very fatiguing & bad walking—having finished these bad Banks, we took along the River & at 5 PM put up at the Herring Rapid, but several did not arrive 'till very late—our Horses are very much fatigued & what is worse they have nothing to eat, the Country affording no Grass.

"No Grass" is typical of this mountainous reach of the Clark Fork. On Thompson's first trip, his horses had endured three days of hard travel with nothing to eat. On his second, they did the same, but they started out in worse shape. One horse was so weak on his pins he had to be left at the post, and it wasn't long before the rest of them were "knocking up." By the fourth day, Thompson was shedding them, one by one, along the trail. The first to go was the *Crème*, "left below the Hills," and the following day, it was the grey, left with "plenty of Grass & water." Last to go was *Poile de Biche* (doeskin), left to fend for himself near "a little Brook."

Thompson's men fared no better. By the time they reached Thompson Falls, they'd had nothing to eat for two days, and after they reached it, not much for four more. Thompson tried his utmost to trade a horse for food (his own were "too poor" to eat), but the Indians refused to part with their horseflesh. There followed a succession of days of "hunting but without Success" and "fishing &c but still without effect." In the midst of this struggle to find food, James McMillan was put out of action.

> By the accidental going off of his Gun Mr McMillan had both the fore fingers of his Hands shot thru by a Ball & much lacerated with the Powder, both of his Fingers are broke & seemingly will with difficulty be kept from falling off. I dressed them the best I could ...

Six days of hunger had left Thompson's men too weak to work, and by November 14, not a log had been cut for the construction of the new post. But on the seventh day, Jaco and his wife arrived at the camp, bringing two parcels of dried meat, twenty-eight beaver tails, forty pounds of beat meat, twenty-one dried beavers, and three pieces of dried meat. With plenty of food in camp, Thompson wasted no time in putting his crew to work. "The men now got something to eat & cut wood for a shed &c." The construction of Saleesh House had begun.

In this corner of Montana, more natural features have been named after David Thompson—a falls, a pass, a river, a forest, and a chain of three lakes—than anywhere else he travelled. Even the town has taken his name, yet Thompson Falls is one place where the site of his trading post has yet to be positively identified.

It's not because no one has tried. As early as 1922, historian Jacob A. Meyer was working on the problem,[9] and in the late 1940s, editor Catherine White puzzled over it with little success.[10] In 1959 Ralph Space came up with a tentative answer, but by his own admission, couldn't prove it. After plotting the distances and making some deductions, he opted for a site upstream of the falls and downstream of the mouth of the Thompson River, a pioneer farm known as the Dubia Homestead.

> I agree with Mr. Meyer that the Dubia place is the site. The writings of Ferris, who visited the abandoned post in 1833, also indicate the Dubia location. He describes it as being a short distance below the mouth of the Thompson River and states that seven buildings were still standing although the Indians were tearing one of them down for fuel.[11]

A find of artifacts seemed to clinch the matter, and the Dubia Homestead came to be accepted as the site of Saleesh House. There remained, however, some controversy about the choice of location. The opposition argued for a site on the far side of the Clark Fork, but Thompson mentioned crossing the river only once: "took a turn across the River, but the Woods are too close for hunting."

The habits of the Nor'Westers also argue for a location on the north side of the river. As a rule, the traders avoided the heavy forest and deep shade typical of the south side and built their forts on the north side, where the open ground was exposed to the sun in the winter and the snow melted earlier in the spring. On his trip down the Clark Fork the following April, Thompson commented on the difference: "Snow along the Sides of the River, but continual & deep on the left Side."

Today the collection of artifacts is housed in the Old Jail Museum, and the Dubia Homestead is an acreage development situated between the Clark Fork River and the Thompson Falls airport. On the east side of town, a road leads into the development, where a commemorative (and noncommittal) sign at the roadside reads:

THE SALISH HOUSE

FOUNDED BY DAVID THOMPSON AND OPERATED FROM 1809–1826. THE FIRST RECORDED CHRISTMAS IN MONTANA WAS CELEBRATED HERE. THIS TRADING POST WAS THE FIRST OF ITS KIND IN MONTANA AND A HAVEN TO ALL TRAVELERS. DAVID THOMPSON WILL NEVER BE FORGOTTEN IN THIS COUNTRY AS OUR TOWN, RIVER & PASS BEAR HIS NAME.

The construction of Saleesh House progressed in fits and starts. Within four days, the men had dug in the posts for Thompson's room, put up three walls, and raised the roofbeams. The next day, being Sunday, they had a day off, but by Monday morning three of them weren't fit to work. "Roberge still quite lame—cannot stand—Mr McMillan's fore finger of the left hand having a bad appearance & no hopes of its joining with the stump I separated it ... Boulard quite ill." After a fashion, the work went on. The remaining men filled in one of the gable ends and mudded the roof while Thompson built himself a stone fireplace.

Over the next month, the men completed the trading hall and Thompson's room (the two separated by a partition) and erected their bunkhouse, James McMillan's quarters, a warehouse to store goods and furs, and an ice house to preserve meat. Ralph Space maintained that these buildings "were made of logs and poles that were of the stockade or vertical type";[12] if so, Saleesh House was the first post Thompson ever built that way. His usual method was to stack the logs horizontally, describing his progress in terms of how high the walls had been raised (two and a half feet one day, six and a half the next), a clear indication he was building from the ground up. He described progress on Saleesh House a little differently: "put up three Sides of the Walls." The change in terminology does suggest he changed his technique, though it's hard to see why he would.

During the first week of construction, Thompson's weather reports invariably involved cold and snow, but then the winter suddenly retreated. The air turned mild, and three days of mist, sleet, and rain ended with the "Snow all melted & scarce any Ice in the River." The temperature continued to rise. November 26 was "a fine day—like Spring every where."

On December 1 Thompson moved into his room. There must have been a thermometer in the packs McMillan brought over Howse Pass, because as soon as Thompson had a place to work, he started keeping track of the temperature—three times a day, every day, for the next eighty-six days, from December 2, 1809, right through to February 22, 1810. At the end of December, he summarized his results for the month.

> Decr 31ˢᵗ, hitherto this month has been mild weather, with
> much light drizzling rain; how different from the east side of the
> Mountains, where the largest Rivers and the Lakes have now thick
> ice on them ... The mean of the Thermometer for the month of
> December from 7½ Am to 9 PM +27, the lowest +13 and the
> highest +44.

Nevertheless, the balmy climate of western Montana was more a curse than a blessing. The river didn't freeze hard enough to travel on, and there wasn't enough birchbark to build a canoe. Whenever it rained or thawed, the pole-and-mud roofs leaked, and it was a rare day when it was cold enough to freeze meat. But Thompson was nothing if not resourceful. He traded some rush mats to cover the leaking roofs, gave up on the ice house and made pemmican instead, and in the absence of birchbark, ultimately had his cargo canoe fashioned from split cedar boards.

As spring approached, Thompson made three flying visits to Dixon, Montana, in less than a month. At the time, Dixon was a large Flathead encampment at the junction of the Flathead and Jocko Rivers, about twenty miles upstream of the mouth of the Flathead. Exactly what he hoped to accomplish by all this to-ing and fro-ing is a mystery, but one result was a detailed survey of the Lower Flathead River and the middle reaches of the Clark Fork.

As mentioned earlier, Thompson considered the Flathead and the Clark Fork one continuous river, which he called the Saleesh. On his map, he handled the Bitterroot River and part of the downstream Clark Fork the same way, labelling the combination *Nemisoolatakoo*. On modern maps, the Bitterroot is a tributary of the Clark Fork that joins the main river at Missoula. (If you examine the word *Nemisoolatakoo*, you'll find the origin of that city's name.)

For a time, Missoula was also the name of the Clark Fork, which went through more aliases than a fugitive from justice before it was finally gazetted as the Clark Fork of the Columbia River. Today the Clark Fork Valley still displays the mild climate encountered by Thompson. A frequent winter weather report is "mountain snows, valley rains," Missoula bills itself as the "Garden City," and outfitters on the river hold out the promise of year-round fishing.

On February 22 Thompson left James McMillan in charge of the trade at Saleesh House and set out on horseback for the Flathead camp at Dixon. With him went three of his men (Mousseau, Forcier, and Boulard) and two Indian hunters. This ride was no afternoon jaunt, but a stiff two-day ride each way. On this trip, however, they were on the road for close to five days, as Thompson stopped to trade with every Indian band they encountered on the way.

As soon as the riders reached Dixon, Thompson went looking for Beaulieu, who was in the area working beaver. Beaulieu had also been searching for birchbark but hadn't managed to find any. Thompson joined in the search, following lead after lead supplied by a helpful band of Kootenays, "but all to no purpose." He finally gave up on the idea of a birchbark canoe and, leaving his crew at Dixon with instructions to start cutting cedar, he set off on the return trip to Saleesh House. Three days later he was back on his horse, headed for Dixon again.

When he arrived, Thompson checked on the progress of his canoe, which "from the bad weather was only begun," then hired two Kalispels to transport him back to Saleesh House in their sturgeon-nosed craft. The trip took them two days. The first day, Thompson laid out a detailed survey of the Flathead; the second day, he surveyed the Clark Fork, scouting rapids and walking portages as he went. The weather had continued to deteriorate, and conditions on the river made surveying difficult. "The constant snowy weather ... has rendered all the Distances very uncertain, as often I could not see ¼ M before me." On March 14 the Kalispels landed him at Saleesh House. Three days later he was on his way back to Dixon again.

Snow in the Night & fine Morn^g but soon changed to Snow ... we had a rough day—At 11 AM set off—hav^g searched for the Horses from day light to 10¼ AM ... went on to ab^t 1 M of the Plains & put

up at 5 PM to be clear of the Indians & their Dogs—In making a
Fire cut my knee very deep with my crooked Knife, close below the
Joint ... [the next day] Hurt my Knee by 2 falls from a Horse vicious
& bad ...

It was March 19 when Thompson reached Dixon, time to start transporting the winter's accumulation of provisions and furs to Saleesh
House. Judging by the volume of trade, and by the new names that
repeatedly cropped up in his journal (Michael, Lolo, Gregoire, Bellaire,
Jacques, Pierre, Ignace, Joseph, Manuel, and many more), Thompson had
been dealing, not just with the Flatheads and the Kootenays, but with
the "White hunters," Iroquois trappers, and free traders who were working in the area.

Work on the canoe was still held up by bad weather, but within four
days of Thompson's arrival, construction was nearly complete. On the
evening of March 23, "had all the horses collected & hobbled ready for
the Morrow." At nine o'clock the next morning, four of his men and two
Indians set off for Saleesh House with a cavalcade of pack horses. By
noon, the *voyageurs* had finished gumming their cedar canoe and were
ready to follow. Thompson travelled with the men handling the canoe,
absorbed once again in his journal, covering page after page with strings
of notations, interrupting himself only to pen a few words on the first
signs of spring.

Warm at times & times Showers of Hail & Snow—Saw a few
Geese & a Flock of Swans with a few Ducks, but killed none, they
are too Shy, & the Canoe too rolling to admit turning in it—the
first Foal in the Saleesh Camp [Dixon] fell abᵗ 6 days ago—there
are several & all do well. The Geese are all paired, the Ducks mostly
the same, but the Swans are still in small Flocks.

Two years later Thompson would spend a second winter at Saleesh
House and devote another week to exploring the country. At the end of
February 1812, he followed the Jocko River upstream and crossed a
height of land to reach present-day Missoula. On the north bank of the
Clark Fork, he climbed a high hill, where he examined Lewis and Clark's
route down the Bitterroot and made a sketch of Missoula's rivers. Tyrrell
identified this landmark as Jumbo Hill,[13] which now overlooks the
University of Montana campus and is easily identified by the giant "L"
on its flanks.[14] On March 1 of the same year, Thompson made his last

trip up the Clark Fork. He rode to Dixon, then turned north to follow the course of the Flathead River. On Polson Hill, at the south end of Flathead Lake, he paused to make another sketch, which may be why the lake's distinctive square shape is so apparent on his map.

On March 25, 1809, the canoe and the pack horses reached Saleesh House, and Thompson started preparing for the spring journey across the mountains. He sent the canoe back to Dixon for another load, set up the press, and started packing furs. As the tally mounted—four packs, eleven packs, twenty-one packs, forty-seven packs—Thompson gave up his room "as the Warehouse is too small" and moved into a tent. The trade that had started so slowly ended with more than two tons of furs packed and ready for shipment to Rainy Lake.

Near the end of March, Thompson reengaged Jaco "in his old capacity as Clerk and Interpreter," and in the middle of April, he devoted a day to visiting with the Flathead, Snake, and Kootenay chiefs arriving at Saleesh House. "They wish to bid us adieux ... gave to each of the Chiefs a little Ammunition & Tobacco." Four days later Thompson and his men portaged the packs of furs around Thompson Falls, reloaded the canoe, and plunged once more into the rapids of the Clark Fork. The next day they reached Lake Pend Oreille and Kullyspell House, where everything went on hold for three days while Thompson made his second failed bid to reach the mouth of the Pend Oreille River.

Up to that point, Thompson had given no sign that this trade run across the mountains was anything but routine. Nevertheless, he'd apparently decided to leave the field and put in a year in Montreal. He gave no reason for this sudden decision, though it's possible he believed it was his turn to "go down on rotation." It's also possible, however, that he was tired of being stonewalled by the Montreal partners and had decided to do something about it.

Thompson could be mulishly stubborn, a side of his character he liked to portray in his *Narrative*, such as the time he walked out on the Hudson's Bay Company, the time he arranged for a fractious horse to destroy his liquor casks, and the time he shipped a collection of mountain goat pelts to Rainy Lake House. On that occasion, the partners had scoffed at the strange-looking "furs" and told him not to bother sending any more. When the pelts proved to be unexpectedly profitable, the partners did an about-face and instructed him to send all he could get. But Thompson (according to Thompson) never shipped another.

It's risky second-guessing his motives, but it's possible the affair of his leave was another of these times. It's apparent his decision to spend a year in Montreal was both unilateral and unannounced. As he was making his way east, not only were the partners voting to renew his appointment as head of the Columbia Division, they were assuming he'd be there to take up the position. They'd made no move to dispatch a wintering partner to replace him, an omission that left the Columbia Division headless for an entire year. It's tempting to speculate that Thompson may have been playing his old "my way or the highway" card, a strategy, as events the following year would show, that extracted a number of concessions from his partners.

Whatever his motive, Thompson turned his back on the Columbia Division on May 9, 1810. He left Finan McDonald in charge of Saleesh House, assigned James McMillan to Kullyspell House, and dispatched Jaco Finlay to build a new post on the Spokane River. Over the next five weeks, he travelled with the fur brigade, along the Pack River Portage to the Kootenai River, up the Kootenai to Canal Flats, and down the upper reaches of the Columbia to the Blaeberry River. At the foot of the Rocky Mountains, he left McMillan and his men to manage the pack horses, and made the climb to Howse Pass alone.

Back to the Brazeau–1810

After only three years in operation, the Columbia Division was flourishing. More men were working west of the Rockies than ever before, their numbers augmented by an army of hunters, trappers, and free traders. Since 1807, fur shipments to Rainy Lake House had doubled in size each year. Despite this promising track record, the summer of 1810 brought the division to the brink of chaos—hastily cancelled plans, another missed rendezvous, fresh trouble with the Peigans, and an abrupt halt to the traffic over Howse Pass.

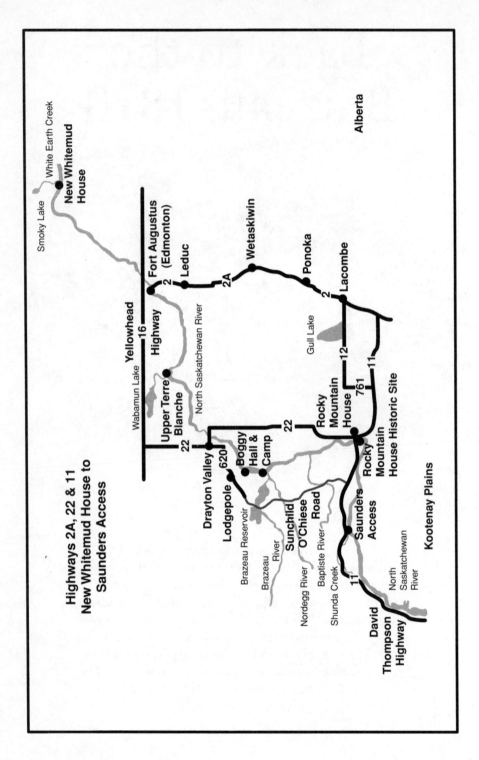

Highways 2A, 22 & 11
New Whitemud House to
Saunders Access

IN THE YEAR 1810 NORTH WEST PARTNER ALEXANDER HENRY SPENT A BUSY spring building a new fort near Smoky Lake, Alberta. Variously called New Whitemud House, Fort White Earth, Lower *Terre Blanche*, and Fort Augustus, the new post stood at the junction of White Earth Creek and the North Saskatchewan River, about seventy miles northeast of the present-day city of Edmonton. Constructed to protect the traders and their families during the Blackfoot-Cree wars, New Whitemud House replaced old Fort Augustus, Fort Vermilion, and the Hudson's Bay Company's Edmonton House, all of which were abandoned for the duration.

When the new fort was ready, Henry shipped his effects upriver on a flat-bottomed boat and set off himself with a cavalcade of "44 horses, 60 dogs, 12 men, 6 women, and 1 blind man."[1] At about the same time, Charlotte Thompson moved with her three youngest children from old Fort Augustus to the safety of New Whitemud House.

Barely a month after his move, Alexander Henry was working on a plan to reopen the abandoned post at Rocky Mountain House. The Nor'Westers had hopes of separating the warring Cree and Blackfoot by offering the Peigans a trading post of their own. Fortunately, Henry found time in his hectic schedule to maintain his journal, as Thompson's own journals for September and October (if there were any) have been lost.

When Thompson emerged from Howse Pass, three *voyageurs* met him at The Forks, and the four men headed for New Whitemud House. It was a run of nearly four hundred miles, but the North Saskatchewan was in full flood from the snowmelt and it was downstream all the way. Near Kootenay Plains they encountered two heavily loaded Hudson's Bay canoes labouring upstream. The Bay, increasingly intrigued by the volume of furs flowing out of the Columbia Division, was sending Joseph Howse across the Rocky Mountains for the winter. Howse and Thompson exchanged news and went their separate ways, but the Bay's move into his territory wasn't lost on Thompson. By the time he reached New Whitemud House on June 23, he'd come to a decision. James McMillan must return to the Columbia as soon as he reached New Whitemud House, with instructions to keep an eye on Joseph Howse.

As it turned out, McMillan was able to keep a closer eye on Howse than anyone expected. Although they'd both managed to slip through Howse Pass, the Peigans were waiting for them on the far side of the Rockies, and the Bay men and the Nor'Westers had to hole up together at old Kootanae House. Eventually, the Peigans let them go, but not without a warning about what would happen if they crossed the pass again. They told the men, reported Howse, that "if they ever again met with a white Man going to supply their Enemies, they would not only plunder & kill him, but that they would make dry Meat of his body."[2]

On June 28 Thompson and Charlotte and the three children started out on their journey east. Alexander Henry wrote that "Mr. Thompson embarked with his family for Montreal, in a light canoe with five men and a *Saulter* [Indian]."[3] Borne along by the swift currents of the North Saskatchewan, the canoe flew by the abandoned posts of Fort Vermilion and Fort George, past the forks of the North and South Saskatchewan, and on to Cumberland House, where Alexander Henry's cousin, William Henry, was in charge. Here the Thompsons stopped to take on provisions, but they were soon on their way again, travelling down the Saskatchewan River, across the portage at Grand Rapids, then into Lake Winnipeg and south along most of its length. Near the middle of July, they reached Winnipeg House, where Charlotte's brother Patrick was stationed, and Thompson left his wife and children with Charlotte's sister-in-law. He started up the Winnipeg River toward Rainy Lake House, and his journal records his arrival there on July 22, 1810, the last entry he made for over three months.

By early August, Thompson was hastening west again. The partners had decided he was needed on the Columbia. "I intended," Thompson later wrote to retired partner Fraser Alexander, "to have paid you a visit at Montreal this last summer, but the critical situation of our affairs in the Columbia obliged me to return. The Americans, it seems, were as usual ... determined to be beforehand with us in the Columbia in ship navigation."

Thompson wrote this letter in December, at a time when the Americans' plans were common knowledge, but it's quite possible he'd heard about their intentions much earlier, well before he reached Rainy Lake. In mid-July, just about the time Thompson and his family reached Winnipeg House, a group of Canadians (many of them former partners or *engagés* of the North West Company) left Montreal and paddled off down Lake Champlain. They portaged into the Hudson River and set their course for the port of New York and the *Tonquin*, a trading vessel owned by American speculator John Jacob Astor. Astor had recruited the Canadians to work in the American fur trade, and the *Tonquin* was set to sail around Cape Horn that fall, bound for the Columbia River.

These events are the source of a story about a so-called "race to the sea." A number of historians interpreted Thompson's precipitous return to the Columbia as a desperate bid to beat the Americans to the mouth of the Columbia River. The "race" pitted Thompson against Astor and the British against the Americans. At stake, so the theory goes, was the future boundary between Canada and the United States. But the Nor'Westers were more interested in commerce than empire. Ever since Simon Fraser had reached the Pacific in 1808, they'd been appealing to Britain for help in developing the new territory. They asked for several concessions, among them an exclusive charter on the Pacific Slope, military and naval support, and a licence to trade into China. For two years, they pressed for an answer, but Britain failed to respond. That silence was probably the main reason David Thompson's explorations went on hold for two years. It wasn't until Astor made his end run to the Columbia that the North West Company decided to go it alone.

If Thompson had received advance warning that his Montreal trip was off, it would explain why he left Charlotte and the children at Winnipeg House instead of taking them to Rainy Lake with him. In any event, once he'd received his marching orders, he left Rainy Lake, picked up his family at Winnipeg House, and headed back up the Saskatchewan River. He may have taken William Henry on board at Cumberland House, since William was at New Whitemud House a few weeks later, ready to take on the job as Thompson's clerk.

By September 5, it was evident that word of Thompson's return was percolating west. On that day Alexander Henry sent two women out to gather gum to repair the Columbia canoes, though it wasn't until the next afternoon "at two o'clock [that] Mr. David Thompson arrived from *Lac la Pluie* [Rainy Lake]."[4] The following morning three more of Thompson's canoes appeared from the east, each one manned by six *voyageurs* and loaded with fifteen hundred pounds of trade goods. As they neared the riverbank, the *voyageurs* unloaded the cargo, carried the canoes ashore, and immediately tackled their repairs. That evening, with whatever energy they had left, they kicked up their heels at a dance, but by morning they were ready to go.

Since the first crossing in 1807, Thompson's men had journeyed over Howse Pass at least twice a year, transporting goods west in the fall and shipping furs east in the spring. But no goods would cross the pass in the fall of 1810. The problem wasn't lack of preparation; the usual logistics were in place. At New Whitemud House, the *voyageurs* were reloading their canoes, Thompson was preparing to ride with the hunters, and Bercier was waiting at Kootenay Plains with the horses they'd need for the portage over Howse Pass. This time, however, an unknown factor was at work. The Peigans had set up a blockade near Saunders and were lying in wait for the canoes.

Thompson had known for years that the Peigans resented the traffic over the pass, but he was unaware that his relations with the Indians had taken a turn for the worse while he was away. In 1807 he'd worried that Finan McDonald, "however well intentioned was by far too unexperienced to act alone in the present unfavorable situation." In 1810 he had little reason to revise his opinion.

McDonald, so far as Thompson knew, had spent the winter in charge of the trade at Saleesh House. Left to "act alone," he'd gone buffalo hunting with the Flatheads and run into a Peigan ambush. The Flatheads had been armed (and some say trained) by Thompson's men, and in the battle that followed, seven Peigans were shot dead, two of them, according to Thompson's *Narrative*, by Finan McDonald himself. Although the Peigans killed five of the Flatheads, they considered the battle a defeat, a humiliation that convinced them of two things: first, that the flow of guns over Howse Pass had to stop; second, that the blame for the guns in the hands of their enemies rested solely with David Thompson.

Meanwhile, Thompson and his crews were in the process of leaving New Whitemud House. Once again, Charlotte and the children would be left behind, this time, though neither Thompson nor Charlotte knew it, for almost two years. Thompson's son Joshua, who was born the following March, would be a year and a half old before his father saw him for the first time.

The *voyageurs* started up the North Saskatchewan on September 6, Alexander Henry noting in his journal that "the Columbia canoes set off with some loads."[5] Two days later Henry recorded the departure of Thompson and his hunting party, who followed the canoes on horseback. "Mr. Thompson and party set off by land, Wm. Henry, Kenville, and 3 women, with Jérome and Gabriel to conduct them to Upper *Terre Blanche*."[6]

Upper *Terre Blanche* was located at the junction of the Wabamun and North Saskatchewan Rivers, about 120 miles upriver of New Whitemud House. The riders set out across the open parkland, travelling at Thompson's usual brisk pace of twenty-three miles a day. Five days later they arrived at Upper *Terre Blanche*, where Thompson and William Henry, accompanied by two Iroquois hunters, immediately set out again. The easy ride across open country lay behind them; they now pursued a tangled trail through the heavy forests of the foothills.

Thompson's ride along the North Saskatchewan River can't be duplicated by car. For one thing, the missing journal ensures we don't know where he was; for another, the roads in the area don't cooperate with modern explorers. The west side of the river is now resource country, and though forestry and oil exploration roads cut through the forest, none that we've ever found parallels the river. Between Rocky Mountain House and the town of Drayton Valley, even approaching the riverside by car is a hit-and-miss business. Travel Alberta's *Reach Reports* for this section of the river indicate that Thompson must have encountered similar difficulty trying to reach it on horseback.

> Although not a true wilderness trip, the lack of access to the river
> and the scenery along the shores gives the impression of isolation.
> The river is surrounded by low hills, so that low densely forested
> banks of poplar and aspen alternate with high, bare sandstone cliffs ...[7]

Most *Reach Reports* offer several "access points" over the course of a canoe trip, but between Drayton Valley and the Baptiste River, this report suggests none. Even the recommended campsites are on islands in the river, rather than on its shores. Despite the lack of access, somewhere between Upper *Terre Blanche* and the Brazeau River, Thompson did meet the canoes to turn over a supply of meat. Although we don't know exactly where he was at the time, there are two likely locations on the west side of the river where both riders and canoes could have reached the riverbank. One was the present-day canoe launch near Drayton Valley, a quarter of a mile upstream of the Highway 39 bridge; the other was the abandoned North West post at Boggy Hall, about twenty-one river miles upstream.

Once the hunting party reached the river, the *voyageurs* loaded the meat into the canoes, agreed to meet Thompson at Rocky Mountain House, and headed up the North Saskatchewan again. Thompson, William Henry, and the two Iroquois mounted their horses, rode back into the forest, and disappeared from the face of the map.

Two days after Thompson and his riders left New Whitemud House, Alexander Henry started packing up for his own move. He dispatched four canoes loaded with trade goods for restocking Rocky Mountain House and sent his own canoe off with his family and his baggage. That done, he saddled his horse and set out with a party of men—not along Thompson's trail, but south through the central Alberta parkland.

Henry's men were apprehensive about undertaking a 190-mile ride across open country, but the route was 60 miles shorter than Thompson's trail along the North Saskatchewan. Even so, Henry and his men were on the road for nine days. Initially, they followed much the same route as today's Highway 2A. They rode past the future townsites of Leduc, Wetaskiwin, and Hobbema; then, just north of Lacombe, they turned west, skirted Gull Lake, and rode the final eighty miles to Rocky Mountain House. When they came within sight of the fort, Henry was amazed to see a plume of smoke rising from the chimney. Unaccountably, Rocky Mountain House was occupied.

He was even more amazed when he discovered the occupants were Thompson's *voyageurs*, who should have been well on their way to Howse Pass. The men explained that Thompson had failed to turn up at Rocky Mountain House, so they'd decided to carry on. They'd paddled up the North Saskatchewan, hoping to rejoin him at Kootenay Plains, but a few miles downstream of Shunda Creek, they'd run into a Peigan blockade. The Peigans hadn't been aggressive, but they had been determined. They'd escorted the *voyageurs* back to Rocky Mountain House and were holding them under guard. Of Thompson's whereabouts, his men knew nothing. They hadn't seen him since he'd left them to go hunting two weeks before.

Alexander Henry had few worries about the Peigans, despite being well aware of their warlike tendencies. "They very frankly tell us," he wrote, "that War, Women and Horses are all they delight in."[8] But the Peigans were also trading partners, and though they'd been quick to torch the abandoned Fort Augustus, Henry figured they were unlikely to jeopardize their source of guns and ammunition (or their supplies of rum and tobacco) by attacking the traders themselves. Needless to say, he knew no more about Finan McDonald's exploits in Montana than Thompson himself did.

At this point, Thompson's story begins to get complicated, particularly since Alexander and William Henry will now share the stage, so to speak. Because they also share the same surname, an already confusing account is in danger of becoming incomprehensible. In the interests of clarity, then, we'll refer to them both by their given names.

Although Alexander's own canoes had yet to reach Rocky Mountain House, in the interests of peace, he raided the Columbia packs and started doing business with the Peigan guards. Two days later, the rest of the Peigans arrived from the blockade. They had with them a pair of blue leggings that belonged to his cousin William, and a horse he recognized as one of Thompson's. The Peigans claimed they'd found the horse wandering three days before. Alexander pretended indifference to this disturbing development, merely noting the news that Thompson and William must be somewhere up the river to the west. He couldn't do much while the Peigans were hanging around, and it wasn't until they lost interest and started to drift away that he made his first attempt to reunite Thompson and his canoes.

The Peigans hadn't gone far, however, and suspicious of the sudden burst of activity, they drifted back again to watch. Finally, Alexander cracked a keg of rum, made a great show of sending the canoes downstream instead of upstream, and proceeded to get the Peigans drunk. While the Peigans were sleeping it off, the Columbia canoes slipped quietly past the fort and headed off up the river toward Kootenay Plains. Satisfied that the *voyageurs* would soon catch up to Thompson, Alexander was able to breathe a little.

But not for long. It was too bad for Alexander, but Thompson wasn't west of Rocky Mountain House at all. He was camped at the mouth of the Brazeau River, fifty miles north of the post. Alexander didn't discover his error until October 12, when his own canoes finally arrived from New Whitemud House, and for some inexplicable reason, his cousin William arrived with them. "I was astonished to hear," Alexander declared, "that he came from below, and had left Mr. Thompson near the North branch [the Brazeau River] waiting for his people." It must have occurred to Alexander that he'd considerably reduced the company's rum supply to no purpose. "I immediately sent Clement to stop the canoes."[9]

By this time, Alexander had given up trying to understand the events going on around him. If one man's leggings and another man's horse have been found west of the fort, wasn't it logical to assume that's where the two men were? How could Thompson possibly be where William insisted he was? Alexander demanded some answers and recorded the explanation in his journal:

> [My cousin] informed me that on their way up they followed an old
> route which they hoped would bring them to the Saskatchewan
> about this place [Rocky Mountain House], where he [Thompson]
> expected to use his canoes; but instead of that, they had sighted the
> river near the First Ridge of Mountains at Jacques brook.[10]

This meant that Thompson had left the course of the North Saskatchewan River, which would have led him directly to Rocky Mountain House, and trusted his luck to an inland trail. The trail led him seriously off course, and he emerged from the bush at Shunda Creek, over fifty miles west of the fort.

Had all gone well, Thompson would have reached Rocky Mountain House less than two weeks after leaving Upper *Terre Blanche*. His men, however, claimed he was out of touch with them for more than three weeks. Since Thompson didn't keep a journal during this period, historians have had a field day speculating on the reason for his absence and, even worse, his motive for failing to record what he was doing.

Thompson and William must have ridden close to 150 miles during the time they were missing. Compared to the ride across the parkland, their pace seems excruciatingly slow, but they were riding through Alberta's Rocky-Clearwater Forest, the virtually impenetrable stands of spruce, poplar, and willow that blanket the Alberta foothills. As anyone who travels the Sunchild O'Chiese Road between the Brazeau Reservoir and the David Thompson Highway will find, this is a landscape to get lost in. There are few vistas (not even the Rocky Mountains are visible), and given just how far off course he was, it's a good bet Thompson's instruments were travelling by canoe.

When the riders found themselves at Shunda Creek, they elected to stay put, even though they were well upriver of the intended rendezvous. They camped to dry the meat of three elk they'd killed and settled down to wait for the canoes. The older Iroquois, alarmed by an ominous dream, left them, and a restless Thompson sent William and the younger Iroquois down the North Saskatchewan to see if they could "discover" any sign of the canoes. What they discovered instead was the Peigan blockade. William went on to describe what happened next.

> This alarmed them and made Mr. Thompson suppose he was watched by the Indians, and that his canoes had been stopped below; he therefore sent an express to Bercier, at the Kootenay Plains, telling him to come down with the horses and follow him quickly to the North branch [the Brazeau River] by the interior route.[11]

The express was probably carried by the younger Iroquois hunter. Thompson's change of plans meant that Bercier would have to leave Kootenay Plains and trail twenty-four horses more than one hundred miles through the Rocky-Clearwater Forest to the mouth of the Brazeau River. Meanwhile, Thompson and William started their trek back to the Brazeau to wait until Bercier could get there.

It was almost the end of the first week of October before the two men reached the mouth of the Brazeau. On a high cliff overlooking its junction with the North Saskatchewan, they pitched their tent and prepared to wait for Bercier. A few days later, they heard an unexpected sound—the songs and shouts of an approaching brigade of *voyageurs*— Alexander's canoes. The two wanderers flagged them down, and William was borne away to Rocky Mountain House to report the collapse of the expedition. Thompson stayed behind to keep a lookout for Bercier and the horses.

Thompson's quick inference about the Peigans' stopping the canoes at the blockade, his prompt decision to change his plans, and his forethought in warning Bercier to avoid the river and use the "interior route" belie the state of indecision he portrayed in his *Narrative*.

> My situation precluded sleep, cut off from my men, uncertain where
> to find them, and equally so of the movements of the Indians, I was
> at a loss what to do, or which way to proceed.

This bleak picture concludes a stirring account of blood on the stones by the river, an ill-advised shot fired in warning, a harrowing flight through the woods with the Indians in murderous pursuit, and three phantom grizzlies that scared the superstitious Peigans off and allowed Thompson to escape into a snowstorm. Since this part of Thompson's journal is missing, the *Narrative* forms the official record of his adventures with the Peigans. The *Narrative*, however, isn't to be trusted. It represents a dramatization of events rather than a factual account. In it, Thompson dropped all mention of his camp on the Brazeau River and (directly contradicting William's version of events) claimed that he rode straight to Rocky Mountain House to meet his men.

Unfortunately, Thompson's elliptical version of events attracted the attention of scholars studying his writings. As early as 1908 (and possibly earlier), tales of the North West Company's "Columbian Enterprise" and the "race to the Pacific" were turning up in the literature. A. S. Morton, writing in the 1930s, picked up on these stories. Suspicious (perhaps justifiably) of the coincidence of the elusive explorer and the missing journal, Morton maintained that Thompson had not only jeopardized the "enterprise" and lost the "race" against John Jacob Astor's ship, but that his lack of persistence resulted in the ultimate loss of the Oregon Territory to the Americans. "No Alexander Mackenzie or Simon Fraser this, but a scholarly surveyor, not without an element of timidity in him. In this crucial hour of his life, David Thompson was weighed and found wanting."[12]

In his turn, Richard Glover, writing in the 1960s, concluded that the critical expedition came unglued because Thompson "lost his nerve."[13] To this day, the notions of these earlier historians turn up in virtually every paragraph, chapter, article, or book devoted to Thompson's explorations. Nowhere is this more clearly illustrated than in Peter C.

Newman's book *Caesars of the Wilderness*, where he presents his version of Thompson's encounter with the Peigan Indians. It begins with William Henry's return to camp after discovering the Peigan blockade.

> The search party promptly came crashing back. [There was no search party—just William Henry and the Iroquois, a hunter whose job description was unlikely to include crashing.]

> At this point, Thompson lost his nerve. [A man who loses his nerve goes home to his family. He doesn't undertake to cross the northern Rockies on foot in the month of January.]

> ... spent the next three weeks cowering alone in the wooded gully in the nearby hills. [a) He wasn't alone; b) he wasn't in a gully; c) he wasn't there three weeks; and d) the nearby hills were more than fifty miles of slogging from where he'd encountered the Peigans.]

> A *voyageur* arrived ... [Actually, it was William Henry.]

> ... and finally located the trembling geographer. ["Trembling" is sheer fiction, as is an earlier line, "paralyzed with terror," and a later one, "still wild-eyed."]

> The grounded explorer had been living mainly on berries for twenty days. [a) Far from being grounded, Thompson had been on the move for the better part of three weeks; b) he'd been dining on elk less than a week before; and c) by mid-October, the bears would have polished off most of the berries.]

> ... and seemed beyond the point of making rational choices. [Except for immediately sending an express to his horsekeeper, deciding to head back to the Brazeau, and changing his route over the mountains to Athabasca Pass.]

> The month-long delay [closer to two weeks], Thompson's refusal to take the easier route, and the three months [actually three weeks] he spent in a winter camp waiting for the weather to yield cost him valuable time. [Northern weather can't be relied on to "yield" in late December. As we'll see, Thompson spent the three weeks building shelters, sleds, and snow-

shoes in preparation for crossing Athabasca Pass. And though facing the angry Peigans would undoubtedly have been "easier," Thompson wasn't in the habit of engaging in gun battles with his customers.]

... having made an unnecessary, six-hundred-mile detour when Thompson chose to avoid Howse Pass and seek a new route to the north.[14] [The question remains: If the detour was unnecessary, why was Thompson's new route followed by the Canadian fur trade for the next half-century?]

The bulk of Newman's account is an exercise in myth-making. There's little evidence Thompson lost his nerve, but, as William Henry's report makes clear, he did lose his way. As soon as William had explained where Thompson actually was, Alexander hitched a ride with the canoe men and headed down the North Saskatchewan to find him.

At 4 Oclock arrived at the spot where Mr. Thompson was camped
on the North side of the River, upon the top of a Hill about 300 feet
from the level of the river, where tall Pines stood so thickly planted
that I could [not] see his tent until I came within ten yards of it.
Here he was starving, and waiting for his people—both his own
Canoes and those men who were coming down with his Horses.
This affair of his Canoes being stopped by the Peagans has induced
him to alter his route and endeavour to open a new road ...[15]

Alexander Henry didn't fall in with Thompson's new plans without an argument. The Peigans, he protested, were harmless. There was no need for extravagant measures like marching off to unknown northern passes in the middle of winter. Not only had Joseph Howse crossed the pass that summer, but so had James McMillan. The Peigans didn't attack Howse and McMillan, so why would they attack Thompson? But these men weren't David Thompson. Despite his long-standing friendships among the tribal leaders, Thompson had finally driven the Peigans too far. He'd traded guns to the enemy, the enemy had defeated them, so Thompson was now an enemy. "The Indians," he noted ruefully, "allow no neutrals."

Realizing the futility of arguing with Thompson, Alexander Henry gave in. "It was therefore determined that the Canoes should be ordered to return below in as private a manner as possible, to avoid all misunderstanding with the Natives." He "bade Mr. Thompson farewell" and headed back to Rocky Mountain House on horseback.

We followed an Assiniboine track of this year ... The country is
overgrown with large and small pines of several kinds, so close
together that a horse can scarcely force his way through ... Our
guide soon went on the track of a moose, and we were left in the
thick wood to find our own way. We frequently lost the track, and
narrowly escaped getting astray.[16]

Alexander Henry arrived at Rocky Mountain House on October 16,
and that night, aided by another keg of rum, he managed to achieve a
"private" departure for Thompson's canoes.

As the Peigans were roaring drunk, the canoes got away unper-
ceived & my Cousin went with them ... I was happy to get clear of
those canoes, that had caused me so much trouble and anxiety ever
since my arrival.[17]

Thompson never did describe his wanderings between the Brazeau
River and the Peigan blockade. One reason might have been something
like "professional pride." It must have been virtually impossible for the
North West Company's geographer, the man who had surveyed more of
North America than any man living, to admit he'd been lost. In this, he
was hardly unique. As Calgary *Sun* columnist Stephen Lautens once put
it: "Men are never lost. Sometimes roads aren't where they should be."

Thompson and his *voyageurs*, and Bercier and the horses, finally got
together ten miles north of the Brazeau at old Boggy Hall. Here the men
unloaded the four canoes, repacked the cargo, and loaded it onto the
horses. Thompson sent two men back to Upper *Terre Blanche* to fetch
sled dogs for the pass and dressed leather for snowshoes. He also sent
four men back to Rocky Mountain House for dried provisions.

Belyea has it that Thompson didn't set out to cross the mountains
either lightly loaded or exceptionally late.[18] In fact, he was both. It was
barely a week after Alexander Henry left Thompson that the men seek-
ing provisions arrived at Rocky Mountain House, evidence that food, at
least, had been lightly loaded. And it was also late. It would be over two
months before Thompson and his party reached Athabasca Pass, which
meant they would cross the Rockies in the depths of winter. By any stan-
dard, this was late. Indeed, Thompson himself figured he was late. By the
time a canoe arrived with the provisions a week later, he was gone.

Athabasca Pass–1811[1]

Thompson's decision to leave Boggy Hall before his men arrived with the provisions planted the seed of discontent that eventually erupted into mutiny. Although there were periods of plenty on the journey to Athabasca Pass, there were also intervals of near starvation; and though physical exhaustion and fear of the unknown played their part in the loss of morale, it was quarrels over how much his men ate and when they ate it that led to Thompson's increasingly irascible handling of his men.

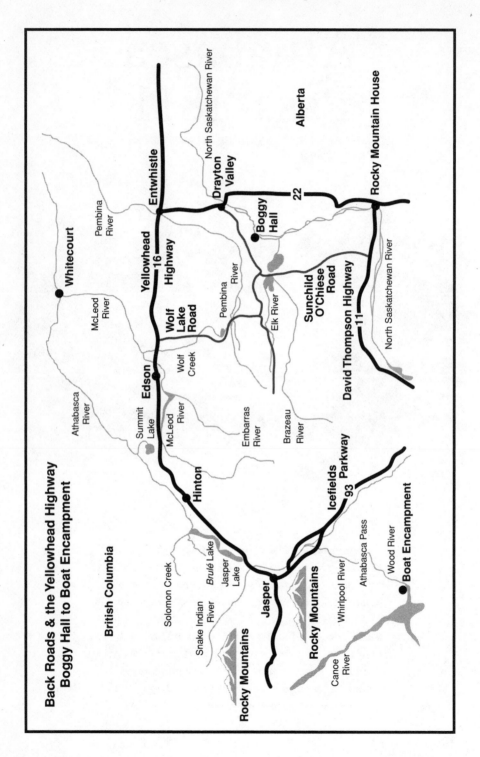

Back Roads & the Yellowhead Highway
Boggy Hall to Boat Encampment

IN TERMS OF MANPOWER, THOMPSON'S OVERLAND EXPEDITION TO ATHABASCA Pass was the largest he'd ever mounted: Thompson himself, William Henry to act as clerk, two men to hunt, two to clear the road, and twelve to manage the horses. Thomas (the Iroquois guide who went with them to conduct them through Athabasca Pass), three women, and the six men who were away getting dogs and provisions completed the somewhat unwieldy party of twenty-five men and three women.

Thompson was equipped with twenty-four of the company's horses, but none of them carried a rider. Since six horses were needed to bear the freight of a single canoe, all of the animals were fully loaded, each carrying 180 to 240 pounds of trade goods. Except for the hunters, who had their own horses, and Thompson, who usually rode with them on his "Cut-tailed Red Horse," all members were mounted on shank's mare.

On October 29, 1810, a cloudy but mild morning, the expedition set out from Boggy Hall. The travellers started west along a small tributary of the North Saskatchewan River, turned southwest to avoid a "morass," then struck an old trail known as the Stone Indian Road. Their route lay between two rivers the Cree called the "Great River of the Plains" (the North Saskatchewan) and the "Great River of the Woods" (the Athabasca). Their direction of travel was northwest, which meant they would have to cross two major tributaries of the Athabasca: the Pembina River, which reaches its confluence with the Athabasca far to the north, and the McLeod River, which joins the Athabasca near today's town of Whitecourt. All four of these rivers have the same name today as they had in Thompson's time.

By the fourth day out, the expedition had covered only eighteen miles of the Stone Indian Road. The travellers set up camp near the Pembina River, and Thompson dispatched two men to Rocky Mountain House to return some horses. The men carried a letter from Thompson to Alexander Henry, who wrote his reaction to it in his journal.

> At 11 o'clock arrived Pichette and Pierre with three horses from Mr. Thompson's Camp. He was then upon the Panbina River with all his property, on his way to the waters of the Columbia, cutting his road through a wretched thick Woody Country, over Mountains and gloomy Maskagues and nearly starving with Hunger, Animals being very scarce in that quarter, and his hunter can only find a chance Wood Buffalo, upon which they subsist; when that fails they have recourse to what flour, and other *douceurs* [sweet things] Mr. Thompson has along with them—in fact, their case is pitiful.[2]

Sometimes Henry's journal is as creative as his spelling. In this account, he's guilty of exaggeration (as we suspect he was when he stumbled on Thompson's camp on the Brazeau River). According to Thompson's journal, on the day he wrote this letter, his hunters (three, not one) had killed a deer, two buffalo cows, and a grizzly bear over a two-day period. Nor had Thompson and his party yet come across any "Mountains," though the "gloomy Maskagues" were real enough. But maybe Henry was prescient. Over the next three days, Thompson's hunters came up empty-handed, and the four men sent for provisions still hadn't turned up.

On November 2, Thompson's party forded the Pembina, and followed the river to where a "bold Brook falls in from the south[d]." This stream was probably Dismal Creek, a tributary of the Pembina River that roughly parallels the river before flowing into it. As they marched west along the Pembina, Thompson's concern over a dwindling food supply increased with every mile. Although his rate of travel was less than eight miles a day, the riders bringing the provisions had still failed to catch up. He decided to camp for a day and wait, and that evening, a week after the expedition had left Boggy Hall, the long-awaited provisions arrived. Thompson's party had been without food since the day they'd forded the Pembina River.

At 11 Pm the Men sent for Meat arrived—they brought 2 Bags of
Provisions, greater part of which we directly distributed among the
Men who, late as it was, made directly a hearty Meal, hav[g] tasted
nothing but a Dram of Rum these 3 days.

Where there was no trail, the *voyageurs* pushed on to make one. This was a job that called for chainsaws and a Cat. Thompson's men tackled it with two-foot axes—hacking their way through a tangle of underbrush, willow thickets, and burnt deadfalls of spruce and alder. Even when the expedition camped, the trailblazers were ahead, splashing across streams, wading through "morasses," slithering down one streambank and scrambling up the other, a job of work unlikely to appeal to men who loved their paddles but despised a portage.

And this was a very long portage. Even if the expedition had followed a straight course, the Athabasca River is almost one hundred miles from the North Saskatchewan. There was no straight course, however, just as there's none now. Thompson's trail led through Alberta's Whitecourt and Edson forests, a wilderness to this day, uncleared and unsettled, with only a few primitive roads to serve the province's mining and forestry industries. It's almost impossible to track Thompson through this maze of bush and swamp, and "maze" is the operative word. In this particular journal, Thompson's numbers are more misleading than informative. He was up to his old trick of recording some of his courses backwards, and the distances he reported reflect a tortured trail not 100 miles long, but 141.

Nevertheless, it's still possible to drive through the wilderness that Thompson travelled. Eighteen miles west of Rocky Mountain House, the David Thompson Highway comes to a junction with the Sunchild O'Chiese Road, the start of a back-country route to the McLeod River. The road runs through crowded stands of spruce and tamarack in the bogs, spruce and poplar on higher ground, and clear-cuts where the forest has been logged. This part of the route is paved, but once the road crosses the Brazeau Reservoir, it tends to degenerate. Five miles north of the Brazeau Reservoir crossing, a turnoff to the west descends into the Elk River Valley. The Elk River Road is currently surfaced in dirt, smooth enough for travel by car, but slippery in wet weather. Eighteen miles farther on is the turnoff to Wolf Lake, where a gravel road leads north along Thompson's trail. The Wolf Lake Road crosses Dismal Creek and the Pembina River, and just north of Wolf Lake, it crosses Wolf Creek, the stream that finally led Thompson to the McLeod River.

On November 6 Thompson and his party left the Pembina River and turned northwest. The next day they left the Stone Indian Road behind as well, a departure that marked the beginning of two weeks of trying to stay on course, camping often, held up by bad weather or waiting for the advance party to mark and clear the trail. Thompson's route lay northwest, but in this watery world, he was constantly forced south for a mile only to turn west for another, trying to find solid ground that would lead him in the right direction.

Back-country Roads

~ The Elk River and Wolf Lake Roads are resource-industry roads that are also used for recreational access to the Wolf Lake and Minnow Lake Campgrounds.

~ Following these back-country roads to the McLeod River involves a drive of over a hundred miles through some of the remotest country in Alberta—no services, no habitations, and scarcely any traffic.

~ Except during the tourist season, the route is sufficiently remote to be hazardous. The rest of the year, the prudent

choice for a drive from Rocky Mountain House to the
McLeod River is north along Highway 22, then west along
the Yellowhead.

We made a Road ab^t 1M farther to the wrd but finding ourselves on
the verge of a large Morass, we turned about to the Rill of water.
Our Hunters, still unsuccessful for want of Snow, say that we
cannot pass to the West^d & it is by this account uncertain if we can
get from where we are, as the Marshes are not froze to any depth
sufficient to bear up the Horses.

The long march through Alberta's forests was hard on the people, but
it was harder still on the horses. On most days, Thompson called a halt
by noon or shortly after, noting "the Horses much fatigued with the badness of the Road." The swampy ground was frozen only in the morning;
by early afternoon, the heavily laden animals were plunging through the
fragile ice. Their only feed was the grass they foraged themselves, and
though they were turned out to graze whenever the expedition camped,
they were steadily losing weight.

Sixty-five miles northwest of the Pembina River, the expedition
reached the banks of Wolf Creek. Thompson doesn't mention Wolf
Creek by name, and it was only because of the work done on
Thompson's route by modern *voyageur* Jeff Gottfred that we were able
to figure out which stream Thompson followed to reach the McLeod
River. Gottfred used Thompson's coordinates to establish where
Thompson was when he reached the Athabasca River, and he published
his conclusions in the *Northwest Journal*.[3] On a map, we identified
Thompson's position on the Athabasca and traced him backwards, first
along the McLeod, then for seventeen miles up Wolf Creek to the point
where he started measuring the stream's width.

When he came to Wolf Creek, Thompson followed its course downstream, crossing and recrossing the stream as it grew from a width of five
yards where he met it, to six yards as it flowed north, to sixteen yards as
it neared its mouth. Here Wolf Creek approaches its junction with a
river Thompson knew by name—the McLeod. It must have been a relief
to Thompson to reach the McLeod River, and it was a relief to us as well.
Once he left the Pembina, he named not a single stream and mentioned
only one landmark, Old Fort Peles, a site that's no longer identifiable.
After the tortured (and often indecipherable) trail from the Pembina to

Wolf Creek, Thompson's description of his approach to the McLeod River is a model of clarity.

> Here we crossed the Brook now 16 Y^{ds} wide for the last time, it
> going off abt N20W. We held on S65W 2M to the place of our
> campment, a small Plain of good Grass. The [McLeod] River is ab^t
> 30 Y^{ds} wide & is fast froze over with Snow on it like the small
> Brooks; the Banks in the obtuse Angles of the River seem to be of
> Grind Stone—of this I shall examine the Morrow.

Today's maps do show Wolf Creek going off to the northwest, suggesting that "the place of our campment" is now the home of the East of Edson RV Park. We drove along the bypass to the park to see whether the banks of the McLeod River there might be composed of "Grind Stone." They were, and though sandstone cliffs are fairly common along the McLeod, their presence here was one more indication that Thompson had reached the river by way of Wolf Creek.

Thompson spent the next day pacing off the width of the McLeod River, measuring its depth, and recording its characteristics in his journal. On November 24, the expedition crossed the river, and Thompson climbed a "knowl" to have a look at the countryside. He estimated that the McLeod exited the mountains about forty miles to the south and disappeared from sight about forty miles to the northeast. He noted that "High Lands" had appeared to the west.

Over that day and the next, Thompson followed the course of the McLeod River west for twenty-two miles, where he reported that a "large Brook by Flats comes in from the right, nearly parallel to the River." It's likely this was the Embarras River, which wanders across its flats to join the McLeod River about six miles south of today's town of Edson. Thompson's use of the word "parallel" is unusual; but in this reach, the McLeod dips sharply south, with the result that the two rivers are flowing along the same axis when they meet.

The next morning Thompson's party continued the trek along the flats of the McLeod, and Thompson finally recorded an identifiable landmark: "a high Hill stretching oblique across our Road ab^t 10M dist[ant] ... Thomas describes our Route of the Morrow to be first ab^t west & then turning around to the SW to fall on the Athabasca River and avoid the Hill." From his position on the flats of the McLeod River, Thompson could have been looking at the hill that forms the summit of the Yellowhead Highway. From the highway, the hill doesn't look high, and it doesn't "stretch" as it once did. Its southern face has been cut back several times—once to accommodate the old highway between Edmonton and Jasper, again for the Yellowhead Highway, and yet again for a pullout where travellers can gaze on a panoramic view of the forests to the south and the mountains to the west.

Just west of this hill lies Summit Lake, a body of water drained to the north by Obed Creek. To reach the lake, Thompson skirted the base of the hill, passed two smaller lakes, then paused long enough to make a sketch of Summit Lake in his journal. It was this sketch, showing the unusual shape of the lake, that gave Gottfred the clue he needed to trace Thompson's final steps to the Athabasca River.[4] From Summit Lake, Thompson followed Obed Creek north for about three miles, then called a halt. "We camped on the Banks of [the] Brook, which winds much—from hence, on climbing a Tree, we see the Athabasca River." They camped for a day, a much-needed rest for both people and horses, and on November 29, exactly one month from the day they set out, followed Obed Creek to the banks of the Athabasca River.

Thompson had high hopes of establishing Athabasca Pass as the main trade route across the Rocky Mountains and was doing some thinking about its possibilities. He was soon measuring the width of the river's channels and making notes about its braided character: "The Athabasca River, like all the Rivers that descend from the east side of the Mountains, has many channels, generally shoal, with gravel flats and sand." Later he estimated the number of days it would take a canoe brigade to travel from the North Saskatchewan River to the Columbia River and recorded the results in his journal.

> Fort Augustus to Pembina River 3 days + 4 days to Athabaska River + 5 days to McLeod's Fort + 13 days to the Mountain Port^{ge} = 25 days + 4 days to the Columbia = 29 days. This is only 2 days more than the other Route [Howse Pass] & avoids much of that tedious & expensive business of Horses, which can never be brought within strict Calculation, being liable to too many Accidents.

Thompson made detailed notes over his entire route from Boggy Hall to the Athabasca River, pausing from time to time to work his "observations." Unfortunately, his notes identify few landmarks, and his observations are often of little use in fixing his position. Although his coordinates for the forts he lived and worked in are accurate, the readings he took at waypoints under difficult field conditions are understandably less so. At the camp he would shortly set up near *Brulé* [burnt] Lake, for example, his coordinates (N53°33'33" and W117°36'34") would have placed him seventeen miles northeast of where he actually was (about N53°21' and W117°50'). Taking Thompson's record literally would lead us to believe he was well north of the Athabasca River (nine miles north and slightly west of today's town of Hinton) in country he'd never seen.

Lacking a precise picture of his trail to the Athabasca River, Thompson's editors have tried to deduce where he was when he reached it. J. B. Tyrrell placed Thompson on the Athabasca " ... a few miles below where the Grand Trunk Pacific Railway now reaches it ... " and claimed that "the next day he crossed the river and continued up along its bank to *Brulé* lake ... "[5] Tyrrell's assessment, however, doesn't account for the days Thompson spent travelling the Athabasca. He allows Thompson only one day of travel to reach *Brulé* Lake, but Thompson didn't sight the lake until five days after he'd reached the Athabasca River.

In her notes, Barbara Belyea maintains that Thompson reached the Athabasca by following Maskuta Creek to the south end of *Brulé* Lake,[6] but this isn't possible. Thompson was moving downstream at this point, and "downstream" on the Maskuta would have led him north, not south. Even if Thompson had followed the Maskuta, he would have ended up only about ten miles north of *Brulé* Lake, too close to account for the mileage he recorded along the Athabasca River.

It seems clear that Thompson was nowhere near *Brulé* Lake when he reached the Athabasca River. Gottfred's argument that Thompson reached the Athabasca far to the east of where either editor placed him seems indisputable.[7] The distinctive shape of Summit Lake, the length and direction of Obed Creek, and the distances Thompson travelled upriver on both the McLeod and the Athabasca all indicate that Thompson was thirty-four miles downstream of *Brulé* Lake when he reached the Athabasca River.

Once the expedition reached the Athabasca, Thompson described crossing the river and following its course upstream, sometimes along the river's banks and sometimes along its frozen surface. The temperature was now dropping precipitously, and the ice of the Athabasca was thick enough to bear the weight of the horses. But once they started travelling on the ice, it was evident the animals were in a bad way, and one of them was finally finished.

> ... rested the Horses & brought the one that was knocked up yesterday, but he is unfit for farther Service; considering the very bad slippery Road that we have had for these 2 days past on the River Ice, we may be thankful that several of the Horses are not killed—they have received many & severe Falls.

Despite the horses' difficulties, the tempo of the journey started to pick up. The riversides of the Athabasca Valley made for easier walking than the awkward trail through the forest, and the people were able to make better time and spend longer hours on the road.

> ... we camped at 2:20 Pm—the People all arrived by 3 Pm. Always
> high Land & Thick woods of Pine & Cypress, mostly the former,
> but green. The Country appears very rude & marshy, mossy & very
> uneven—no appearance of either Animals or Plains ... Boussé &
> Du Nord did not join us.

This wasn't the first time Thompson's hunters had failed to join them. Belyea comments on the men's increasing reluctance to stick together, interpreting it as a sign of declining morale.[8] Several of the men had no love for Thompson and may have "slept out" simply to avoid his company. But they didn't have a hope of avoiding that other major irritant—the weather.

The next morning a wind swept in from the south, bringing with it one of the Athabasca River's notorious sandstorms. The wind blasted the sand from the river's shoals and flats and whirled it down the valley, smothering everything in its path in grit. Almost two hundred years later, these storms still persist, compelling CN Rail to use snowploughs in the summer to clear the sands of the Athabasca from the rail line's tracks. With typical understatement, Thompson recorded the effect of the sandstorm on his people: "The Sand brought by the Wind from the Trees & Flats covered the Snow & was very distressing to us, filling our Eyes & Mouth."

The day they reached *Brulé* Lake, Thompson gave the first sign his temper was beginning to fray. Over the choice of a winter campsite, he was uncharacteristically critical of his guide, one of the few men he could trust. Thomas knew the country, knew where he was going, and seemed never to raise any difficulties about getting there. Thompson, however, was displeased with his taste in accommodations.

> The Iroquois insisted on our going to an old Hut on the Lake—we
> went ... and camped there ... in a most disagreeable Place: the Hut is
> small & very dirty, besides being without Windows, badly situated
> & no Grass for the Horses.

The next morning Thompson had his people pack up and backtrack about five miles, where he found a campsite more to his liking. They set up their winter camp "near a small Fountain of Water among Pines & Aspins, with plenty of Grass for the Horses." This campsite was probably on Oldhouse Creek, a small tributary of Solomon Creek, near the site of a North West Company fort that was built there in 1813. Today Oldhouse Creek is unrecognizable as the stream it once was. Although it may flow at some times of the year, when we visited it one fall, it looked more like a rock dump than a streambed, and the railway's engineers had ensured that Oldhouse Creek hadn't a trickle of water in it.

The choice of a winter campsite was important, as the expedition was to stay there for three weeks, preparing to cross Athabasca Pass. There was a lot of work to do. Thompson's people had to cut wood for building materials, erect sheds for storing trade goods and meat, and put together eight sleds and thirteen pairs of snowshoes for the crossing. The snowshoes were another irritant for Thompson: "... the Line for the Snow Shoes is very bad," he complained, "from the awkwardness of the Women." To do the women justice, the thermometer was now hovering around minus 32°F, not the best of conditions for leatherwork.

On December 14, Thompson sent seven men to Rocky Mountain House to request, according to Alexander Henry, "provisions, dogs and horses, all of which they were entirely destitute."[9] This was patently not true, as Thompson at the time still had more than twenty horses, fourteen dogs, and sufficient meat to require a shed to store it. According to Thompson, the men were sent for "Pemmican & the Goods that had been left there, with Letters &c." Since he later set out for Athabasca Pass with only four horses, the men must have taken the rest of the pack string to Rocky Mountain House to carry the goods and pemmican back to the camp. Still, the rest of Henry's story is illuminating.

> At 5 p.m., seven men arrived from Mr. Thompson ... It is 17 days since they left Mr. Thompson on Athabasca river at the foot of the mountains. On their way here they ate an old horse and five dogs, but had been some time without food and were worn out with fatigue and hunger ... We have no more meat in store than will answer for eight days' rations, and of other provisions not a mouthful. Our hunters are lazy; and when we shall see an Indian to bring a supply, God knows.[10]

Having nothing to send, Henry sent exactly that, and the seven *voyageurs* (along with the horses) never did return to the Athabasca. This was characteristic of the pattern of attrition on this trip. With rare exceptions, no one who departed with messages ever returned to the expedition. In addition, William Henry, who eventually maintained a supply line for the expedition, stayed behind on the Athabasca to build a supply post. The post was named "Henry House," and though no sign of its location remains today, Jasper's local historians believe it was built on Old Fort Point, just across the river from Jasper townsite.

Somewhere along the way, the three women seem to have disappeared as well, and by the time Thompson was ready to load the sleds, his party had shrunk to twelve men, four horses, eight sleds, and twelve dogs. On December 21 he paused in his work to write to his old friend Fraser Alexander. Apparently Thompson, now past forty and with twenty-seven years in the field behind him, was beginning to feel the strain.

> If all goes well and it pleases good Providence to take care of me
> I hope to see you and a civilized world in the autumn of 1812. I am
> getting tired of such constant hard journeys; for the last 20 months
> I have spent only barely two months under the shelter of a hut, all
> the rest has been in my tent, and there is little likelihood the next
> 12 months will be much otherwise.

Christmas Day passed without comment by Thompson. By the closing days of 1810, his men were loading the sleds—120 pounds of goods on the sleds hauled by two dogs, 70 pounds on the sleds hauled by one. The four horses carried a load of fresh meat and what remained of the supplies—208 pounds of pemmican, 35 pounds of grease, and 60 pounds of flour. By seven the next morning, Thompson was ready to leave.

But first the *voyageurs* had to have their breakfast. In the past, it had been Thompson's habit to have his men push on for a couple of hours before stopping for breakfast; however, these weren't Thompson's usual men, and they had their own ideas. Every day two or three hours went by before they finished their morning repast and were ready to make a move. Thompson found both the delays and the quantities of food they put away a continuing source of irritation, and his journal shows it.

Over the first days of the journey up the Athabasca River, Thompson made no fewer than ten entries about his men's eating habits. At first his tone is mildly acid: "My men did not forget to destroy all the Marrow Bones, as if they were so many Wolves ... Having well filled their Bellies, the men set off at 9 Am ... As usual the Men made a good Kettle of Meat to eat ... " Finally, however, his comments culminate in an indignant outburst: "In the last 36 Hours the Men have eat 56 lbs of Pemmican, more than ¼ of our whole Stock; they are a set of the most improvident, thoughtless Men I ever saw."

Once his men could be induced to move, Thompson herded them up *Brulé* Lake, following the same general direction the Yellowhead Highway follows today. The weather was bitterly cold and a stiff gale was blowing, but so far the snow wasn't very deep. Although it's hard to know whether either men or dogs had any experience in the job ahead, the dogs seemed reluctant to pull, and the men's notion of encouragement was to beat them. Thompson's journal rarely records any sound effects, but between the cursing of the men and the yelping of the poor dogs, the noise must have been appalling. Within two days, despite the beatings (or because of them), the dogs couldn't pull the sleds another inch. To reduce the weight, Thompson offloaded two hundred pounds of goods and left them behind in a hoard.

New Year's Day of 1811 found them well into the mountains, surrounded on every side by the peaks that line the Athabasca Valley.

> The Country from our entrance into the Mountains hereto has
> been tolerable good for such northerly Mountainous Lands: there
> are very many low rocky Hills, with plenty of wild Sheep but saw no
> Goats, & the many Defiles in the Mountains & Brooks with the Isl^{ds}
> &c afford room & rude pasturage for a few Buffalo, Red Deer & a
> chance Moose.

Thompson's party passed the mouth of the Snake Indian River, and a mile or so later, reached Jasper Lake. Here they camped for two days, then set off again. On January 4, they passed the junction of the Athabasca and Maligne Rivers, and soon after, left the route of the Yellowhead Highway to follow the Icefields Parkway south. The next day they arrived at the junction of the Whirlpool and Athabasca Rivers and turned west up the Whirlpool.

> ... this Branch is abt 40 to 50 Y^{ds} wide & not deep, say 2½ feet at a
> mean. Our Road was bad among large Stones, close to the water
> Edge—we were obliged to have our Sleds always on our Hands to
> prevent them sliding into the River. The Horses cut the Point within
> & the Men with them said the Road was very bad from thick Woods.

On the travellers' right was Mount Edith Cavell, a mountain the *voyageurs* referred to as *La Montagne de la Grande Traverse*. Ten miles later, they were forced to abandon the horses (now down to three), as this was the last chance for grazing and Thompson judged the trail ahead unfit for horses. "The Dogs," he wrote, "may be said to swim in the fresh beat Road made by the Snow Shoes—the Snow is getting ab* 2 feet deep."

As they followed the Whirlpool River toward the final ascent to Athabasca Pass, more tempers than Thompson's started to fray. A *voyageur* named Du Nord beat one of the dogs senseless. Thompson recorded the incident, but aside from noting that somehow "the sled got broke" made no comment. Both dog and sled were thrown aside, and the climb to the pass continued.

The snow was now seven feet deep, and a Chinook had started to blow. The temperature soared to plus 32°F, an increase of 65°F from the day they'd set out from Oldhouse Creek. "Very bad hauling," commented Thompson. "The Sleds I may say stuck to the Snow." They turned up the left fork of the Whirlpool, and on their twelfth day out reached the Continental Divide. This time Thompson didn't linger to rejoice in the rills that ran to the Pacific Ocean. He had more serious matters to deal with.

> Du Nord threw his Load aside, saying he would not haul it any more altho' he has only 80 lbs to 2 good Dogs ... I ordered Du Nord to return [leave] for his bad behaviour, but accusing himself I permitted him to continue, altho' in my opinion he is a poor spiritless wretch.

Thompson relieved the rebel of his sled and sent him off to hunt instead. Two hours later, Du Nord turned up looking for something to eat "and finding no Meat was ready, was answered by Francois that they did not expect him so soon." Thompson recorded Du Nord's response: "What, said he, do you take me for a Horse to go for so long without eating?" and then added his own editorial comment: "Such is this famous FDP Man." Thompson's scorn for the "FDP Man" arose because it was the *voyageurs* from the *Fort des Prairies* Division (Du Nord, D'Eau, and Le Tendre) who were the main source of dissent among his men. They didn't know Thompson, had never been near the mountains before, and didn't like where they were going. In contrast, Pareil and Coté, the "Montreal men," had a lot more heart than the men from the FDP, and Thompson was to increasingly rely on them.

On the western side of the Rockies, they started the descent down the Wood River, a stream Thompson called "Flat Heart Brook" to reflect the mood of his men. The mild weather had the dogs wallowing in the soft snow, barely able to haul their loads, so Thompson cleared the sleds of all but the tents, food, and clothing, and had everything else "hung up." But rather than being relieved by the lighter loads, his men grew increasingly reluctant to carry on. Thompson writes of their problems with a sympathy not untinged by sarcasm.

> The Courage of part of my Men (those from FDP) is sinking fast. They see nothing in its proper Colour—the soft Weather is a thing, it seems, they never felt before. The Snow, now reduced to 3 & 3½ feet is beyond all thought, yet they talk of 6 & 7 feet Snow at Montreal, but that was in Canada, where there are a great many People. I told them it was no matter the Snow was 20 ft deep, provided we went well over it, & had they been with me last Spring they would have carried Packs & Canoes over much deeper—but when Men arrive in a strange Country, fear gathers on them from every Object.

Thomas, his job done, returned east in mid-January. A *voyageur* named Vaudette went with him, carrying letters, and vanished forever from the expedition. Thompson and his remaining men continued their descent, zigzagging across the channels of Flat Heart Brook, drenched to the skin from dunkings in the river and the rain that had started to fall. On January 19 they reached the point where the Wood River flows into the northernmost bend of the Columbia River (which Thompson still called the Kootanae, though he knew better). On the narrow flats between the Wood and Canoe Rivers, they camped for the night.

The next day Thompson was urging his men along the banks of the Columbia, anxious to reach Kootanae House, about two hundred miles to the south, where they could wait out the winter in relative comfort. The FDP men, however, were now dragging their heels in earnest. At one point, much to Thompson's disgust, they took two and a half hours to negotiate forty yards of riverbank, even though Pareil made four trips helping them get their loads past the difficulty. After they had camped for the night, Thompson went off by himself "to see how the country was." And possibly get a little peace.

When he returned with a description of many large cedars and a steep rock "not passable without imminent Danger" and full of an ambitious plan to build a raft and ferry the loads around it, Du Nord and the FDP men decided they'd had enough. The three of them, "having long been dispirited & useless as old Women," told Thompson they would "return"; Thompson, "heartily tired of such worthless fellows," concluded he'd be better off without them. Realizing he was under-staffed and poorly equipped, he abandoned his plan to reach Kootanae House and turned back for the camp at Flat Heart Brook.

The return journey couldn't have been a pleasant one, with the demoralized men "sitting down" every half-mile and three of them plan-ning to desert as soon as they were in a position to do so. Thompson, however, seemed quite cheerful at the thought of getting rid of them: "A very mild light snowy Morn^g, fine Day," he wrote the day they reached the camp. "Du Nord, Le Tendre & D'Eau deserted." He sat down on his sled and, lacking paper to write on, wrote some letters on boards. He gave the departing men half his remaining supply of pemmican, and recorded their leave-taking ("they went off") with little sign of regret.

In all, seven men left the expedition that day: the three FDP men; François, who was booking off sick; and Coté, Pareil, and Villiard, who were to deliver Thompson's letters to William Henry for transcription onto a more conventional writing surface and bring back more goods. Two men named Vallade and L'Amoureux stayed with Thompson, and the three of them started to build the shelter that would house the men for the winter and provide storage for the goods and provisions. "We have," Thompson wrote, "ab^t 35 lbs of Pemmican, 25 lbs of Flour & a lit-tle of the other Provisions, & trust in the Mercy of Kind Providence to preserve us & find us Food."

On February 17 the ever-reliable Coté and Pareil, accompanied by Villiard, arrived back from William Henry's post with the goods and some much-needed supplies.

> Pareil & Coté & Villiard arrived from the Athabasca River where
> Mr Wm Henry is in care of the Goods—they have 78 lbs of Fat,
> 42½ lbs of Powder, 1 tin Kettle of 5½ lbs, 1 fm of HB Blue Strouds
> [woollen cloth] & ab^t 20 lbs of Lead, with Provisions to make a Bag
> of Pemmican, I think. Thank Heaven for their safe arrival.

Since the departure from Boggy Hall the previous October, more than twenty men (and three women) had vanished from the expedition, and now Thompson, Coté, Pareil, and Vallade were the only ones left. The four of them spent the next two months living in the shed, dining on moose meat, and building a cedar canoe. They called the place "Boat

Encampment," a name that persisted until 1973, when the Mica Dam was built on the Columbia and the site disappeared under the waters of Kinbasket Lake.

It could be argued that Thompson may as well have spent the winter with his family in the comfort of New Whitemud House. But that wouldn't have been Thompson. He was not, as P. J. Vesilind pointed out, a mellow man: "He wore out everyone around him."[11] It was probably best for everyone that he stayed where he was—wintering in a shed in the mountains rather than waiting it out in a fort on the Prairies— domestic comforts notwithstanding. At Boat Encampment, at least he could see the Columbia and know that he was halfway to solving the riddle of its course.

The Spokane River–1811[1]

*Thompson returned to the Columbia Division in
the spring of 1811. By that time, not only had the partners
given him permission to explore the Columbia, they were
considering sending in a replacement so he could "prosecute
his plans of discovery." But the explorer didn't shake the trader
that easily. Once again, Thompson turned aside from the
Columbia to devote his energies to the fur trade, and
for two months after he left Boat Encampment, his trail
was essentially a detour. Not until he'd logged another
six hundred miles overland was he finally free to
undertake his long-deferred "Voyage to the Sea."*

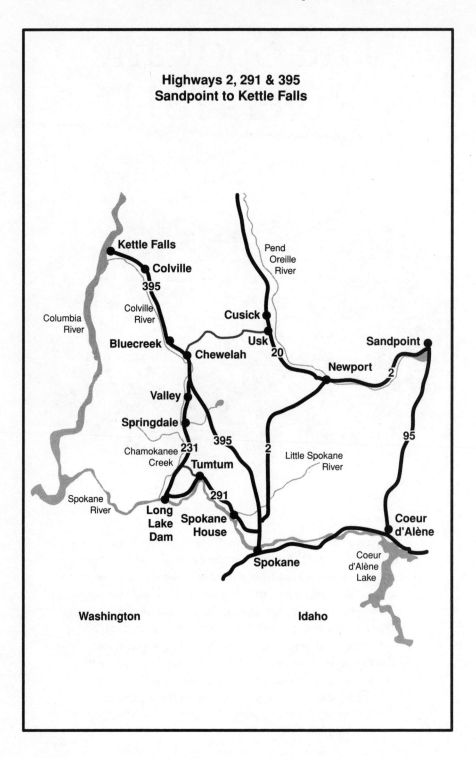

Highways 2, 291 & 395
Sandpoint to Kettle Falls

DURING THE SUMMER OF 1810, A NEW NORTH WEST POST WENT UP ON THE east bank of the Spokane River, about a mile upstream of its confluence with the Little Spokane. A century after the post was constructed, J. B. Tyrrell visited the site, and in his notes to the *Narrative* recalled his impressions: "The peninsula at this confluence is a beautiful protected flat, triangular in shape, and was always a favourite gathering-place for the Indians to catch and dry fish."[2] On that peninsula, Jaco Finlay built Spokane House, the first European settlement in the present state of Washington.

The site of Spokane House lies nine miles northwest of downtown Spokane, Washington, just past Riverside State Park on the Nine-Mile Road (Highway 291). Largely through the efforts of private individuals, 160 acres of historically significant land were set aside, land that was later acquired by the Washington State Parks and Recreation Commission. Today the once-bustling hub of the western fur trade is a delightful place for a walk on a hot summer day. The meadows of the peninsula are dotted with ponderosa pine, and thickets of Saskatoon and gooseberry crowd the grassy paths. Here and there among the rushes that line the river, a drift of yellow iris blooms by the water.

The remains of the post that Jaco built have yet to be found. In 1812, John Clarke of Astor's Pacific Fur Company built a rival post on the same flat, the more permanent (and more luxurious) Fort Spokane, but Astor's men enjoyed its amenities for only one winter. During the War of 1812 between Britain and the United States, the Nor'Westers took over the post, bought out the inventory at fire-sale prices, and renamed their new quarters Spokane House. It was the remains of this second Spokane House that were discovered and excavated during the 1950s and 1960s. One corner of the peninsula is now occupied by the Spokane House Interpretive Center. The center documents the history of the fur trade in the American northwest and displays the artifacts recovered from the site. It also interprets the complex history of the post. At one point, the second version of Spokane House underwent three changes of ownership—from the Pacific Fur Company to the North West Company to the Hudson's Bay Company—in less than ten years.

As the winter of 1811 gave way to spring, the Columbia Division was still struggling along without its head. Jaco Finlay was based at Spokane House, James McMillan was at Kullyspell House, and where Finan McDonald was, only Finan knew. Thompson was still at Boat Encampment, where March 22, 1811, found him busily engaged in knifing timbers for his clinker-built canoe. A thousand miles downstream, the sailing ship *Tonquin* had ended her seven-month voyage around Cape Horn and was standing off the mouth of the Columbia. On March 25, Thompson felled a giant cedar and started turning wood for gunwales; the same day, the *Tonquin* sailed across the bar, repeatedly struck bottom, then lifted into Baker's Bay on the swell of the incoming tide. On April 16, Thompson sealed the last seam on his canoe. Astor's men were on the south shore of the Columbia hacking Fort Astoria out of the rain forest. Only a three-week dash down the Columbia separated the Nor'Westers from the Astorians, but, though he may have been tempted, Thompson didn't head downstream.

In his *Narrative,* he gave a logical reason for his decision: he and his three men were "too few" to put up a bold front if the Indians along the Columbia proved unfriendly. A second reason (which he didn't mention) was the size of his cargo. According to the inventory he made on the Upper Columbia, he'd accumulated twenty-six packs of trade goods over the winter. Thompson didn't make a big deal of all that merchandise, but it was a big deal nonetheless. The record of his count gives us some idea of the size of the load he was carrying.

It was staggering. Inside the packs, horse belting rubbed shoulders with gartering, iron hoops with looking glasses, axes with a bottle of peppermint. But these were mere incidentals. Even a partial summary indicates that Thompson and his *voyageurs* had brought a full complement of goods across Athabasca Pass:

Two steel traps, 8 guns, 8 kettles, and 47 knives; 144 awls, 200 flints, 858 buttons, 1,573 rings, and 2,753 hawk bells;

Twelve pounds of beads (blue and white), 47 pounds of bird shot, 60 pounds plus of lead balls, 86 pounds of gunpowder, and 141 pounds of tobacco twist;

A stock of men's "equipments" (blankets, shirts, jackets, breeches, belts, and caps), 2 yards of Hudson's Bay cloth for Jaco, and a curious assortment of drygoods earmarked for Thompson himself: a fine jacket (the only item in the packs that wasn't new), a cape, a pair of gray cotton "trowsers," 2 wool twill vests, 3 calico shirts, 3 handkerchiefs, 2 pairs of worsted stockings, 2 3/4 pieces of China ribbon, 2 yards of green cloth, 4 yards of checked cotton, 4 1/2 yards of white linen, 6 yards of flannel, 7 1/2 yards of blue calico, and a flowered blanket.

The cargo raises some knotty questions. When the North West partners sent Thompson west, did they insist he burden himself with the usual shipment of trade goods? Or did Thompson himself feel obliged to supply his posts? Was delivering trade goods part of his itinerary, or was he stuck with the job after so many of his men deserted? Was his journey a desperate race to the sea or merely a routine check on the competition invading his territory? Thompson's journal doesn't answer any of these questions, but there's little doubt the load of goods dictated his choice of route. No one but a madman would have tackled a thousand miles of unknown river in an untried craft with a crew of three and a ton of excess baggage.

On the morning of April 17, 1811, Thompson and his men pushed off from Boat Encampment. "We are," he wrote, "Rene Vallade Steersman, Pierre Pareil & Jos Coté middlemen & myself the foreman." Also on board was an anonymous canine Thompson had taken to calling "my Dog." Conditions on the Columbia hadn't improved since February, and for the first hundred miles, the canoe was more hindrance than help. The men paddled and poled and towed it through rock-riddled rapids, packed it across stretches of frozen river, and wrestled it along the riverbank on snowshoes. When miles of solid ice sealed the river, they huddled in wretched camps, waiting for a sign of a thaw. Winter drizzled into spring, then blustered into winter again—rain and fog, sleet and snow, and deep in the Rocky Mountain Trench, always more shadow than sun. For Thompson, the trip had only one consolation: he'd never seen this stretch of the Columbia before and was absorbed in charting another hundred miles of its course.

At one time, a road followed this stretch of river. It was called the Big Bend Highway, so-named because it arched around the northern loop of the Columbia River. Although the name was appropriate, that twisted, dusty, rock-strewn, mosquito-infested gravel track never did merit the term "highway." That's not to say the Big Bend wasn't important. For more than thirty years it was the only road between Golden and Revelstoke, B.C., as well as an indispensable link between Highway 1 East and Highway 1 West.

Today the TransCanada Highway links Golden and Revelstoke, and the old highway lies in pieces. In 1973 the Mica Dam severed the loop of the Big Bend, backed up the Columbia River for a hundred miles, and inundated most of the road. In the late 1960s, there was a rumour that a mysterious "they" wanted to dam the Columbia and fill the Rocky Mountain Trench with water, a notion that bordered on the ridiculous at the time. But a few years later, there it was—twenty million acre feet of water stored in the Rocky Mountain Trench. The new body of water inherited the name of a former widening in the Columbia—Kinbasket Lake.

Long and narrow and deep, Kinbasket Lake has an enormous capacity, a spectacular mountain setting, and a reputation as an ecological disaster. In 1990 author Robin Cody described forty vertical feet of exposed shoreline at high water and learned that the drawdown can expose 155 feet of shoreline at low water.[3] Eight years later, little had changed. At the Kinbasket Lake Resort, a forlorn-looking wharf lay canted over in the spring mud, though the owner assured us that by mid-summer, there would be sixty feet of water underneath it.

Cody, who paddled the entire length of the Columbia River, described the history of the Mica Dam. When the dam was built, BC Hydro wasn't required to log the land. As a result, the lake's depths are infested with deadheads, its surface waters scattered with debris, its shores littered with twisted stumps and toppling trees. The flooding led to the loss of thousands of animals (grizzly, moose, deer, mink) and the wholesale destruction of habitat once utilized by fish and waterfowl. Even the mosquitoes, Cody noted grimly, are gone.[4]

Once Thompson and his men passed the mouth of the Blaeberry River, they put the hazards of winter behind them. The snow had retreated to the slopes of the mountains, and only a skim of ice clung to the margins of the Columbia. They paddled through the wetlands, portaged across Canal Flats, and launched their canoe on the Kootenay. At the river's confluence with the Fisher, Thompson laid up the canoe, loaded his packs onto fourteen horses he'd borrowed and bartered from the Kootenays, and set off down the Kootanae Road.[5]

On this trip, probably because his guides were the Kootenays themselves, Thompson got the road right. He headed south along the Fisher River for eighteen miles, cut off the river's southward loop by crossing a height of land, turned east past the chain of Thompson Lakes, then turned south again to follow the Thompson River for thirty miles. There he left the river, turned markedly southeast, and rode the last thirty miles to the present-day site of the town of Plains.

Today forestry roads through the Kootenai and Lolo National Forests mimic the route of the Kootanae Road. The first, which follows the Fisher River, is a paved road that begins at the David Thompson Bridge on Highway 37. Initially, it's numbered 763, changes to 535 at its midpoint, and ends at Highway 2 just west of a roadside landmark called Happy's Inn. The second, which follows the Thompson River, is a gravel road that begins seven miles east of Happy's Inn and ends at Highway

200. This road, called the Thompson River Road, is numbered 556.

In its upper reaches, the Thompson River is a lazy brook meandering across broad, grassy flats, in its middle reaches, a fast-moving stream running in multiple channels, and in its lower reaches, a whitewater river charging through a narrow rocky channel. The road follows the river for about thirty miles, then divides. The west fork stays with the river all the way to Thompson Falls (roughly another twenty-five miles); the east fork follows Thompson's trail to Plains (about thirty miles). Since logging roads are often confusing (we ended up in Thompson Falls instead of Plains), a forestry map well marked with a highlighter is strongly recommended.

From Plains, Thompson turned west onto his usual trail along the Clark Fork River. His immediate destination was Saleesh House, where he hoped to recruit more men for the journey to the mouth of the Columbia. Although he'd hired two Iroquois—Charles, "an excellent canoe man" to act as bowsman, and Ignace, "to be Steersman of my Canoe"—the Athabasca mutiny had left him desperately short of men. All during his stay at Boat Encampment, he'd waited for his *voyageurs* to recover from their "Panic" and venture across the pass. The day he launched his canoe, he was still waiting. Soon after leaving Boat Encampment, he'd met a band of Nipissing trappers heading north and hired two of them to "find my People & guide & hunt for them," a mission that was never accomplished.

Nor would there be any men at Saleesh House, and if Thompson had planned to turn over his cargo to Finan McDonald, the news along the Kootanae Road wasn't good. A group of free traders working the area filled him in on McDonald's dustup with the Peigans, and a Kootenay named L'Originale informed him that Finan had abandoned Saleesh House and moved twenty miles west. Forewarned, Thompson wasn't surprised to find the post empty, but he must have wondered whether the Columbia Division was coming apart at the seams.

> I examined the old Ho[use]—but found no Letter nor writing of
> any kind to inform me what had become of the people who had
> wintered there. Wrote a few Lines in Charcoal on a Board in case
> the Americans should pass—purporting that we had left the Ho
> on acc' of the War with the Peegans ...

The "Americans" were members of the second arm of Astor's expedition, this one travelling overland to the Columbia along the route pioneered by Lewis and Clark. Thompson's use of the word "purporting" is suggestive. As a rule, he was precise in his choice of words, and "purporting" carries an air of deceit that's lacking, for example, in the word "explaining." When Thompson left Rainy Lake for the Columbia, he was carrying a letter of agreement between his wintering partners and John Jacob Astor. The agreement covered the purchase by the Nor'Westers of a one-third share in Astor's Pacific Fur Company. When Thompson left Rainy Lake, he was aware that the Montreal partners hadn't formally approved the deal, but he didn't know that they'd subsequently cancelled it. His uncertainty about the status of the agreement may have led to his rather cagey handling of the Astorians. This wasn't the only occasion he seemed to be trying to outfox a potential competitor.

An empty Saleesh House was of little use to Thompson. He moved twenty miles down the Clark Fork looking for cedar to build another canoe, and incidentally for the elusive Finan. A week later, McDonald still hadn't shown up, and Thompson and his men were loading the canoe for the run to Lake Pend Oreille. On June 6 they reached Kullyspell House, but there was no hope of dropping the load of goods there. James McMillan had left on his annual trek over the Rockies, and Kullyspell House was deserted.

They paddled across Lake Pend Oreille and started down the Pend Oreille River. At Cusick, Thompson learned that his missing clerk was at Spokane House. He hired two Kalispels to take a message to the post, and four days later, McDonald arrived with thirteen horses to carry the trade goods over the last fifty miles. On June 14, 1811, two months after he'd left Boat Encampment, Thompson finally reached Spokane House. There (in a masterpiece of understatement) he offloaded "a small assortment of goods."

Although Thompson would eventually stay at Spokane House on several occasions, he never spent more than a few nights there. In contrast, Finan McDonald and Jaco Finlay were associated with the post for more than a decade of tumultuous change. West of the Rockies, there'd been no rivalry with the Hudson's Bay Company for ten years (Joseph Howse had abandoned his post on Flathead Lake after one nerve-wracking winter), but on the Prairies, confrontations between the two firms had grown so violent that they were both on the verge of bankruptcy. In 1821, at the order of the British Parliament, the North West partners were forced into a merger with the Hudson's Bay Company. The new firm spanned the North American continent from the Atlantic to the Pacific and turned Spokane House into a Hudson's Bay post staffed by a crew of Nor'Westers.

Finan McDonald joined the new company and, the year after the merger, was busy tearing down the stockade to enlarge the Hudson's Bay warehouse. But as the trade route across the Rockies shifted from Howse Pass to Athabasca Pass, Spokane House was stranded in a backwater. McDonald stayed on for five years, but in 1826, when the Bay moved its operations to Kettle Falls, he retired to eastern Canada. At age sixty-six (by which time you'd think he'd have mellowed a bit), he was lodged in a Toronto jail, apparently as a result of a dispute over his brother's estate.

There's no record of Jaco Finlay signing on with the Bay, but he was still living in a stripped and desolate Spokane House the year the post was closed. That was the year David Douglas brought his gun in for repairs and found Jaco living in the abandoned buildings.[6] At the time, Jaco was only in his late fifties, but within two years, he was dead. His dying wish was to be buried at the foot of one of the bastions of Spokane House, a wish that somebody granted. Today a glass wall in the interpretive centre overlooks Jaco's grave.

Two days after Thompson reached Spokane House, he was saddling up to leave. He knew the Spokane River joined the Columbia less than sixty miles downstream of the trading post, but he dismissed the Lower Spokane for the same reason he'd dismissed the Lower Kootenay and the Lower Pend Oreille: the river's headlong rush to its mouth rendered its lower reaches unnavigable. On Thompson's map, the Spokane River and Coeur d'Alène Lake (which the river drains) are labelled "Skeetshoo River and Lake." In his journal, however, he often referred to the river as the Spokane. Over its 110-mile descent to the Columbia, the river's falls and rapids have attracted the attention of modern dam builders at six different locations, but the chief obstacle for Thompson was a towering falls that poured into the chasm now filled by the Long Lake Dam. About thirty miles downstream of Spokane House, the dam sits in a twisted canyon, its spillway crabwise to the river, the bulk of its structure the solid rock of the gorge. Apparently there was no way to portage these falls, since neither Thompson nor the traders who came after him ever challenged the Lower Spokane.

Thompson's alternative was to ride sixty-eight miles along an Indian trail that led north through the Colville Valley. Some sections of his trail are hard to define, but today's roads tend to mirror his route, and once he entered the Colville Valley, there was only one way he could go. When Thompson and his riders left Spokane House, they headed northwest, following a trail above the Spokane River for twelve and a half miles. Over this part of the ride, only the names have changed. The route is now known as Highway 291, and this reach of the river as Long Lake.

Near the present-day town of Tumtum, the riders turned away from the Spokane to cross a "Ridge of Knowls," probably along the route now followed by the Rail Canyon Road. The road leads northwest out of Tumtum, winds through a landscape of parched grass, open-grown pine and gravel slopes for about seven miles, and ends at its junction with Highway 231. To the left, the highway leads to the Long Lake Dam; to the right, it follows Thompson's trail up the valley of Chamokanee Creek.

Here the riders turned northeast up the valley, following the same general direction as Highway 231. Near the present-day community of Springdale, they came to a river that Thompson classed as a "Brook" and trotted out onto the flats of the Colville River Valley. He was immediately struck by the contrast between the dry country they'd passed through and the fertile lands that lay ahead. In his *Narrative*, he wrote: "I noticed a great change in the soil which hitherto has been a light sandy loam, today a fine vegetable mould on a rich clayey loam very fit for agriculture." He later added that the Colville Valley was "a country of open Woods and Meadows with Ponds and Brooks of Water; all fit for cultivation and cattle."

As the agricultural landscape of today's Colville Valley shows, Thompson was quite right in his assessment, though he wasn't the only trader to foresee its potential. Fifteen years later, the Bay's George Simpson declared: "An excellent Farm can be made at this place where as much Grain and potatoes may be raised as would feed all the Natives of the Columbia and sufficient number of Cattle and Hogs to supply his Majestys Navy."[7] Today broad fields of grain and alfalfa flourish in the valley, and sizeable herds of cattle graze its pastures. Through the middle of it all winds the Colville River, still no bigger than a brook, ambling from one field to the next as it makes its way to the Columbia.

From Springdale, Highway 231 follows Thompson's route to the town of Valley, where it joins Highway 395 to pursue his trail past Chewelah, Bluecreek, and Colville. It ends at his launch point on the Columbia—Kettle Falls. Thompson had his own name for the falls. He called them "Ilthkoyape," a name so uniquely Thompsonian that even Tyrrell was unable to figure out how he came up with it. Eventually, Tyrrell tracked down historian Jacob A. Meyers, who explained that the term derived from *Ilth-hape*, the Salish word for "kettle," and *Hoy-ape*, the Salish word for "trap."[8]

Even so, the origin of the modern name remains a matter of some speculation. There's no disagreement about the term "falls" (a thirty-foot drop within half a mile is sufficiently stupendous to forestall any argument), but the word "kettle" is another matter. Some maintain it refers to great bowls scoured out of the Columbia's substrates by the falls, others advance the more likely explanation that it refers to the basket traps the Colvilles used to capture salmon. Still others point out that the *voyageurs* called the falls *La Chaudière*, which is the most graphic of the three options. The term translates as "boiler" and is related to the French term for "cauldron."

Today Kettle Falls is merely the name of a town on the Columbia River. The falls themselves lie ninety feet beneath the waters of Franklin D. Roosevelt Lake, the reservoir created by the construction of the Grand Coulee Dam. Once in a while, as happened in 1997, the level of the reservoir drops and the falls make a curtain call, inspiring a flurry of picture-taking among local residents. But most years, the original falls, and the Indian fishery they once supported, appear only in the early photos and paintings that hang on the walls of the Kettle Falls Interpretive Center.

Grand Coulee Dam

~ Completed in 1942, the Grand Coulee Dam delivered much-needed water to the Columbia Plateau, generated the power to support the U.S. World War II effort, and created a monument to rival the pyramids.

~ It also cut off the spawning run of Chinook salmon, wiping out not only the Native fishery at Kettle Falls, but the entire Chinook fishery in the Canadian part of the Columbia.

~ Grand Coulee was the third dam on the Columbia, but it was the first to be built without fish ladders.

Although the interpretive centre's museum has a variety of themes, its volunteers are well acquainted with David Thompson. Jack Nisbet, author of *Sources of the River*, once gave a talk there, and the gift shop still features the David Thompson T-shirt that marked the occasion. A short walk from the centre, a lane carpeted in pine needles traces part of the old portage past the falls; nearby, a small cemetery commemorates the traders and Colvilles who lived and died there. On the south edge of town, a historic walk records the story of the Bay's grist mill, its great waterwheel once powered by the Colville River's final drop to the Columbia.

Thompson and his men reached Kettle Falls on June 19. There they found a large village of raised split-cedar lodges that did double duty as living quarters for the Colvilles and as racks for drying salmon. The spawning run of Chinook had just begun, and only one fisherman was working the river, though Thompson maintained there were enough salmon leaping the falls to occupy thirty more. He was intrigued by the Colvilles' description of the life history of the Chinook, but he had trouble believing that none of the fish would survive their upstream journey. He puzzled over their freshwater origins, their seaward migration, their eventual return to the streams of their birth to spawn and die. Although he carefully recorded all the Colvilles told him, he was only half-convinced of its truth.

For two days after they arrived at Kettle Falls, Thompson and his men searched for enough cedar to build another canoe. Finally recalling they'd passed a stand of the trees on the trail, they retreated seven miles up the Colville, where they managed to cut enough wood to construct a craft for their journey. By that time, Thompson had recruited a full crew for his venture. His two Montreal men, Pierre Pareil and Joseph Coté, stayed on with the expedition, as did the two Iroquois canoe men, Charles and Ignace. In addition, he'd taken on a hunter named François Grégoire, a free trader named Michel Bourdeaux, and his old summer hand, Michel Boulard. Two Sanpoil translators completed the crew, and by July 3, 1811, Thompson was ready to launch his canoe on the Columbia. Destination: the Pacific Ocean.

The Great River of the West–1811[1]

David Thompson's most memorable contribution to the geography of the northwest was a complete survey of the Columbia from its headwaters to its mouth. As of the spring of 1811, he'd explored only two hundred miles of the river; by the end of the summer, he'd covered the remaining thousand. The feat was his greatest accomplishment, not because the journey was exceptionally difficult—the weather was mild, the route a given, his crew experienced and loyal—but because he went so far, moved so fast, and completed a survey of such precision it stood for one hundred years.

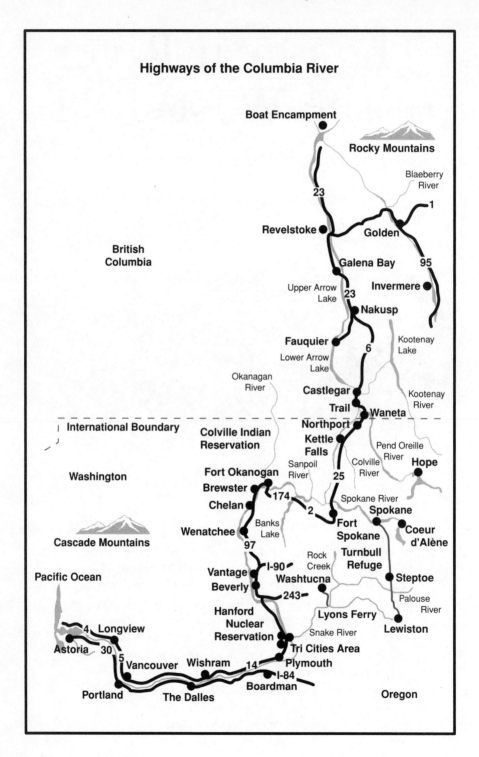

Highways of the Columbia River

JUST WHY THE NORTH WEST PARTNERS DISPATCHED THOMPSON TO THE Pacific is one of the haziest spots in his history, yet the notion that he lost the "race to the sea" is often treated as certainty. The original source of the tale may have been Washington Irving, who, as early as 1836, published a book on events at Astoria. Well known for his other fairy tales, Irving laid out a summary of Thompson's journey, complete with an account of his motives.

Originally, Irving maintained, Thompson was dispatched to "anticipate Mr. Astor," and "pushed on his course in great haste." But when the Athabasca mutiny defeated his purpose, Thompson "descended the river simply to reconnoitre and ascertain whether an American settlement had been commenced." And when Thompson finally reached Astoria: "Mr. Thompson could be considered as little better than a spy in the camp."[2]

The author was no fan of Thompson's, partly because Irving was naturally on the side of the Americans and partly because Thompson had refused him access to his journals. Neither excuse will do for the twentieth-century historians who polished the tale and lent it fresh credibility. And there's another side to the story—Thompson's own.

On July 3, 1811, the day he left Kettle Falls, Thompson wrote: "Set off on a voyage down the Columbia River, to explore this River, in order to open out a Passage for the Interior Trade with the Pacific Ocean." Here we have his view of the journey, and there's little reason to suppose it differed from that of his partners. Assuming, however, that the North West Company actually meant to pit Thompson against Astor, the only reason for doing so was to establish a post at the mouth of the Columbia before the Astorians could get there.

If, however, the partners had stressed "great haste," Thompson would have pushed the pace. Instead, he stopped to visit and smoke with every Indian band on the river—Sanpoil, Nespelem, Methow, Wenatchee, Yakima, Shawpatin, Umatilla, Klickitat—he visited them all. If the partners had instructed him to build a new post, he'd have loaded his canoe with trade goods. Instead, he took only enough goods to buy in provisions and loaded his canoe with furs ("49 Beaver, 15 Black Bear, 5 grisled d°, 5 yellow d°, 3 brown bears, 1 Otter, 12 Cats"). And if he'd arrived to find Astoria already established (which he did), he'd have done what traders had done for decades—built a post of his own next door. Instead, he dropped in on the Astorians, hung around for a week, and behaved like a tourist on holiday.

At no time did he behave like a man in a race. Visiting the Indians cost him a lot of time, which he justified by the need to make friends with the people who lived on the river. He'd taken the furs along "as an adventure," but it's unlikely he planned to deliver them to Astoria. He had no way of knowing whether there was a post at the mouth of the Columbia or not, and even if he had, he wouldn't have wasted his time carrying coals to Newcastle. If, however, by an "adventure," he meant "on spec," he may have been gambling on meeting a ship bound for China, in which case a canoeful of furs would make sense.

Taken together, Thompson's actions suggest a man on a trial run, a pathfinder whose main concern was not a collection of huts on the lip of the Pacific, but the route he followed to get there. Within two months of leaving Astoria, he'd opened that route from the Columbia's Big Bend to its mouth. Coupled with his crossing of Athabasca Pass (a long portage, but almost three hundred miles shorter than Lewis and Clark's), he'd connected the Prairies to the Pacific and the North West Company's fur brigades to the ships sailing the ocean. That Thompson accomplished what his partners intended became apparent the following year. The deal they offered him bore the obvious stamp of a reward for a job well done.

During the summer of 1811, Thompson logged over two thousand miles of travel. The run from Kettle Falls to Astoria represented seven hundred of those miles, which (despite all the socializing along the way) his *voyageurs* disposed of in a scant thirteen days. On average, they covered sixty miles a day, with a record of eighty-six. In 1990 Robin Cody took almost fifty days to paddle the same stretch of river. His average was fourteen miles a day, and his record thirty-five. The difference wasn't merely the one between a full crew and a man on his own. Most of it was dictated by change in the Columbia itself.

Cody paddled a river stilled by the works of man, a long string of lakes bracketed by concrete dams: Grand Coulee, Chief Joseph, Wells, Rocky Reach, Rock Island, Wanapum, Priest Rapids, McNary, John Day, The Dalles, and Bonneville. Eleven in all, each one forced him off the river or into a lock before he could continue his paddle to the sea.[3] He had little help from the Columbia. For seventy-five percent of its length, the modern river is slackwater. Where it isn't still, it offers only the sluggish pull of a barely perceptible current.

The historic Columbia was never still. Thompson launched his canoe on a brawling river that seethed with a ten-mile-an-hour boost. The *voyageurs* dodged eddies and whirlpools that "bore the canoe from side to side," plunged into whitewater ("Last 1/2 mile very strong dangerous rapids"), and charged between "high Rocks on the right" and "high Rocks on the left." While his men challenged the river, Thompson was trying to chart it. "The Courses are not so correct as I could wish ... the Compass was always vibrating."

Today the Colville Indian Reservation borders the west side of this reach of the Columbia, and the Lake Roosevelt National Recreation Area, the east side. From Kettle Falls, Highway 25 runs south through the recreation area to the mouth of the Spokane River, a distance of about sixty miles. Along the way, the small communities of Bradbury Beach, Daisy, Gifford, and Hunters provide access to the campsites and boat launches scattered along the shore of Lake Roosevelt. Although the present lake is much tamer than Thompson's river, its setting still fits his description: "the country always wears a pleasing romantic view ... Hills, Vallies &c, with partly wooded thinly & partly Meadow."

By late afternoon, the *voyageurs* had romped through Grand Rapids and Spokane Rapids and were eighty-six miles down the Columbia. Turning into the Sanpoil River, they paddled a quarter of a mile upstream and put ashore near a Sanpoil village.

> On our Arrival at the Simpoil Camp, we pitched our Tents. No one approached us 'till we sent for them to come & smoke—the Chief then made a speech & the Men all followed him in File & sat down round the Tent ... the Smoking being done & the news being all told, I then told the Chief what I had to say, of my Voyage to the Sea &c &c ...

Thompson and his men stayed at the Sanpoil camp until noon the next day, visiting and smoking and exchanging gifts. Thompson's description of the Sanpoil people and their customs ran on for two pages, a pattern he was to repeat at every village on the Middle Columbia. As the first white man to record information on these villages, Thompson may have considered his observations important, but it's equally likely he was assessing the river's potential for trade. Once he reached the Lower Columbia, where Lewis and Clark had preceded him, his cultural descriptions were cursory, but he conducted a detailed census all the way to the mouth of the river. By counting the men and multiplying by seven to account for the women and children, he calculated a riverside population equal to that of a small city—"13,615 Souls."

South of the Spokane River, the Columbia turns west into a country that's virtually devoid of landmarks. Between Fort Spokane (originally a military post near the mouth of the Spokane River) and Fort Okanogan (once a Pacific Fur Company post at the mouth of the Okanogan), rejoining Thompson's route down the Columbia requires a hundred-mile cross-country detour to the west. In the meantime, his canoe disappears to the north, following the Columbia into the remote hills enclosing present-day Rufus Woods Lake.

On the afternoon of July 4, the canoe reached Box Canyon, where the Columbia once rose to squeeze through a "deep narrow Channel" and spilled over Kalichen Falls. The men scouted the rapids and decided to run them, but "in doing so," wrote Thompson, who had prudently removed himself and the cargo to shore, "they run too close to a drift-wood Tree on a Rock, which tore part of the upper lath away and struck Ignace out of the Stem of the Canoe." Ignace managed to keep his head above water until the men could turn around, but the accident ended the day. Resigned to a night on a rockpile, Thompson left the canoe in the river and administered his usual form of first aid: "I bled Ignace."

Since leaving the Sanpoil camp, Thompson had watched the countryside shrivel before his eyes. As he moved west and south, he commented on poor soil—"white grey earth of a kind of impalpable Powder mixed with Stones"—and sparse vegetation—"Grass in Tufts" and "strong-scented Shrubs." The shrubs were, of course, sagebrush, still typical of lands that lie in the rain-shadow of the Cascades. These mountains divide a rain-drenched coast from a parched interior, and whoever dubbed Washington "the Evergreen State" must never have ventured east of them. Here, green gives way to the faded gold of treeless hills, the stark black of rocky outcrops, and, running like ribbon through the landscape, the brilliant blue of the Columbia.

After their uncomfortable night on the rocks, Thompson and his crew were rescued by a band of mounted Nespelem, who immediately set to work getting the packs past the remaining rapids. They escorted the strangers back to their village and presented them with five roasted salmon, a bushel of berries and two of roots, and "4 small dried fat Animals which I take to be the Marmot." Thompson accepted the salmon and berries, declined the roots and the marmots, and spent the balance of the day visiting.

> Having smoked a few Pipes discussed of the Country, which they
> described as a hilly Meadow with very few Trees of Fir from hence to
> the Occhenawga [Okanogan] River. Of course there can be no
> Beaver; they have Bears & Rats, with a few sheep & black-tailed Deer;
> Horses they have many & the Country appears good for them.

Early in the morning, Thompson and his men set off from the Nespelem camp, and, about fifteen miles downstream, they encountered the Foster Creek Rapids. These rapids were near the site of today's Chief

Joseph Dam, named in honour of a Nez Percé chief defeated by the U.S. Army in 1877. In their flight from the army, the Nez Percé almost reached Canada, where Chief Joseph had hoped to find a haven for his people. His famous oration at the time of his surrender mourned the dead and the lost and the starving, and ended with the oft-quoted words: "Hear me, my chiefs; my heart is sick and sad; from where the sun now stands Joseph will fight no more forever." Chief Joseph spent his last years in exile on today's Colville Indian Reservation.

Downstream of the dam, the Columbia turns briefly north, and there Thompson sighted the "high woody Mountains" of the Okanogan National Forest. The *voyageurs* paddled across the flooded flats opposite the mouth of the Okanogan River, followed the curve of the Columbia south, then put ashore at an encampment of Methows. After the customary civilities, Thompson made his usual request for information.

> They said the River was tolerable from hence to another Tribe
> & that they would inform me of some dist^ce beyond that again, as
> their Knowledge reached no farther. Having accepted part of the
> Present they brought, 3 roasted Salmon & ab^t ½ Bushel of Arrow
> Wood Berries, I made them a present of 2 ft of Tob, 6 Rings, 1 fm
> of Gart^g, 6 Hawks Bells, & 2 Awls—& 4 In to the Chief.

Two hours later, the chief and four young men helped the visitors portage the two-mile length of the Methow Rapids, and for the rest of the day the *voyageurs* pursued a southward course. Late in the afternoon, they ran the Entiat Rapids, and at seven in the evening, put up for the night not far from a Columbia campground now known as Wenatchee Confluence.

Today Highway 97 meets the Columbia at its junction with the Okanogan River and follows Thompson's route down two long narrow lakes named Pateros and Entiat. Pateros Lake lies behind the Wells Dam; Entiat Lake, behind Rocky Reach. Thompson described this valley as "bare of Wood," which may have been true then but isn't the case now. The ledges of the modern Columbia are dense with apple trees— Delicious and Winesap, Gala and Rome, Jonagold and Fuji and Cameo. For just over seventy miles, Highway 97 winds among Washington's apple towns—Brewster, Chelan, Orondo—until both road and river reach the "Apple Capital of the World," Wenatchee.

Early the next morning, Thompson and his crew made the ten-mile run to the head of the Rock Island Rapids, where a Wenatchee village, eight hundred strong, stood on the banks of the river.

> They received us all dancing in their Huts ... it was 20' before we
> could get them all to sit down ... A very old respectable Man sat
> down by me, thankful to see us & smoke of our Tobacco before he
> died—he after felt my Shoes & Legs gently as if to know whether
> I was like themselves. A Chief of the Countries below offered to
> accompany me; he understood the Language of the People below,
> which I gladly accepted ...

They stayed visiting and smoking with the Wenatchees for three hours, then set off again with the chief and his wife and their baggage. "We had much trouble to get away, as they very much wished to detain us all night ... " While Thompson "walked down" the Rock Island Rapids, "the Canoe ran it close on the left." By nightfall, they'd passed today's riverside resort of Crescent Bar, descended a deep gorge ("a vast wall of Rock bounding the River on the right, also much of the same on the left"), and paddled the "long Reach" upstream of the Wanapum Dam.

South of Wenatchee, Highway 28 follows Thompson down the Columbia, but only as far as Crescent Bar. No other highway borders the river until just north of Vantage, where Interstate 90 picks up the trail again. From Vantage, Highway 243 runs south to the Wanapum Dam near Beverly, which is where Tyrrell thought the expedition camped on the night of July 7.[4] If so, Beverly has much to answer for: "Passed a bad Night with Musketoes & high Winds."

The next morning the *voyageurs* put an ill wind to good use. They rigged up a mast, raised a sail, and flew through the Priest Rapids, over-shooting by half a mile a village of four hundred Wanapum. Never one to pass up a chance to go visiting, Thompson pulled in and waited.

> Here the Chief came to visit us on Horseback, then returned with
> word to the Camp ... He returned with another, & with them an old
> white headed Man, with the handle of a Tea Kettle for an ornament
> ab* his Head ... he was quite naked & ran nearly as fast as the
> Horses—we could not but admire him. I invited them to call all
> their People to smoke, which they set off to do on a round Gallop, &
> the old Man on foot ran after them & did not lose much ground.

When Thompson left these people, he immediately turned northeast, indicating the Wanapum lived then where they still live now—in the shadow of the Priest Rapids Dam. The old man's ornament was the first sign of contact with Europeans, though probably not direct contact, since Thompson was still 350 miles upstream of the mouth of the Columbia. For the rest of the afternoon, the *voyageurs* paddled the reach of the river that now skirts the Hanford Nuclear Reservation.

Hanford Reach is forty-seven miles of natural river, a rarity on the Columbia, and the ironic outcome of the radioactive contamination of its waters. From the bridge between Highway 243 and the Hanford site, you can see the current picking up speed, and if you're equipped with a canoe, you can run the Coyote Rapids with the *voyageurs* who ran them two hundred years ago. But the roads across Hanford remain resolutely remote from the river. Highway 24 sets off to the south, bisecting a hard-scrabble plain of grass and sagebrush. To the west, bare hills clad in the wrinkled hide of a Sharpei; to the east, sun-scalded flats to the horizon. The forty-mile drive ends in Washington's Tri Cities Area, where Richland, Kennewick, and Pasco cluster around the Columbia's conflu-ence with the Snake River.

Thompson's canoe approached the Tri Cities Area late in the after-noon of July 8. Half a mile north of the mouth of the Snake River, he saw a large camp of Yakimas a short way ahead and decided to put up for the night.

> 4 Horsemen came ahead—they smoked & I sent them to invite all the Indians to come & smoke also, which they did, bringing a Present of 4 Salmon ... We discoursed much, 3 Chiefs repeating after each other what I said. They say ... there are plenty of Chevreuil ... They have no Berries &c whatever, nor did we see any Roots. Salmon is plenty with them in the Seine ... they give a little Oil in the Kettle, the very first that have done so & have a trout like taste.

For almost a week, Thompson had been fretting about the accuracy of his survey. His complaint that the compass was "always vibrating" was only the first of many. At Beverly, "The whirlpools keep the Compass continually agitated; at Hanford, " ... last two courses by the Watch ... as the low Pts are so dist that I cannot determine the dist[ce] by them ...;" at Pasco, "I found my instrument had got shaken quite out of adjustment to the left ... I do not know when the Sextant got this shake." Thompson hoped to make the courses more accurate on his return, but he never did return to the Middle Columbia. Even so, he needn't have worried about the accuracy of his map.

Modern renderings of the Columbia between the Okanogan and Snake Rivers outline the profile of an Indian gazing west. Near the man's forehead, the Okanogan joins the Columbia, and over his cheeks course the canals that irrigate the Columbia Plateau. At the tip of his nose is the city of Wenatchee, and tucked under his chin, Hanford. Few identifiable landmarks appear on Thompson's map, but the shape he gave to the Indian's profile is the same shape we find on our maps today.

It was just after six the next morning when the expedition reached the junction of the Snake and the Columbia. Thompson promptly "erected a small Pole with a half sheet of Paper well tied about it," and laid formal claim to a large chunk of the future state of Washington.

> Know hereby that this Country is claimed by Great Britain as part of it's Territories and that the NW Company of Merchants from Canada, finding the Factory for this people inconvenient for them, do hereby intend to erect a Factory in this Place for the Commerce of the Country around. D. Thompson. Junction of the Shawpatin [Snake] River with the Columbia, July 8th, 1811.

That morning Thompson's route intercepted that of Lewis and Clark for the first time, and near the Walla Walla River, he encountered a man who'd met his American counterparts six years before. Thompson knew him as Chief Yellepit, "Principal Chief of all the Tribes of the Shawpatin."

> ... he had an American medal of 1801 Thos Jefferson & a small Flag of that Nation—he was a stately good looking Man of ab.t 40 years old, well dressed ... I found him intelligent; he was also very friendly, & we discoursed a long time & settled on the Junction of the Shawpatin River for a House &c.

We had to chuckle at Thompson's cheek in referring to President Jefferson as "Thos," to say nothing of his bland assumption that he could claim a jointly occupied territory on behalf of Great Britain. Alexander Ross, one of Astor's clerks, chanced upon Thompson's "half sheet of Paper" a couple of weeks later and was outraged. "That he should have attempted to incite the Indians against us, in our helpless and almost forlorn state, was conduct which the world must condemn."[5]

South of the Tri Cities Area, the Columbia curves through the Wallula Gap and flows into the two-hundred-mile-long Columbia Gorge. The gorge was born many millions of years ago in a firestorm of volcanic eruptions that repeatedly flooded the region with molten rock. The lava flows cooled into thick layers of basalt, and more millions of years later, as the Cascade Range uplifted, the Columbia cut through the layers of ash and lava and rock and mud until its bed lay just above sea level. In the process, the river carved out the Columbia Gorge, now a mecca for historical tourists and the subject of countless brochures on walking trails and driving tours; heritage museums and discovery centers; hydro dams, locks, and fish ladders; campgrounds, hotels, and the occasional resort.

As the Columbia swings west, it forms the boundary between Washington and Oregon, both of which have a highway that runs through the gorge. In Oregon, a busy Interstate 84 follows the river from Boardman to Portland; in Washington, a more leisurely Highway 14 links Plymouth and Vancouver. A third route through the gorge is the river itself, known here as the Columbia-Snake Inland Waterway. The waterway carries the river traffic—cruise ships and pleasure craft, and tugs pushing long tows of barges—between the coast and Lewiston, Idaho, 465 miles inland. Not all the traffic on the river is headed upstream or down. Offshore of Hood River, fleets of colourful sailboards chase back and forth—easy on the eyes but hard on the nerves of river pilots, who consider the playthings a menace.

In Thompson's time, the gorge supported a major salmon fishery, a bustling marketplace crowded with Indian families fishing and trading and exchanging the latest news. Some had what Thompson called the "Sea Look"; others, the features of the Plains. Most were as friendly as the isolated bands upstream, though a few were inclined to be less so. Overall, they were so numerous Thompson resorted to travelling in short bursts punctuated by even shorter visits.

As the Columbia narrowed to crowd through the gorge, it erupted in a tumult of rapids. Most formidable were those at Celilo Falls, The Dalles, and the Cascades, and all three required an extended portage. At Celilo Falls, the Columbia poured over a complex of basalt slabs that spanned the river, and even at high water, almost cost Thompson his canoe. Celilo's salmon fishery rivalled that of Kettle Falls, and once upon a time, was the lifeblood of Wishram, a large Native settlement that occupied both sides of the gorge.

From the base of Celilo Falls, Thompson described the Columbia as churning west for nine miles, then suddenly contracting from half a mile wide to sixty yards: "imagination can hardly form an idea of the working of this immense body of water under such a compression, raging and hissing as if alive." These rapids were called *dalles* (French for "paving stones"), the *voyageurs'* term for the flat basalt rock of the Columbia.

Although they named other rapids "The Dalles," those in the gorge were four miles upstream of the Oregon city that now bears the same name.

For two days, Thompson had been recording glimpses of snow-mantled mountains: Mount Hood to the south; Mount St. Helens to the north. Both are part of the string of volcanoes that make up the Cascade Range. As he entered the Cascades, Thompson started recording the change from inland to coastal vegetation, the same change we see today on the drive west. He noted "the first Ash," then isolated groves of trees, and finally rugged mountainsides "well wooded with red Fir, smooth Poplar, Willows & a few Ash &c & Cedars." The changing scene is the result of a change in rainfall, from fifteen inches a year at The Dalles to seventy-five inches at the Cascades, only forty-five miles downstream.

The Cascade Rapids

~ The Cascade Rapids were created five hundred years ago, when the top of Table Mountain slipped from its perch and slid into the Columbia Gorge.

~ For a time, a wall of debris two hundred feet high blocked the Columbia, and until the river breached the barrier, the original inhabitants could cross it on foot.

~ The landslide gave rise to an Indian legend about "The Bridge of the Gods," now the name of a graceful span near the site of the Bonneville Dam.

As late as the mid-1860s, the Cascade Rapids were still a barrier to navigation, and for thirty years, steamboats plying the river had to portage around them. Freight and passengers were laboriously unloaded and the whole kit and kaboodle transported overland, six miles by rail on the Washington shore, fourteen by road in Oregon. Once past the obstacle, everyone and everything had to be loaded again, this time on a different ship. In 1896 this cumbersome arrangement was replaced by the Cascade Locks, now a historic site at the south end of the Bridge of the Gods. At the north end of the bridge, you can still see the fractured cliffs and piles of debris that mark the path of the Table Mountain landslide.

With the completion of the Bonneville Dam in 1938, the Cascade Rapids disappeared. Forty-two years later, The Dalles Dam claimed both the Dalles and Celilo Falls. Today Lakes Bonneville and Celilo have replaced the river that was, and the fisheries that once bordered its rapids are gone. In a small riverside community on the Washington side of the gorge, someone foresaw the need for a memento. Covering one wall of an abandoned building in Wishram is a mural of the Columbia, cascading in all its former glory over the rocks of Celilo Falls.

On July 12 Thompson reached the head of the Cascade Rapids. There he met an old chief who'd picked up a few words of English from the ships. "Some of them," remarked Thompson, "not the best." A more forthright Meriwether Lewis cited a few examples: "musquit, powder, shot, nife, file, damned rascal, sun of a bitch, &c."[6] The next morning the chief and his men helped the travellers carry the canoe and the packs over the two-mile portage, and by eight that evening, the *voyageurs* had put forty miles of river behind them. "A little above Point Vancouver," Thompson called a halt for the night.

The following day their course lay north toward Longview, where the Columbia turns west for the last time. That night, the "tide fell ab[t] 2 ft," and on the morning of July 15, "after shaving and arranging our-selves," Thompson and his crew cast off on the last leg of their journey. They avoided the heavy winds off Tongue Point by portaging across its neck, then paddled the last mile and a half to Astoria. From his posi-tion on shore, a mystified Gabriel Franchère watched the arrival of a strange craft.

> Toward midday we saw a large canoe with a flag displayed at her stern, rounding the point which we called Tongue Point. We did not know who it could be ... The flag she bore was the British, and her crew was composed of eight Canadian boatmen or *voyageurs*.
> A well-dressed man, who appeared to be the commander, was the first to leap ashore; and addressing us without ceremony, he said that his name was David Thompson, and that he was one of the partners of the North West Company.[7]

Thompson described his welcome as "most polite," and he was most polite in turn. He presented Astor's partners with a letter that began, "Gentlemen: Permit me to congratulate you on your safe arrival & building in the mouth of the Columbia River ... " and went on, "I have only to hope that the respective parties at Montreal may finally settle the arrangements between the two Companies which in my opinion will be to our mutual Interest." The next day, Duncan McDougall, the Astor partner who was in charge of the post, wrote a noncommittal reply couched in virtually the same terms. Then began a curious minuet between two men who really didn't know whether they were colleagues or competitors.

Two weeks before Thompson's arrival, McDougall had heard (a

rather exaggerated) rumour about a party of thirty white men building a post near The Dalles. He concluded that the men must be Nor'Westers, and by the time Thompson reached Astoria, McDougall was in the process of having three dugout canoes loaded for a trip upstream "in case of an opposition."[8] McDougall informed his visitor that the canoes were meant to meet Astor's overland expedition, a story Thompson wouldn't have believed for a minute. When it became apparent that the Nor'Westers would be accompanying the Astorians upriver, McDougall was forced to admit their real mission was to set up a post "somewhere below" Celilo Falls, a story no closer to the truth than the first one. Although David Stuart and his crew of Astorians *paused* below Celilo Falls, as soon as Thompson's canoe was safely on its way, they continued upriver for 350 miles and built a trading post at the mouth of the Okanogan.

Thompson countered these half-truths with a few of his own. Gabriel Franchère maintained that he was guilty of exaggerating "the dangers and difficulties" of the country upstream.[9] Given Thompson's peaceful progress down the Columbia, the accusation was probably justified. Moreover, Thompson was no more frank about his destination than the Astorians were about theirs. On the day of his departure, he told McDougall he was headed "direct to Montreal." If by "direct," he meant "after I've finished exploring the Columbia River and spent another six months trading furs at Saleesh House," he was being truthful. Otherwise, not.

Alexander Ross, who disapproved of McDougall and mistrusted Thompson, watched this double-edged game with a cynical eye. He considered the visitor's welcome far too warm—"M'Dougall received him like a brother ... nothing was too good for Mr. Thompson"—and came within an ace of accusing his boss of disloyalty to Astor. In the end, however, Ross backed off and declared the contest a draw: " ... for in point of acuteness, duplicity, and diplomatic craft, they were perhaps well matched."[10]

Thompson's account of the Columbia's rendezvous with the Pacific was curiously tame. He wrote no description of the river's angry collision with the ocean and made no mention of the eight *Tonquin* crew members drowned four months before. It's possible he caught the Columbia in a mild mood and didn't hear about the lost men, but three years later, he was forcibly reminded of the river's power. In 1814 Alexander Henry was drowned when his landing craft capsized off Astoria. Over the course of history, the mouth of the Columbia has claimed so many lives, it's known as "the graveyard of the Pacific."

From Portland, Oregon, Highway 30 sets off to the west, past the towns of Scappoose, St. Helens, Rainier, and Clatskanie. The road follows a broad, flat Columbia, now moving at the stately pace befitting an aging river. Pulp mills, factories, and grain elevators spring up along the shore, and ocean-going tankers and container ships berth at the docks on the riverside. Here the Columbia flows once more through a green countryside, the wetlands along its shores reminiscent of those in its headwaters. Ninety-six miles downstream of Portland, the highway comes to an end at the port of Astoria.

Although several miles from the sea, there's no mistaking Astoria for an inland city. It's the home of a marine museum that harks back to the days of the sailing ships. Some of its displays are so massive you'd think the museum was built around them; others are as diminutive as a delicate model of Captain Vancouver's ship. Downtown, the docks that once housed a canning industry are preserved as a picturesque boardwalk of restaurants and bakeries and seafood markets. In the water below, sea lions bob among clusters of abandoned pilings, hoping for a handout of fish scraps.

Astoria was built on a small point of land at the base of a steep hillside, its unique houses climbing upward because there was no other way to go. Early drawings indicate that the Astorians built their trading post on the banks of the Columbia, probably on the same ground now occupied by the city's downtown. But the only reminder of its presence is a few blocks up the hill, where a replica of a log bastion sits in a residential park, and informative plaques outline the history of the settlement. Otherwise, there are few signs of the Astorians in their namesake city; of David Thompson, there's no sign at all.

That's hardly surprising. The dramatic story of Lewis and Clark's Corps of Discovery overshadows the story of the Astorians, and if it weren't for the journals of the fur trade, no one would have known that Thompson was ever there. Except for his half sheet of paper, he left no trace of his presence, and whether his source was the Indian people, Lewis and Clark, or Captain Vancouver, every name on his map appears just as he found it. Unlike explorers before him, he named not a single feature on the Columbia after himself or one of his men.

On July 22, 1811, the North West and Astorian canoes set off up the Columbia together. When they were headed downstream, Thompson's *voyageurs* had covered the distance between the Snake River and Astoria in five and a half days. On the return upstream, with the wind with them but the current against them, the trip took them a full two weeks. On their own, the Nor'Westers would probably have moved faster, but the dugout canoes of the Astorians were not only awkward under sail, but they were also burdensome to carry, making the travellers overly dependent on the Indians at the portages. One of the bands, characterized by Thompson as "a mixture of Kindness & Treachery," demanded exorbitant pay for their services and backed up their demand with two-bladed daggers. Thompson's technique (to paraphrase Theodore Roosevelt) was to "speak softly and carry a big gun." The chiefs responded by ordering their young troublemakers away.

By the time the Nor'Westers and the Astorians parted company at Celilo Falls, it was July 31. Thompson and his men continued upstream to the mouth of the Snake River. There, Thompson hired a horseman to take a message to Spokane House, telling Jaco to meet the canoe with horses and provisions. Three days later, Thompson and his crew were fifty-six miles up the Snake River, where they landed to wait for Jaco.

> ... put ashore at the mouth of a small Brook & camped, as this is the Road to my first Post in the Spokane Lands. Here is a Village of 50 Men—they had danced 'till they were fairly tired & the Chiefs had bawled themselves hoarse—they forced a present of 8 Horses on us ... [The next day] they declared they did not wish for any return for the present of Horses, but that they knew the nature of a Present— I gave each of them Notes for the Horses, to be paid when the Canoes arrive.

These people were the Nez Percé, and the "Brook" was a stream that Lewis and Clark had named after George Drouillard, a civilian member of their expedition. Drewyers River is now known as the Palouse, a narrow stream that flows from a vast tract of land of the same name. By extension, the name attached to the colourful Appaloosa horse, a breed developed by the Nez Percé who once occupied the lands of the Palouse. Today cruise ships on the Columbia-Snake Inland Waterway anchor off the mouth of the Palouse River—an incongruous sight in this near-desert landscape—and in Lyons Ferry State Park, tour buses wait to carry the passengers a few miles upstream for a view of the Palouse Falls.

Now that he was equipped with horses, Thompson decided to leave without waiting for Jaco, and on August 9, he set off for Spokane House. The post lay about eighty miles northeast, and for approximately half that distance, Thompson and his men rode up a series of valleys that lay in a rough gash in the Palouse called the Channelized Scablands.

The Land very rocky & full of rocky Hills cut perpend wherever
the Rocks show themselves, & exactly of the same kind of Rocks as
along the Columbia, with much fragments in splinters &c, very bad
for the Horses, & the Soil a sandy fine impalpable Powder which
suffocated us with Dust.

The first day on the road, the riders followed the valley of the
Palouse River; on the second day, they rode almost due north up the valley of Rock Creek. On the third day, they passed Rock Lake and entered
a countryside "much mended ... tho' parched up for want of rain." They
trotted across a "wide Plain without a Tree," and camped for the night
where "firs are thinly scattered along a kind of Ravine." On the fourth
day, they came to "a few Ponds & good grassy Lands with their Woods,"
and there they stopped to feed and water the horses.

There are few landmarks in this country, but the bands of terrain
Thompson and his riders covered—the Scabland valleys, the open plain,
the grassy woods—are still apparent today. As a result, it's possible to
figure out where Thompson was. His northerly direction, however, is at
odds with the main highways of the Palouse, which tend to run east and
west. Particularly on Thompson's ride through the Scablands, it's easier
to intercept his trail than to follow it.

Toward the southern end of Thompson's route, Highway 26 between
Colfax and Washtucna crosses the Palouse River,[11] the ground there so
rocky that half the fence posts are propped up in barrels. Farther north,
Highway 23 between Steptoe and Sprague crosses Rock Creek, its valley
grass-covered but heavily scarred with outcrops of black rock. Linking
the two highways is a long country road that begins just north of
Washtucna. This road rambles for more than fifty miles past the farming
communities of Benge, Winona, and Lancaster, and ends near St. John on
Highway 23. Although the road roughly parallels Thompson's route, it
avoids the craggy valleys of the rivers and winds instead through a
gentler landscape.

The pioneers called it "Paradise," but the *voyageurs* called it *pelouse*
(French for "lawn"), their attempt to describe a treeless expanse clad in
a smooth coat of short-grass prairie. But the most startling feature of the
Palouse is its hills. Great mounds of wind-blown loess, they're pressed
so close and piled so high, there's no room left for a horizon. Early settlers ignored these dry hills in favour of the irrigable valleys, but today,
every inch of the fertile Palouse has been sculpted into hillside farms. In
this country, there are no fences, no windbreaks, no visible boundaries
at all. Roads curve at random among contoured slopes, dull brown in the

spring, but by late summer, wrapped in green wheatfields and the yellow glow of canola. This is a landscape of close-ups, but Steptoe Butte, its road curling upward like peel from an apple, offers a rare bird's-eye view of the panorama of the Palouse.

From the community of Ewan on Highway 23, the paved Rock Lake Road follows Thompson's trail north. Once past Rock Lake, signs of the Scablands diminish, and the road passes through a band of Palouse hills. About eleven miles north of Ewan, the "wide Plain" that Thompson described appears; five miles farther on, the scattered pines; and within another six miles, the ponds and grass and woods where the riders rested their horses. At that point, they were probably inside today's Turnbull National Wildlife Refuge.

The Cheney Plaza Road, mostly smooth gravel, runs through the wildlife refuge and ends in the city of Cheney. Thompson's own route here isn't entirely clear, but he and his men were still headed more north than east. By the afternoon of their third day on the road, they were riding "a large Plain without Water," quite possibly the present site of the Spokane airport. Thompson didn't mention crossing the Spokane River, which they had to do, but they could have forded it the following morning, when a single hour of travel brought them to Spokane House.

Thompson arrived to find everyone present and accounted for, except, of course, Jaco, who was still wandering the Palouse with the "Provisions and Horses." Luckily, Jaco must have encountered someone who warned him the riders had passed because (no thanks to Thompson) he was back at the post before nightfall. Thompson's stay at Spokane House was brief. Four days after his arrival, he left for Kettle Falls, where he stayed for the next two weeks, preparing for the journey upstream. He sent three men up the Colville to look for cedar, and Finan McDonald up the Columbia to search for the men from Athabasca Pass. So far as we can tell, these were the same men Thompson had been waiting for since April, but though McDonald ascended the river for over two hundred miles, he returned "short" on August 27, "hav[g] seen nothing of the Men & Canoes."

On September 2, 1811, Thompson and his crew launched their canoe on the Columbia, a mile upstream of where they'd set off for the Pacific two months before. Ahead lay a journey that's recorded in Thompson's journal but for some reason is missing from his *Narrative*. In that work, he claimed he'd completed his survey of the Columbia once he reached the Pacific Ocean, which wasn't precisely the case. He still had almost three hundred miles to go.

For seventeen days, the *voyageurs* took up their paddles at six in the morning and laid them down at six at night. As they paddled north, the Columbia narrowed and the surrounding hills rose, woody and rocky and "more rude than before." Forty miles upstream, they crossed the forty-ninth parallel into Canada, and moments later were battling the swirling currents off the mouth of the "Saleesh River."

Today Highway 25 follows the Columbia north from Kettle Falls to Northport, where a side road leads to the border crossing at Waneta. This crossing is tucked away in the middle of nowhere, the only signs of human occupancy a customs' shed the size of a toll booth and the towering Waneta Dam. Here the Pend Oreille River pours into the lower end of a twenty-six-mile stretch of free-flowing Columbia, as narrow and turbulent and noisy now as it was then. Eleven miles upstream, the canoe passed the site of today's city of Trail, B.C., and twenty-six miles farther on, the mouth of "McGillivray's River." The travellers camped for the night just north of the confluence Thompson had hoped to reach four years before—the meeting of the Kootenay and Columbia Rivers—now the site of the city of Castlegar.

Castlegar's downtown is situated within a deep bend of the Columbia, and at the foot of Columbia Avenue, a stone cairn dedicated to Thompson once stood near the city's ferry landing. When the ferry was replaced by the Robson Bridge, the cairn was moved to the grounds of the Kootenay Art Gallery, an out-of-the-way spot high up on the flats near the airport, and about as far as you can get from the river. Nevertheless, Castlegar's cairn is an important historical site. Aside from the one at Invermere, it's the only monument on the Columbia River that acknowledges David Thompson's existence.

The next day, Thompson and his *voyageurs* started up a widening in the Columbia known as the Arrow Lakes. The open water offered a break from the Columbia's rapids, but it also generated powerful headwinds and high waves, and the men paddled north in a mixture of spray and rain. Their first camp on the lakeshore was under a cloudy sky lit by lightning, but the next night, the sky was clear and Thompson spotted a comet. "It's size is that of a Star of the 1ˢᵗ Mag, it's train of Light 2° long to the NEᵈ." As they continued paddling north, he noted "steep ugly rocks" and "good Shore" by turns, and later on, wooded hills and glimpses of snow-streaked mountains. On September 11 the canoe re-entered the river proper, and the expedition put ashore near the present-day city of Revelstoke.

Today the Hugh Keenleyside Dam, one of three Columbia River Treaty dams on the Canadian segment of the Columbia, has widened, deepened, and lengthened the Arrow Lakes, so they now fill the river upstream of Castlegar almost as far as Revelstoke. Most of Lower Arrow Lake has no road on its lakeshore, and a visit to Upper Arrow Lake requires an eighty-seven-mile drive through the back country of the West Kootenays.

Twelve miles northeast of Castlegar, Highway 6 sets off for Nakusp, a charming town on the shores of the upper lake. For those who prefer to live out of the world, Nakusp is an ideal choice. Although it's the only community of any size on the lakes, its residents can't head west unless they drive thirty-four miles south or twenty-nine miles north and reconnect to the world by ferry. To the south, the Fauquier-Needles ferry carries vehicles travelling on Highway 6 across Lower Arrow Lake; to the north, the Galena-Shelter Bay ferry carries those on Highway 23 across Upper Arrow Lake. Highway 23 then follows the Columbia to Revelstoke and beyond. It passes the Revelstoke Dam, continues along Lake Revelstoke to the Mica Dam, and ends just west of the inundated site of Boat Encampment.

On September 12, Thompson's men tackled the Columbia River upstream of Revelstoke. For three days, they lined, handed, and carried the canoe up the lower Dalles ("very bad") and the upper Dalles ("very dangerous"). The upper rapids were so deadly that they'd one day be christened *Dalles des Morts*. Thompson, however, summed them up with his usual penchant for understatement: "I suppose loaded canoes must line down much of the Dalles." On the morning of September 18, 1811, the expedition reached Thompson's old hut at Boat Encampment. For the *voyageurs*, it was the end of a 300-mile upstream battle; for David Thompson, it was the conclusion of a 1200-mile survey of the Great River of the West.

Despite Thompson's explorations (or possibly because of them), the ownership of the Columbia remained a bone of contention for the next thirty-five years. In 1844 James Knox Polk ran for (and won) the American presidency under the sabre-rattling slogan "54–40 or Fight!" Fifty-four-forty was a line of latitude that would have awarded the Americans the entire drainages of both the Columbia and Fraser Rivers, the future cities of Vancouver and Victoria, all of Vancouver Island, and the Queen Charlotte Islands as well. In other words, President Polk had decided to acquire every square inch of the territory America was then sharing with Britain. But when he found himself embroiled in a similar dispute with Mexico, his attention was diverted to his southern flank, and the northern boundary became a non-issue. In 1846 Britain and the United States settled the matter with an arbitrary stroke of the pen. From the Rocky Mountains to the Pacific, the international boundary would follow the forty-ninth parallel and end in a southward quirk around the tip of Vancouver Island.

The new boundary ignored the course of the Columbia, and the result was a river divided—its headwaters in Canada, its mouth in the United States. In a way, the split was appropriate. Captain Gray had discovered the mouth of the Columbia and Thompson had discovered its headwaters. Thompson, however, always considered the settlement unjust, and the notion that Canada lost out because he failed to move faster is probably unjust as well. The dispute over Oregon Country was long and complex, and Thompson's brief visit to the river's mouth influenced the outcome as much as the years he devoted to exploring its basin, which is to say, not at all. Despite the settlements he'd built and the trade he'd established throughout Idaho, Montana, and Washington, the British ceded the territory to the Americans. An ironic footnote to the whole business is that the line drawn in 1846 was a westward extension of the one Thompson himself had drawn forty-eight years before.

Once Thompson reached Boat Encampment, the job he'd been sent to do was done. He seems, however, to have been intent on tying up a few loose ends. While he waited for the men from Athabasca Pass (they still hadn't turned up), he explored the Canoe River as far upstream as Valemont, and after they arrived, rode across the pass to retrieve the goods they'd left behind. At William Henry's post, he received a letter from McDonald of Garth that contained a clearly impossible request for Thompson to meet him at Kootenay Plains. By that time, it was October, too late to take on a journey that was hundreds of miles out of his way.

Unable to acknowledge or fulfill the request, Thompson recrossed the pass to Boat Encampment, hoping McDonald would have the wit to turn upstream once he hit the Columbia. McDonald didn't. Thompson waited a week, then on October 21, gave the order to launch the canoe, and he and his men headed downriver with a load of trade goods. On their arrival at Kettle Falls, they found the village deserted, so they walked the sixty-eight miles to Spokane House to fetch some pack horses. A few days later they delivered the goods to Spokane House, and on November 11, set out again, this time along the overland trail that led to Saleesh House.

Thompson spent the winter of 1811–1812 rebuilding Saleesh House, trading furs with the Flatheads and the Kootenays, and completing his explorations of the Clark Fork and Flathead Rivers. When spring arrived, he made the return journey to Boat Encampment with the fur brigade, and on May 6, 1812, he set out on foot to walk across Athabasca Pass. He never saw the Columbia River again.

Epilogue

DAVID THOMPSON SPENT THE REST OF HIS LIFE IN UPPER AND LOWER CANADA, now the provinces of Ontario and Quebec. There, he was finally free to work on his map of the northwest, an enormous undertaking that took him over two years to complete. For once, he had the full support of his partners. They allowed him his share in the North West Company while he worked on the map, gave him an annual allowance to cover his drafting supplies, and once the map was done and mounted in the dining hall at Fort William, granted him a seven-year pension.

During his first years in eastern Canada, Thompson was quite well off financially. He'd earned good money during his years in the fur trade, he had his pension from the North West Company, and for ten years, he held the position of astronomer with the International Boundary Commission. But a series of unfortunate investments eroded his capital, and as his money dwindled, the size of his family grew. In addition to the five children born in the West, Charlotte had eight more, and by the time the last child was born in 1829, Thompson's capital was gone.

When he was in his sixties, he attempted to raise money by selling his maps and his memoirs, but the publishers of the time weren't interested. Since retirement wasn't an option, he continued to work as a surveyor until his failing eyesight ended his career. When he was seventy-six, he and Charlotte moved in with one of their daughters. They lived there for eleven years—Charlotte watching her grandchildren grow up, Thompson writing draft after draft of his *Narrative.*

David Thompson died at the age of eighty-seven on February 10, 1857. Within three months, Charlotte followed him to the grave. They'd been married for fifty-eight years and are buried beside each other in Montreal's Mount Royal Cemetery.

Thompson used to worry that his entire life's work—his journals, his maps, his *Narrative*—was fated to disappear. But more by chance than design, almost everything he drew or wrote has survived. It was 1887, thirty years after Thompson's death, before J. B. Tyrrell acquired the handwritten *Narrative*, and twenty-nine more years passed before it was finally published. As for Thompson's original journals, almost all of them are housed in the Archives of Ontario in Toronto, and most of the western volumes have been transcribed, edited, and published by modern scholars. And at the entrance to the archives, you can still see David Thompson's great map—ten feet long and six-and-a-half feet high—miraculously intact almost two centuries after he created it.

MAP
OF THE
NORTH-WEST TERRITORIES
OF THE
PROVINCE OF CANADA
From actual Survey during
The years 1792 to 1812

This Map made for the North West Company in 1813 and 1814
and delivered to the Honorable William McGillivray then agent
Embraces the Region lying between 45 and 60 degrees North Latitude
and 84 and 124 degrees West Longitude comprising the Survey's and
Discoveries of 20 years namely the Discovery and Survey of the
Oregon Territory to the Pacific Ocean the survey of the Athabasca
Lake Slave River and Lake from which flows McKenzie's River to
the Arctic Sea by Mr Philip Turner the Route of Sir Alexander
McKenzie in 1792 down part of Fraser's River together with the
Survey of the River to the Pacific Ocean by the late John Stuart
of the North West Company

By David Thompson
Astronomer & Surveyor

NOTES

NOTES TO PROLOGUE

1. J.J. Bigsby. *The Shoe and The Canoe*, Vol. I (London: Chapman & Hall, 1850), 113–114.

NOTES TO THE RED DEER RIVER

1. B. Belyea, ed., *Columbia Journals: David Thompson* (Montreal: McGill-Queens University Press, 1994), 3–11.
2. E. Coues, ed., *New Light on the Early History of the Greater Northwest* (New York: F.P. Harper, 1897), 701.
3. Belyea, *Columbia Journals*, 188.
4. Ibid, 190.
5. D. Scott and E. Hanic. *East Kootenay Chronicle* (Langley, BC: Mr. Paperback, 1979), 44.
6. E.W. Nuffield. *The Pacific Northwest* (Surrey, BC: Hancock House, 1990), 172.

NOTES TO THE BOW RIVER

1. B. Belyea, ed., *Columbia Journals: David Thompson* (Montreal: McGill-Queens University Press, 1994), 12–20.
2. J.C. Jackson. *Children of the Fur Trade: Forgotten Métis of the Pacific Northwest* (Missoula, MT: Mountain Press Publishing, 1996), 3.
3. Belyea, *Columbia Journals*, 197.
4. A.A. Milne. "At the Zoo," *When We Were Very Young* (Toronto: McClelland and Stewart Limited, 1925), 48.
5. P. Cowley. "Interview with Brian Cargill," *Central Alberta Life* (Red Deer), July 29, 1998.
6. J.G. MacGregor. *Peter Fidler: Canada's Forgotten Explorer 1769–1822* (Calgary, AB: Fifth House Publishers, 1998), 70.
7. A.C. Isenberg. *The Destruction of the Bison: An Environmental History, 1750–1920*. (Cambridge: Cambridge University Press, nd, as quoted in a review by W.H. McNeill, "Goodbye to the Bison," *The New York Review of Books*, July 2000, 26.
8. J.O. Whitaker, Jr. *The Audubon Society Field Guide to North American Mammals* (New York: Alfred A. Knopf, Inc., 1980), 672.

9. J.D. Speth. *Bison Kills and Bone Counts: Decision-Making by Ancient Hunters* (Chicago: University of Chicago Press, 1983), 150.
10. B. Gadd. *Handbook of the Canadian Rockies* (Jasper, AB: Corax Press, 1995), 115.

NOTES TO THE NORTH RAM RIVER

1. B. Belyea, ed., *Columbia Journals: David Thompson* (Montreal: McGill-Queens University Press, 1994), 22–34.
2. E. Coues, ed., *New Light on the Early History of the Greater Northwest* (New York: F.P. Harper, 1897), 592.
3. J.C. Jackson. *Children of the Fur Trade: Forgotten Métis of the Pacific Northwest* (Missoula, MT: Mountain Press Publishing, 1996), 201.
4. G.M. Trevelyan. *English Social History: A Survey of Six Centuries, Chaucer to Queen Victoria* (London: Longmans, Green and Co. Ltd., 1944), 489.
5. Belyea, *Columbia Journals*, 103.
6. F.W. Howay, ed., *Voyages of the "Columbia" to the Northwest Coast, 1787–1790 and 1790–93* (Boston: Massachusetts Historical Society, 1941) as quoted in Belyea, *Columbia Journals*, 103.
7. Travel Alberta. *Reach Reports of the North Saskatchewan River System*, Booklet No. 4 (Edmonton: Travel Alberta, n.d.), 9.

NOTES TO NORTHERN EXILE

1. P.C. Newman. *Caesars of the Wilderness* (Markham, ON: Penguin Books, 1987), 9.
2. R.S. Kidd. *Fort George and the Early Fur Trade in Alberta (1792 to 1800)*, Publication No. 2 (Edmonton: Provincial Museum and Archives of Alberta, 1970), 6.
3. M. Wilkins-Campbell. *The Northwest Company* (Toronto: Douglas & McIntyre, 1983), 103.
4. R.E. Pinkerton. *The Gentlemen Adventurers* (Toronto: McClelland and Stewart Limited, n.d.), 227.

5. Ibid, 225.
6. J.C. Jackson. *Children of the Fur Trade: Forgotten Métis of the Pacific Northwest* (Missoula, MT: Mountain Press Publishing, 1996), 6.
7. Ibid.

NOTES TO HOWSE PASS

1. B. Belyea, ed., *Columbia Journals: David Thompson* (Montreal: McGill-Queens University Press, 1994), 36-53.
2. Adapted from A. and J. Salisbury. *Lewis & Clark: The Journey West* (New York: Promontory Press, 1950), 197–203.
3. E.Y. Arima. *Blackfeet and Palefaces: The Pikani and Rocky Mountain House* (Ottawa: The Golden Dog Press, 1995), 49.
4. M. Wilkins-Campbell. *The Northwest Company* (Toronto: Douglas & McIntyre, 1983).
5. H.R. Gardner. *The Canadian Canoe* (Surrey, BC: Hancock House Publishers, 1994), 14,15.
6. J.B. Tyrrell, ed., *David Thompson's Narrative* (New York: Greenwood Press, [1916] 1968), xlix.
7. Belyea, *Columbia Journals*, 210.
8. Travel Alberta. *Reach Reports of the North Saskatchewan River System*, Booklet No. 4, (Edmonton: Travel Alberta, n.d.), 10.
9. J. Ross. and D. Kyba. *The David Thompson Highway: A Hiking Guide* (Calgary, AB: Rocky Mountain Books, 1995), 47.
10. A.R. Verberg. "Adventure on the Hoof in the Howse, Where Legends Live and Dreams Die Hard," *Alberta Report* (Edmonton), August 19, 1996.
11. Belyea, *Columbia Journals*, 215.
12. J.C. Jackson. *Children of the Fur Trade: Forgotten Métis of the Pacific Northwest* (Missoula, MT: Mountain Press Publishing, 1996), 36.
13. Ibid.
14. A.C. Laut. *The Conquest of the Great Northwest*, Vol. II (New York: The Outing Publishing Company, c. 1910), 110.
15. Ibid, 84–86.

NOTES TO THE COLUMBIA RIVER HEADWATERS

1. B. Belyea, ed., *Columbia Journals: David Thompson* (Montreal: McGill-Queens University Press, 1994), 54–74.
2. "Roll on Columbia" was the most popular of a series of songs that Woody Guthrie was hired to write during the late 1930s. Their purpose was to justify the construction of dams on the Columbia River.
3. B. DeVoto. *The Course of Empire* (Boston: Houghton Mifflin Company, 1952), 334.
4. Belyea, *Columbia Journals*, 222.
5. Ibid, 220.
6. Windermere Valley Museum Archives (Invermere, BC).
7. Ibid.
8. Ibid.
9. D.V. Lemaster. *Columbia Valley Guide* (Banff, AB: Luminous Compositions, 1997), 53.
10. *Merck Veterinary Manual*, 6th ed. (Rahway, NJ: Merck & Co. Inc., 1986), 332.
11. Ibid, 332–333.
12. J.B. Tyrrell, ed., *David Thompson's Narrative* (New York: Greenwood Press, [1916] 1968), 379–380.

NOTES TO THE KOOTENAY/ KOOTENAI RIVER

1. B. Belyea, ed., *Columbia Journals: David Thompson* (Montreal: McGill-Queens University Press, 1994), 76–95.
2. E. Coues, ed., *New Light on the Early History of the Greater Northwest* (New York: F.P. Harper, 1897).
3. J.B. Tyrrell, ed., *David Thompson's Narrative* (New York: Greenwood Press, [1916] 1968), lxv–xcviii.
4. R. and M. Parent, eds., *Arrow Lakes Indians: An Introduction to Their History and Culture* (Nakusp, BC: Arrow Lakes Historical Society, 1991), 9.
5. Belyea, *Columbia Journals*, 236.
6. J. Nisbet. *Sources of the River* (Seattle: Sasquatch Books, 1994), 128.
7. Belyea, *Columbia Journals*, 239.
8. W.S. Wallace, ed., *Documents Relating*

to the North West Company (Toronto: The Champlain Society, 1934), 499.

NOTES TO LAKE PEND OREILLE

1. B. Belyea, ed., *Columbia Journals: David Thompson*, 104–116.
2. R.C. Carriker. *The Kalispel People* (Phoenix, AZ: Indian Tribal Series, 1973), 4.
3. Ibid, 27.
4. Belyea, *Columbia Journals*, 247.

NOTES TO THE CLARK FORK

1. M.C. White, ed., *David Thompson's Journals Relating to Montana and Adjacent Regions, 1808–1812.* (Missoula: Montana State University Press, 1950), 43–111.
2. B. DeVoto. *The Course of Empire* (Boston: Houghton Mifflin Company, 1952), 536.
3. W.S. Wallace, ed., *Documents Relating to the North West Company* (Toronto: The Champlain Society, 1934), 262.
4. R. Cox. *The Columbia River: A Journey across the American Continent*, Journey up the Clark Fork, October/November, 1811, ed. E. and J. Stewart (Norman: University of Oklahoma Press, [1831] 1975).
5. Information on the community of Noxon courtesy of Moira Vanek, Noxon, MT.
6. White, *David Thompson's Journals*, 49.
7. J.B. Tyrrell, ed., *David Thompson's Narrative* (New York: Greenwood Press, [1916] 1968), 541.
8. R.J. Space. "David Thompson in Montana." In *David Thompson Sesquicentennial Symposium* (Sandpoint, ID, 1959), 15.
9. Ibid, 17.
10. White, *David Thompson's Journals*, 61, 62n.
11. Space, "David Thompson In Montana," 17.
12. Ibid.
13. Tyrrell, *David Thompson's Narrative*, xcvii.
14. Information on identifying Jumbo Hill courtesy of the University of Montana, Missoula.

NOTES TO BACK TO THE BRAZEAU

1. E. Coues, ed., *New Light on the Early History of the Greater Northwest* (New York: F.P. Harper, 1897), 602.
2. J. Nisbet. *Sources of the River* (Seattle: Sasquatch Books, 1994), 180.
3. Coues, *New Light*, 608.
4. Ibid, 626.
5. Ibid, 627.
6. Ibid.
7. Travel Alberta. *Reach Reports of the North Saskatchewan River System*, Booklet No. 4 (Edmonton: Travel Alberta, n.d.), 15.
8. B. Belyea, ed., *Columbia Journals: David Thompson* (Montreal: McGill-Queens University Press, 1994), 182.
9. Coues, *New Light*, 651.
10. Ibid.
11. Ibid.
12. Belyea, *Columbia Journals*, xiv.
13. Ibid, xv.
14. P.C. Newman. *Caesars of the Wilderness* (Markham, ON: Penguin Books, 1987), 122–123.
15. Coues, *New Light*, 652.
16. E.Y. Arima. *Blackfeet and Palefaces: The Pikani and Rocky Mountain House* (Ottawa, ON: The Golden Dog Press, 1995), 75.
17. Coues, *New Light*, 654.
18. Belyea, *Columbia Journals*, 249.

NOTES TO ATHABASCA PASS

1. B. Belyea, ed., *Columbia Journals: David Thompson* (Montreal: McGill-Queens University Press, 1994), 118–141.
2. Ibid, 251.
3. J. Gottfred. "The Location of David Thompson's 'Goods Shed' on the Athabasca River," *Northwest Journal* IX:7–14.
4. Ibid, 11.
5. J.B. Tyrrell, ed., *David Thompson's Narrative* (New York: Greenwood Press, [1916] 1968), xciii.
6. Belyea, *Columbia Journals*, 253.
7. Gottfred, "David Thompson's 'Goods Shed,'" 14.
8. Belyea, *Columbia Journals*, 252.
9. Ibid, 253.

10. Ibid.
11. P.J. Vesilind. "David Thompson: The Man Who Measured Canada," *National Geographic* May 1996, 112–137.

NOTES TO THE SPOKANE RIVER

1. M.C. White, ed., *David Thompson's Journals Relating to Montana and Adjacent Regions, 1808–1812* (Missoula: Montana State University Press, 1950), 127–174.
2. J.B. Tyrrell, ed., *David Thompson's Narrative* (New York: Greenwood Press, [1916] 1968), 464.
3. R. Cody. *Voyage of a Summer Sun: Canoeing the Columbia River* (Seattle, Sasquatch Books, 1995), 48.
4. Ibid, 60.
5. Much of this journey is a repeat of earlier ones. See the chapter maps in "The Columbia River Headwaters," "The Kootenay/Kootenai River," and "The Clark Fork."
6. J. Davies, ed., *Douglas of the Forests: The North American Journals of David Douglas* (Seattle: University of Washington Press, 1980), 65.
7. J.E. Ferris. "David Thompson in Washington: Spokane House," *David Thompson Sesquicentennial Symposium* (Sandpoint, ID, 1959), 45.
8. Tyrrell, *David Thompson's Narrative*, 465.

NOTES TO THE GREAT RIVER OF THE WEST

1. B. Belyea, ed., *Columbia Journals: David Thompson* (Montreal: McGill-Queens University Press, 1994), 143–178.
2. W. Irving. *Astoria, or Anecdotes of an Enterprise Beyond the Rocky Mountains* (New York: G.P. Putnam's Sons, [1836] 1897), Chapter X.
3. R. Cody. *Voyage of a Summer Sun: Canoeing the Columbia River* (Seattle: Sasquatch Books, 1995).
4. J.B. Tyrrell, ed., *David Thompson's Narrative* (New York: Greenwood Press, [1916] 1968), 485.
5. Belyea, *Columbia Journals*, 271.
6. Ibid, 275.
7. J. Nisbet. *Sources of the River* (Seattle: Sasquatch Books, 1994), 211.
8. R.E. Jones, ed., *Annals of Astoria: The Headquarters Log of the Pacific Fur Company on the Columbia River, 1811–1815* (New York: Fordham University Press, 1999), 14.
9. Nisbet, *Sources of the River*, 213.
10. Ibid, 212.
11. The scale of this chapter map is too small to accommodate all the roads of the Palouse. They can be found on any Washington State road-map.

BIBLIOGRAPHY

Arima, E.Y. 1995. *Blackfeet and Palefaces: The Pikani and Rocky Mountain House.* Ottawa, ON: The Golden Dog Press.

Belyea, B., ed. 1994. *Columbia Journals: David Thompson.* Montreal: McGill-Queens University Press.

Canadian Encyclopedia. 1985. Edmonton, AB: Hurtig Publishers Ltd.

Carriker, R.C. 1973. *The Kalispel People.* Phoenix, AZ: Indian Tribal Series.

Chance, D.H. 1986. *People of the Falls.*

Kettle Falls, WA: Kettle Falls Historical Center, Inc.

Cody, R. 1995. *Voyage of a Summer Sun: Canoeing the Columbia River.* Seattle: Sasquatch Books.

Conley, C. 1982. *Idaho for the Curious.* Cambridge, ID: Backeddy Books.

Coues, E., ed. 1897. *New Light on the Early History of the Greater Northwest: The Manuscript Journals of Alexander Henry, and of David Thompson, 1799–1814.* New York: F.P. Harper.

Cowles, V. 1979. *The Astors.* New York: Alfred A. Knopf.

Cowley, P. 1997. "Interview with Brian Cargill." *Central Alberta Life* (Red Deer), July 29.

Cox, Ross. 1831. *The Columbia River: A Journey across the American Continent.* Facsimile edition, 1975. Edited by E. and J. Stewart. Norman: University of Oklahoma Press.

Dary, D.A. 1975. *The Buffalo Book.* New York: Avon Books.

Davidson, G.C. 1918. *The North West Company.* Facsimile edition, 1967. New York: Russell & Russell.

Davies, J., ed. 1980. *Douglas of the Forests: The North American Journals of David Douglas.* Seattle: University of Washington Press.

DeVoto, B. 1952. *The Course of Empire.* Boston: Houghton Mifflin Company.

Dietrich, W. 1995. *Northwest Passage: The Great Columbia River.* New York: Simon & Schuster.

Ferris, J.E. 1959. "David Thompson in Washington: Spokane House." *David Thompson Sesquicentennial Symposium,* 35–47. Sandpoint, ID.

Franchère, Gabriel. 1969. *Journal of a Voyage on the North West Coast of North America During the Years 1811, 1812, 1813, and 1814.* Edited by W.K. Lamb. Translated by W.T. Lamb. Toronto: The Champlain Society.

Gadd, B. 1995. *Handbook of the Canadian Rockies.* Jasper, AB: Corax Press.

Gardner, H.R. 1994. *The Canadian Canoe.* Surrey, BC, and Blaine, WA: Hancock House Publishers.

Glover, R., ed. 1962. *David Thompson's Narrative.* Toronto: The Champlain Society.

Gottfred, J. 1996. "The Location of David Thompson's 'Goods Shed' on the Athabasca River." *Northwest Journal* IX: 7–14.

Guterson, D. 1999. "The Kingdom of Apples: Picking the Fruit of Immortality in Washington's Laden Orchards." *Harper's Magazine,* October, 41–56.

Harden, B. 1996. *A River Lost: The Life and Death of the Columbia.* New York: W.W. Norton & Company.

Heflick, D. 1998. *Back Roads Cycling Guide: Greater Spokane & Palouse Region.* Orient, WA: Silcox Productions.

Irving, W. 1836. *Astoria, or Anecdotes of an Enterprise Beyond the Rocky Mountains,* 2 vols. Facsimile edition, 1897. New York: G.P. Putnam's Sons.

Jackson, J.C. 1996. *Children of the Fur Trade: Forgotten Métis of the Pacific Northwest.* Missoula, MT: Mountain Press Publishing.

Jones, P.N. 1992. *Columbia River Gorge: A Complete Guide.* Seattle: The Mountaineers.

Jones, R.E., ed. 1999. *Annals of Astoria: The Headquarters Log of the Pacific Fur Company on the Columbia River, 1811–1815.* New York: Fordham University Press.

Jordon, M.E. 1957. "Canada Remembers David Thompson." *Canadian Geographical Journal* LIV(3): 114–17.

Karamitsanis, A. 1991. *Place Names of Alberta,* Vol. I. Calgary, AB: University of Calgary Press.

Kidd, R.S. 1970. *Fort George and the Early Fur Trade in Alberta (1792 to 1800).* Publication No. 2. Edmonton: Provincial Museum and Archives of Alberta.

Landers, R., and D. Hansen. 1998. *Paddle Routes of the Inland Northwest.* Seattle: The Mountaineers.

Laut, A.C. c. 1910. *The Conquest of the Great Northwest,* Vol. II. New York: The Outing Publishing Company.

Lemaster, D.V. 1997. *Columbia Valley Guide.* Banff, AB: Luminous Compositions.

MacGregor, J.G. 1998. *Peter Fidler: Canada's Forgotten Explorer 1769–1822.* Calgary, AB: Fifth House Publishers.

Merck Veterinary Manual. 1986. 6th ed. Rahway, NJ: Merck & Co. Inc.

Milne, A.A. 1925. "At the Zoo." *When We Were Very Young.* Reprinted, 1983. Toronto: McClelland and Stewart Limited.

Morton, A.S. 1936. "The North West Company's Columbia Enterprise and David Thompson." *Canadian Historical Review* 17: 266–88.

Nelson, S., & T. 1997. *Exploring the Columbia-Snake Inland Waterway*. Kenmore, WA: Epicenter Press.

Newman, P.C. 1987. *Caesars of the Wilderness*. Markham, ON: Penguin Books.

Nisbet, J. 1994. *Sources of the River: Tracking David Thompson across Western North America*. Seattle: Sasquatch Books.

Nuffield, E.W. 1990. *The Pacific Northwest: Its Discovery and Early Exploration by Sea, Land, and River*. Surrey, BC: Hancock House.

Parent, R. and M., ed. 1991. *Arrow Lakes Indians: An Introduction to Their History and Culture*. Nakusp, BC: Arrow Lakes Historical Society.

Pinkerton, R.E. n.d. *The Gentlemen Adventurers*. Toronto: McClelland and Stewart Limited.

Ray, A. 1974. *Indians in the Fur Trade: Their Role as Trappers, Hunters and Middlemen in the Lands Southwest of Hudson Bay, 1660–1870*. Toronto: University of Toronto Press.

Roe, J. 1992. *The Columbia River: A Historical Travel Guide*. Golden, CO: Fulcrum Publishing.

Ross, J., and D. Kyba. 1995. *The David Thompson Highway: A Hiking Guide*. Calgary, AB: Rocky Mountain Books.

Salisbury, A., & J. 1950. *Lewis & Clark: The Journey West*. New York: Promontory Press.

Scott, D., and E. Hanic. 1979. *East Kootenay Chronicle*. Langley, BC: Mr. Paperback.

Sebert, L.M. 1981. "David Thompson's Determination of Longitude in Western Canada." *The Canadian Surveyor* 35(4): 405–14.

Smith, S. 1996. *Canadian Rockies Whitewater: The Central Rockies*. Jasper, AB: Headwaters Press Ltd.

Space, R.J. 1959. "David Thompson in Montana." *David Thompson Sesquicentennial Symposium*, 14–22. Sandpoint, ID.

Speth, J.D. 1983. *Bison Kills and Bone Counts: Decision-Making by Ancient Hunters*. Chicago: University of Chicago Press.

Stenson, F. 1985. *Rocky Mountain House: National Historic Park*. Toronto: Parks Canada and New Canada Publications.

Travel Alberta. n.d. *Reach Reports of the North Saskatchewan River System*. Booklet No. 4. Edmonton: Travel Alberta.

Trevelyan, G.M. 1944. *English Social History: A Survey of Six Centuries, Chaucer to Queen Victoria*. London: Longmans, Green and Co. Ltd.

Tyrrell, J.B., ed. 1916. *David Thompson's Narrative*. Facsimile edition, 1968. New York: Greenwood Press.

Van Kirk, S. 1983. *Many Tender Ties: Women in Fur Trade Society, 1670–1870*. Norman: University of Oklahoma Press.

Vesilind, P.J. 1996. "David Thompson: The Man Who Measured Canada." *National Geographic,* May, 112–37.

Wallace, W.S., ed. 1934. *Documents Relating to the North West Company*. Toronto: The Champlain Society.

Whitaker, J.O., Jr. 1980. *The Audubon Society Field Guide to North American Mammals*. New York: Alfred A. Knopf, Inc.

White, M.C., ed. 1950. *David Thompson's Journals Relating to Montana and Adjacent Regions, 1808–1812*. Missoula: Montana State University Press.

Wilkins-Campbell, M. 1983. *The Northwest Company*. Toronto: Douglas & McIntyre.

Windermere Valley Museum Archives, Invermere, BC.

Index to People and Places